Ethics and Excellence

Ethics and Excellence

COOPERATION AND INTEGRITY IN BUSINESS

□ □ □

ROBERT C. SOLOMON

New York   Oxford
OXFORD UNIVERSITY PRESS
1993

Oxford University Press

Oxford New York Toronto
Delhi Bombay Calcutta Madras Karachi
Kuala Lumpur Singapore Hong Kong Tokyo
Nairobi Dar es Salaam Cape Town
Melbourne Auckland Madrid
and associated companies in
Berlin Ibadan

Library of Congress Cataloging-in-Publication Data
Solomon, Robert C.
Ethics and excellence : cooperation and integrity in business /
by Robert C. Solomon.
p. cm.—(The Ruffin series in business ethics)
Includes index.
ISBN 0-19-506430-5, 0-19-508711-9 (pbk)
1. Business ethics. I. Title. II. Series.
HF5387.S614 1992
174'.4—dc20   91-32363

9 8 7 6 5 4 3

Printed in the United States of America
on acid-free paper

For Kathy

ACKNOWLEDGMENTS

A book such as this grows through experience, and in particular the delightful experience of working and talking with a number of exceptional and fine individuals. As business ethics becomes a recognized and valued field in the corporate and academic worlds, it is largely due to the support of excellent people and outstanding institutions. My special thanks, therefore, to Ed Freeman, Pat Werhane, and Joanne Ciulla, three wonderful colleagues without whom this book could not have gotten off the ground. I also want to thank the good people I have worked with at Chemical Bank, IBM, AT&T, and other companies who take the subject and their people seriously. My gratitude and regards, accordingly, to Kathleen Ford, Bill Linderman, Donna Garcia, Laura Mindek, Jim Dixon, Melinda Murphy, Bill Johnson, Sylvia Stern, Walter Shipley, and Tom Johnson. Paul Nelson got the project started many years ago, and Kristine Hanson got me interested in the first place. I also want to thank the business schools at the University of Texas, the University of California, and the School of Commerce at the University of Auckland for their support and their terrific students. Thanks too to Bill Shaw, Tina Hanna, Mark Kraft, Nick Imparato, Peter French, Bill Cunningham, Bob King, Larry Carver, Carol Whitcraft, Paul Woodruff, Shirley Hull, Judith Sanders, Tim Ruefli, and Robert Witt. Special thanks to Quincy Lee of San Antonio. I also want to thank the Ruffin series editor, Ed Freeman (again), and, at Oxford University Press, Herb Addison, Mary Sutherland, Cynthia Read, and my excellent editor, Paul Schlotthauer. I am grateful to Clancy Martin for helping with the proofs and index. My thanks to the Ruffin Fund and the Olsson Center for their support. Above all, my thanks for the support and patience of Kathleen Higgins.

Austin, Texas   R. C. S.
March 1992

CONTENTS

FOREWORD

Robert Solomon points our thinking about business ethics in a new direction with this book. The last twenty years of scholarship have been concerned primarily with adjudicating the conflicting claims of business and society, or with hammering out a consensus on difficult social issues such as pollution, political action committees, or unionism. Solomon shows us a different way.

By proposing a theory of business virtues Solomon enables us to view more accurately the reality of business life. Friendship, honor, loyalty, trust, and justice are present in every successful corporation in the world. Likewise, resentment and envy are powerful forces that every executive must face. For the first time, we have a clear and compelling defense of the virtues and vices that are at work in today's business world. Managers and scholars alike will be amply repaid by entering into the conversation that Solomon has begun here.

This is a very practical book on two counts. First, it addresses the metaphors that we use in business, such as competition, warfare, and business as a game, and shows us the limitations of the way we see the corporation. By asking us to think about joining the corporation as a partner in a marriage as a citizen, Solomon makes us notice the human shortcomings of our current business jargon. Second, there is a great deal of practical wisdom in this book, from his discussion of competition as a moral force that makes us be more honest with ourselves, to his analysis of the virtues that really make corporate life worth living.

The purpose of the Ruffin Series in Business Ethics is to publish the best thinking about the role of ethics in business. In a world in which there are daily reports of questionable business practices, from financial scandals to environmental disasters, we need to step back from the fray and understand the large issues of how business and ethics are and ought to be connected. The books in this series are aimed at three audiences; management scholars, ethicists, and business executives. There is a growing consensus among these groups that business and ethics must be integrated as a vital part of the teaching and practice of management.

There is no better example of the kind of thinking that must be done than that found in Robert Solomon's book. He has continued the current trend towards making business and ethics go together. And he has given us an important new thread—the virtues—in a conversation that seeks to revitalize the corporation.

R. Edward Freeman

Ethics and Excellence

For in the fatness of these pursy times,
Virtue itself of vice must pardon beg.
WILLIAM SHAKESPEARE, *Hamlet* (III, iv)

Introduction:
Can Ethics Be Taught?

> I strongly sympathize with any businessman who thinks it something of an impertinence for a professor to lecture to businessmen on business ethics; if such a businessman were to ask, "Why should I not give lectures to professors on academic ethics?" the only appropriate reply would be, "Why not indeed?"
>
> ALASDAIR MACINTYRE,
> "Why Are the Problems
> of Business Ethics Insoluble?"

What is Ivan Boesky doing these days, in his ample spare time? He is studying ethics and his own religious tradition. "Too late" chortles the chorus of critics, but would such studies have made any difference before? It must seem obvious, especially to Mr. Boesky, that a modicum of attention to ethics might have interrupted the greedy obsession with gain of the notorious 1980s. Of course, some people would still bend the rules (or even flout them), but most of the wrongdoing in business that now fills the newspapers is due to moral myopia, not wickedness.

Business ethics, accordingly, has finally become an established subject and concern. Courses are now given and often required in virtually every business school in the country. It is a subject that is debated almost daily in such somber business publications as the *Wall Street Journal, Business Week,* and *The Economist.* Elementary textbooks and a few classic case studies have given way to sophisticated theories and hands-on problem solving. The once-separate concerns of the humanities and business have started to meet, cooperate, and consolidate their interests and their efforts. Business, we are once again reminding ourselves, is first of all a human enterprise.

Business ethics is a field that has grown in only ten years from a poor joke ("isn't that a contradiction in terms?") to a "hot topic."[1] "Business ethics" is no longer jeered as an oxymoron. Indeed, it is treated in

1. R. Edward Freeman, *Corporate Strategy and the Search for Ethics* (Englewood Cliffs, N.J.: Prentice-Hall, 1988).

3

some business circles with solemnity, even reverence, as a kind of magic that distinguishes the best and most successful corporations. Undergraduate business majors and M.B.A. students crowd into classrooms, curious what all the fuss is about. They've all seen *Wall Street* and watched the fall of Milken and Boesky. They've heard the often self-righteous cries for "more ethics" and, even if they aren't sure what's intended, they know that a preemptive strike isn't going to hurt them. At the very least, the title of such a course on their transcript cannot but do them some good.

But can ethics be taught? Is there really anything to write or think about?[2] We are still reading monthly essays in business publications and op-ed pages wondering, 2,400 years after Plato (and often oblivious to Plato's musings on the subject), whether ethics can be taught or thought at all. One recent such opinion piece, by neoconservative gadfly Michael Levin in the *New York Times*, proclaims that ethics courses are "useless."[3] Levin insists (half rightly) that "moral behavior is the product of training, not reflection," that it is a good upbringing, not a late-in-life college or corporate course, that teaches the difference between right and wrong. "Bicyclists don't have to think about which way to lean and honest men don't have to think about how to answer under oath," he argues.

Of course, it is true, as Aristotle told us 2,400 years ago, that ethics begins with a good upbringing. But it continues, Aristotle also told us, with practical experience, including the vicarious experiences provided by literature and what we now call "case studies," and it culminates in reflection and a deeper understanding of the practices in which one is and has been engaged. This reflection and deeper understanding of business practices are what business ethics, in conjunction with business experience, seek to provide. It is this deeper understanding and reflection, too, that are the subject of business ethics writing, and the aim of this book.

The aim of ethics, whether for students or seasoned executives, is not to "teach the difference between right and wrong" but to make people more comfortable facing moral complexity, what Mark Pastin has rightly called the "hard choices" of management.[4] But those hard choices are not unique to business life, and the habits and ways of thinking that make many of them so hard have much to do with the artificial nature of business language and business thinking. Business is not just "business" and most "business" decisions are ethical as well.

---

2. Ken Goodpaster once deliciously suggested (with credit to William May), "[Applied ethicists] carry water from wells they have not dug to put out fires they cannot find" (Applied Ethics Conference, University of British Columbia, 1990).

3. Michael Levin, *New York Times*, "Ethics Courses Are Useless," Nov. 27, 1989.

4. Mark Pastin, *The Hard Choices of Management* (San Francisco: Jossey-Bass, 1986).

When a middle manager faces conflicting obligations or loyalties, it is simply not true, as Professor Levin argues, that "telling right from wrong in everyday life is not that hard; the hard part is overcoming laziness and cowardice to do what one perfectly well knows one should." Professor Levin has evidently never had to "downsize" a staff of good dedicated employees because of a cost-cutting policy established by those above him.

What the study of ethics provides is not new knowledge, much less a belated attempt to "teach the difference between right and wrong," but a renewed sense of purpose and vision. In the state of business today, nothing could be more timely or more practical. After all of the cost-cutting, the down-sizings, the strategic bankruptcies and restructurings, the mergers and take-overs, the question will be laid bare: What is a corporation? Is it a decent place to work in and plan a life? What happens to loyalty and integrity when every job seems like a temporary position? What happens to merit and quality and progress and innovation? What do we have left once the company is "lean and mean" and survival is the only value?

The call for ethics in business does not come primarily from an outraged public, the polemics-hungry press, or publicity-minded congressional committees. It comes from executives themselves who want the opportunity to think through and clarify the conflicts in which they find themselves on a daily basis. I teach business ethics in university and corporate classrooms, and I must say that I rarely meet a manager who isn't concerned about ethical issues and doesn't want to talk about them, albeit with some discomfort. Every reflective executive recognizes the danger of "tunnel vision"—"*pleonexia*" Plato called it, a sickness of purpose. Michael Maccoby, author of the best-selling book *The Gamesman,* described it as "careerism": "The individuals' sense of identity, integrity, and self-determination is lost as he treats himself as an object whose worth is determined by its fluctuating market value."[5] It is hard to find a manager who does not feel the pressures of careerism or suffer some contradiction between obligations to the company and his or her sense of personal integrity. Business ethics is the reflective sanctuary where these pressures and problems can be shared and discussed, understood and resolved.

The question of what the study of business ethics is supposed to provide for us remains unanswered, however. Reflection and discussion are essential to successful business, but is there a need for anything like a "theory" of business ethics? That is what this book is about. Business ethics is not a piece of specialized philosophy or just another forum for debating public policy, nor is it (as it so often appears to be) an odd

5. Michael Maccoby, *The Gamesman* (New York: Pocket Books, 1975).

byproduct of the social sciences.[6] Business ethics is a kind of "understanding" but it is also an essential part of a practice, in which we cultivate certain kinds of character to fit into certain kinds of organizations
and a certain kind of society (archaically called "capitalist").[7] Here, as
elsewhere, the thin divide between socialization and indoctrination is
hard to discern, and some will complain that any kind of cultivation
amounts to brainwashing programming for the establishment, while
others will insist that the cultivation of character under capitalism is
deficient. But the fact is that what we call capitalism does provide a
certain kind of culture which requires certain kinds of characters and
certain specific virtues, and business ethics is one way of describing those
virtues. So, too, the supposed line between theory and practice turns
out to be dubious at best, for to understand and to articulate the nature
of one's role (in the company or the community) are both essential to
and often sufficient for the proper performance of that role. Of course,
there is always the bigger picture in which one understands one's role
and contributions, and it is here that business ethics makes a decisive
difference. Knowing what one is doing is obviously not unimportant to
doing it well. Business ethics, I keep arguing, is not the superimposi-
tion of foreign values on business but the understanding of the foundations of business itself.

This is not to say, of course, that managers who know what they are
doing won't cheat or that knowledgeable executives won't deal under
the table. Teaching crooks a little Aristotle won't make them better
managers or human beings, and reading a book in business ethics certainly will not make up for a deficient or vicious upbringing. Indeed,
there is nothing so sinister as the language of ethics skillfully employed
by a Machiavellian executive who sees the value of a noble demeanor.
We all know that the most dangerous crooks are *not* those who openly
extoll "the bottom line" but those who bend the rules to their own purposes. A good deal of wrongdoing in business, however, is due to im-

6. One of the odder features of the current literature is the number of "scientific"
studies obsessed with the supposed affect of business ethics courses on students. Whether
a single course "makes any difference," however, is a depressing and self-indulgent distraction as well as a misunderstanding of what business ethics is all about and what its
study is supposed to do. The aim of business ethics and the "study" of business ethics are
not merely to change one's response to an ethics questionnaire ("Would you agree to
. . . if . . . ?)" but to instill an eventual sense of confidence in one's ability to face and
handle practical situations.

7. It is worth a moment's attention to note that the ideology of "capitalism" thus puts
its emphasis on "capital," whereas the emphasis of its rival ideology of "socialism" puts
its stress on the "social." Whatever the relative virtues and weaknesses of these two supposedly antagonistic economic systems, the opponents of business are way ahead in the
war of words, replacing the cold, calculating language of "cost/benefit analysis" with the
far more passionate language of morality, fairness, and exploitation. I will, accordingly,
have very little to say about capitalism in this book but this should not be confused with
any sort of rejection of free enterprise.

poverished language, one or another faulty conception of business life, and a lack of adequate understanding rather than outright greed or wickedness. For example, if one thinks of business as a "dog-eat-dog" fight for survival or calculates all business decisions in the limited language of cost/benefit analysis, unethical behavior is bound to follow. If, on the other hand, one thinks of social responsibility, one will probably act socially responsible. Business ethics so conceived is social self-awareness writ large, a clear sense of purpose in business and of the importance of virtue and honor and ethics. I want to develop that conception of business ethics here. For reasons that I will make clear as I go, I call it "an Aristotelean approach to business."

In this book I want to develop a theoretical framework for thinking about business that is neither abstract nor formal but based upon and encouraging active engagement in the business world. Such engagement eliminates the distance necessary for a thoroughly critical, abstract theory, and so I should be frank from the beginning that what I want to develop here is a theory which the free enterprise system is taken as a starting point and not itself subjected to scrutiny. Business ethics is meaningful only as it is part of and appropriate to the business world. I do not pretend to have a God's-eye view, and I do not see myself as the instrument of radical change, no matter how many such fantasies may be entertained in college libraries and the reading room of the British Museum. What a business ethicist can do is to enter into the business world and improve its perspectives and conceptions of its own activities—and make an enormous difference to the corporate community and its members by doing so.

No one in the corporate world today will deny that there are deep problems concerning business, and, although these are not usually discussed in terms of "ethics," they are, nevertheless, profoundly ethical and philosophical: questions about the very nature of business and the corporation. For example, the very conception of the corporation as a "legal fiction" defined in terms of obligations to its stockholders implies that corporations are not moral or morally responsible agencies and suggests (at best) a morally ambiguous sense of responsibility for the executives and employees of the corporation. It is not surprising, then, that some major, once respectable companies find themselves riddled and ruined by scandals in which the rubber check of corporate responsibility bounces up and down the hierarchy and seems to get cashed out nowhere.

So, too, business activity itself is misconceived in an amoral way, subsumed (or hidden) under the all-purpose imagery of "competitiveness." But "competition" is but one of a large number of relationships that companies have with one another and with other members of the community, and an overemphasis on competition can be disastrous for the sense of community and for the underlying cooperation that are necessary for any successful business activity. The need to be more "competitive" is more often than not better cast as the need to be more cooperative, to earn the loyalty and understanding of one's customers and one's employees. The combination of our amoral conception of the corporation and our emphasis on competition, however, is doubly disastrous, feeding a frenzy of self-serving but (for the corporations and communities involved) ruinous attacks on corporate stability and the personal security of employees. Its results are short-term thinking and an impoverished sense of innovation, an inevitable loss of productivity, and poor employee morale.[8]

Almost all of my attention in this book will be focused on business life in large corporations, but ethical problems are, nevertheless, "people problems." The repetitive emphasis on the virtues of competitiveness and toughness that are supposed to provide the solution is in fact the very problem. The corporate raids and hostile takeovers that are waged in the name of stockholder rights betray a monstrous distortion of the very idea of corporations and the purpose of business. The consequent "downsizing" bloodbaths (as a defense against such raids and takeovers) have crippled some of our best corporations and hurt hundreds of thousands of people. What we do not need is more "tough" management and more emphasis on the economics of competition. What we need is more attention to those deep ethical (and not just "bleeding heart") concerns that touch on the very care of the corporation and its ability to function as a vibrant, creative organism in society. The practical problem of business ethics is how to alter our conception of business and of the corporation to make our businesses more successful. The theoretical problem that will be the concern of this book is how to frame discussions of business ethics to maximize our understanding of business and ethics and best approach our practical problems.

My answer to these questions and concerns is based on more than a decade of consulting, lecturing, and writing on business ethics. I have spent much of this time in corporations and business schools listening and talking to managers and executives as well as business students, young and old. I have become friendly and sympathetic to their needs and pressures and impressed with their thoughtfulness and sensitivity, and I have become extremely suspicious of the hostility expressed toward business and corporate life by those who know little or nothing about it. I have also become increasingly dissatisfied with those who are more sympathetic but nevertheless insist on remaining "above" the actual conflicts and controversies that people face in everyday life. Life is not

---

8. "It seemed that every time we were beginning to form teams we were reorganized. I was to learn later in life that we tend to meet every situation by reorganizing, and a wonderful method it can be for creating the illusion of progress while producing confusion, inefficiency and demoralization" (Gaius Petronius Arbiter, Proconsul of Bithynia, first century A.D.).

just a convenient set of examples or data for our ethical theories; it is the source and justification of our ethical concerns. Corporations are not abstractions or monoliths; they are real communities of people working together. The impact of such collective activity is formidable. Most of the time, that impact is benign; at best it transforms and improves the life of the nation and, even at its not-so-best, it provides jobs, a sense of community, new resources, and more choices for the consumer. Sometimes, of course, the impact is disastrous, with massive destruction of the environment and innocent deaths. These, unfortunately, are the situations in which the call for "business ethics" is heard the loudest and most frequently, but business ethics is not just about scandals and disasters. It is also about business success and day-to-day business life and the integrity of the people who "do" business.

I have divided the book into three parts. The first is primarily concerned with clearing the ground of myths and metaphors that have been largely responsible for the misunderstanding of business and much of the hostility and criticism of the past century or so. In the second part I will discuss the sort of theory appropriate to business ethics and lay out the basic framework of what I call the Aristotelean approach, starting with the idea that business is first of all a social practice. In the third part I will discuss the heart of the Aristotelean approach to business, the nature of the virtues, and, in particular, those virtues essential to life in the corporation. Some of this will be mere groundbreaking, an invitation to others to develop these themes in much more detail. But my overall aim is to make familiar a healthy and satisfying way of thinking about business that my own experience and many conversations have confirmed.

I have tried to write a book that is as sophisticated as my audience and, I hope, lacks the usual combination of cheerleading and dull prose that mars so much business writing. I have tried to be thoroughly practical in the sense that I always have my own business and corporate constituencies and their questions in mind, but there will be no bulleted lists in the pages that follow and no numbered pearls of witty, homespun advice. I expect that my readers would find it patronizing and offensive (as I would) if in a treatise in ethics I tried to pretend that there are simple recipes or easy answers to the enormous variety of ethical issues that present themselves in everyday business life. "Practical," for me, does not mean abstaining from speculative or literary language in the name of hard-headed "pragmatism." In the pages that follow, there will be quite a bit of philosophy. I will also drop a number of names and discuss those whose thoughts have shaped our current conceptions, among them Aristotle, Adam Smith, and John Stuart Mill. If my experience in corporate seminars is any evidence, I have found that most of the executives I talk to appreciate and often grow enthusiastic about the life of ideas that is inevitably a part of any reflective enterprise. Business ethics is not just solving problems or moralizing about the company code; it is, first of all, an essential exercise in self-understanding. And it is that mix of self-understanding, on-the-job concern, and intellectual adventure that I have tried to capture here, and I believe that old Aristotle, even though he didn't like business, could not but approve.

I

BUSINESS MYTHS AND METAPHORS: VICES PARADING AS VIRTUES

1

Bonfire of the Virtues

The social responsibility of business is to increase its profits.

MILTON FRIEDMAN
"The Social Responsibility of Business"

In the ensuing anarchy the bad drove out the good, the big drove out the small, and the brawn drove out the brains. There was a single trait common to denizens of the back row, though I doubt it ever occurred to anyone: They sensed that they needed to shed whatever refinements of personality and intellect they had brought with them to Salomon Brothers.

MICHAEL LEWIS, *Liar's Poker* [1]

According to Milton Friedman, the trading floor on the forty-first floor of Salomon Brothers must have been the very epitome of social responsibility. The company was, by almost any accounting, one of the most profitable firms on Wall Street, and the financial industry it so well represented became the paradigm of American business. Thousands of the best and brightest college graduates, M.B.A.'s, and other young wizards applied for every single position on the trading floor and in the equally lucrative investment banking business next door. Those who succeeded were amply rewarded. Young traders barely out of college made hundreds of thousands of dollars, in some cases millions. They were not breaking any laws. Indeed, they were doing just what they had been taught to do, with the enthusiastic approval of society—at least, as demonstrated by that one indisputable monetary measure with which this society usually seeks to show its approval.

And yet, with the benefit of only a few years' hindsight (and a fiscal crisis in the astronomical thirteen-figure range) it is obvious that something was very wrong on the forty-first floor. Perhaps the harsh case can be made out that these young traders were in effect selling out their country, undermining the securities industry and the monetary

---

1. I am indebted to Mr. Lewis for his witty exposé of his brief life on Wall Street and will refer to his account freely in the pages to follow.

system while their colleagues in investment banking were developing strategies to make life insecure and unbearable in virtually every other industry. There is no doubt that the milder case can be made that they produced little or nothing and ultimately served no one but themselves and their firm. As Lewis puts it, "never before have so many unskilled twenty-year-olds made so much money in so little time. . . . There has never before been such a fantastic exception to the rule of the market-place that one takes out no more than one puts in."[2] By any measure, the Salomon Brothers traders were overpaid for what they did and for what they contributed to society. Theirs was a travesty of the age-old business wisdom that only hard work and perseverance lead to success. They provided living disproof of Adam Smith's celebrated teaching, that individual initiative, even if only self-interested, will lead to general prosperity. Smith was talking about grocers and pin manufacturers— people who *produced* something for consumption and, however motivated, *contributed* to the larger society. He wasn't talking about institutionalized greed or speculative boom-building. He wasn't talking about the trading room floor.

Now it can be argued that I am being unfair; that, whatever the motives or the character of the traders, capitalism requires capital. Innovation and development require investment, and the bonds that provide investment capital must be bought and therefore sold. The traders thus provide a vital function and, as Adam Smith famously said of his grocer, it does not matter that they do not do it out of benevolence or love of their fellow man. But it is a slippery argument from such truisms to the activity in the trading room. I want to be very careful in delineating my diagnosis here. I am by no means attacking the financial industry as such. I am not disputing the importance of corporate bonds to raise money for product development or a new factory or of municipal bonds to raise money for a growing city's new airport or improved water treatment system. Nor am I questioning the broker who actually brings together venture capital and a bright young idea and then takes a piece of the successful product. But I am questioning the ethics of a system that becomes wholly abstracted from society, productivity, and people, a "game" in itself. After all, what does a bond trader do? Kurt Vonnegut tells us: "There is a magic moment, during which a man who has surrendered a treasure, and during which the man who is about to receive it has not yet done so. An alert [bond trader] will make that moment his own, possessing the treasure for a magic microsecond, taking a little of it and passing it on."[3] Those takings are substantial, proportionate to the sum and unrelated to time, effort, skill, or service. The Greek philosopher Aristotle, writing over two thousand years be-

---

2. Michael Lewis, *Liar's Poker* (New York: Norton, 1989), p. 9.
3. Quoted in Lewis, *Liar's Poker*, p. 34.

fore Wall Street, called people who engaged in such activities "parasites." Capitalism may require capital, but it does not require, much less should it be defined by, the parasites it inevitably attracts.

Moralists may lament that the trading game, like so much else in the Eighties, was little more than a display of rampant, unadulterated greed. But I think that the story deserves a deeper interpretation than that. Wall Street has always been described as sharklike (by Henry Adams in the nineteenth century, for instance, and by his grandfather in the century before that), but Wall Street has not always been taken as the paradigm of business activity and business thinking. Indeed, the financial community and its analysts were somewhat shocked when the economy as a whole stayed quite stable during and after the so-called "crash" of October 1987. What conception of business (as well as changes in the policies of the Fed, for example) had to become prevalent in order for the financial economy and the traders on Wall Street to attract so much attention? How did we so shift our attention from the classic business virtues of productivity and prosperity to the dubious virtues of the trading floor? Moreover, it is not as if the trading floor attracted any particular breed of amoral monsters. There were no congenital Midas-like symptoms evident in most of the trainee traders-to-be. They were, like most just-graduated students, happy to have a new job, anxious to fit in, ready to learn the rules and to take whatever rewards were appropriate to a job well done. What they learned in training and on the job, however, was a rather spectacular form of self-serving irresponsibility. What they learned to do, in a phrase, was to "make money."

The large questions raised by the success of these young (and the not-so-young) traders have to do with the very nature of business and success in business. By any measure, these young college graduates did not *earn* what they made, no matter how skillful they became at manipulating the market and their customers. As Lewis puts it, "I felt not like I was going to work but rather picking up my winnings at a lottery."[4] It is not obvious that they made any significant contribution to society in their work in return for these "lottery winnings"; indeed, it has been persuasively argued that they cost their country billions and, with the help of an ironically "pro-business" federal government, threatened its preeminent place in the financial world. But worst of all—as the backlash against the Yuppie phenomenon has made publicly evident, the success of these young traders represented and richly rewarded the wrong virtues and values in business—among them a kind of self-righteous selfishness, a purely monetary measure of worth, a fraudulent celebration of risk-taking (with "O.P.M."),[5] a gamesman's approach to

4. Ibid., p. x.
5. The prevalence of the phrase "Other People's Money," condensed into such a convenient acronym, says in itself all that has really to be said about the relationship between classic capitalism and the so-called capitalism of Wall Street.

life devoid of interest in the impact on others outside of the game, and a kind of crass ruthlessness that came to be seen as a hallmark of success. Lewis describes some of his most successful colleagues: "Some of [them] were truly awful human beings. They sacked others to promote themselves. They harassed women. They humiliated trainees. They didn't have customers. They had victims. . . . Bad guys did not suffer comeuppance in Act V on the forty-first floor. They flourished."[6]

When the Scottish gentleman Adam Smith first proposed the virtues of free enterprise two hundred years ago, could he have imagined such creatures as the beneficiaries of his system? When Milton Friedman so praised the profit motive and excoriated those who insist on social responsibility, could he have been thinking about the forty-first floor? Indeed, what must he have thought of the popular movie *Wall Street*, in which the profit motive and social responsibility are shown to be at such odds?[7] And when those several presidents proudly proclaimed that "the business of America is business," are these the people they had in mind?

ETHICS AND EXCELLENCE: BUSINESS AND THE VIRTUES

> Once again, modern business is paying the price for conceiving of itself as representing an abstract species of "economic man," rather than as men and women engaged in a fully human activity.
>   IRVING KRISTOL, "Ethics Anyone? Or Morals?"

It is business as "a fully human activity" that is my concern in this book. There has always been the danger, anticipated by Adam Smith and threatened by Karl Marx, that overzealous business activity would narrow our focus and bring out the worst in us, but the 1980s have displayed a degree of greed and an obsession with financial fetishism that would have stunned even the most militant Marxist. Such quaint notions as integrity and virtue have been put in the back files, and such macho mock values as ruthlessness and raw ambition have been promoted to the status of ideals. Thus Lewis describes the ideal of the

---

6. Ibid., p. 69.

7. Friedman does not praise the pursuit of profits without qualification, of course. He plainly states that one should "make as much money as possible while conforming to the basic rules of society, both those embodied in law and those embodied in ethical custom" *New York Times*, Sept. 13, 1970). But it is precisely some of those "ethical customs" of contemporary business that should concern us, along with the practices that support and sanction them. As for the law, we might note that the acclaimed movie *Wall Street* cheats, for moralistic effect: the dark figure of Gordon Gekko doesn't stop at legitimate financial power-mongering—which presumably would fit Friedman's guidelines to a *T*: he has to step over the line to insider trading in order to legally deserve his comeuppance. In the drama of Michael Milken, life again imitates art.

trading floor: "A new employee, once he reached the trading floor, was handed a pair of telephones. He went on-line almost immediately. If he could make millions of dollars come out of those phones, he became that most revered of all species: a Big Swinging Dick. . . . Everyone wanted to be a Big Swinging Dick, even the women."[8]

To put the Aristotelean thesis of this book with merely quoted crudity, I want to argue that it is no virtue in business to be a Big Swinging Dick, and the adolescent conception of business that would support such a notion is not a conception of business that is worth defending or retaining. Business, I want to insist in language that is as old as civilization itself, is an essential part of our culture just because it depends upon and presupposes the virtues and that basic sense of community and minimal mutual trust without which no activities of production or exchange or mutual benefit would be possible. It is not only Tom Peters and a few fellow cheerleaders who insist that ethics is essential to excellence and that business requires integrity and the virtues. That is the unsung story of the history of business itself. Capitalism has succeeded not with brute strength and not just because it has made many people rich but because it has produced responsible citizens and—however unevenly—prosperous communities. It cannot long tolerate a conception of business that focuses solely on income and vulgarity and ignores the traditional virtues of responsibility, community, and integrity.

There are other nasty things being said about traders (Tom Wolfe has said or displayed most of them in his *Bonfire of the Vanities*) but what is so shocking and revealing is the extent to which some of Lewis's traders are happy to display and boast about their own vices. Male high-school lockerroom sensibilities are elevated as golden keys to success. Sentence-clogging profanity is employed as a mark of sophistication. Contempt for education is conflated with wisdom, and contempt for the client is converted into a strategy for doing business. Money alone becomes the measure. But it is not just in Lewis's book or in the trading world that we find this one-dimensional attitude. We see it in our students, and one reads it in the popular press. The pure pursuit of profit (formerly known as the "sin of avarice") has been generalized. And somehow this false ideal of business got us sidetracked from the productivity and the prosperity that Adam Smith and Andrew Carnegie bragged about and led us into a cynicism and vulgarity that exceed even the accusations leveled by Marx and Engels. Business life is reduced to the thrill of the market and its "lottery winnings." There is no pride in one's products (they are just new and better instruments for making money), no sense of dignity or "service" in one's services. Indeed, service to and [in the barnyard sense] the "servicing" of one's

8. Lewis, *Liar's Poker*, p. 46.

customers become almost indistinguishable.[9] True, businessmen have long been chastized for their lack of finesse and public spiritedness, but they used to fight this image, even becoming aristocratic philanthropists and reform-minded politicians in the process. Never before have they endorsed it with a kind of pride, as if all insensitivity and vulgarity is not only excused but admired if enough cash is coming in the door.

Twenty-four hundred years ago, the great Greek philosopher Aristotle attacked virtually all commercial activities and the people who prospered from them. He thought it unnatural to make money from money and established the prejudice against usury (that is, any such profitable financial activity) that lasted for two millennia. Living in an agrarian, militaristic, slave-supported society, Aristotle, too, readily concluded that profit-oriented commerce—is opposed to mere exchange—was both antisocial and unethical, not to mention undignified. Aristotle's mistake (with two-millennia hindsight) was to generalize his indictment of certain superfluous and non-productive financial practices to virtually all of what we call "business." It is even more of a mistake, however, to dismiss Aristotle as ignorant of and irrelevant to the contemporary business world.[10] He anticipated, centuries before there were investment bankers, bond traders, Fannie or Ginnie Maes, the source of some of the worst ills of our economy. True, he did not understand the notion of a productive economy, and he mistakenly thought that all profit had to be exploitation or theft. But in his attack on an archaic form of commerce, he provided the ethical grounds that are still assumed by most people in business today. In fact, his charges are especially appropriate to our own high-flying financial paradigms, where business is wrongly reduced to making a profit, making money, any way that one can. But this is, as anyone outside the game can see, a reductio ad absurdum of what had to be a bad idea to begin with. If that were business, then business indeed would have no proper place in civilized society, except perhaps as a marginal entertainment, like dog racing or roller derby. But business is, first of all, social interaction and a sophisticated sense of cooperation, not vulgar competition. It is productivity and not mere profit seeking. It is an essential part of our society and not a merely parasitic or marginal activity, a self-enclosed game of concern only to its "players."

I am using the trading floor as a stepping stone into the ethical problems that face business and people in business today not because I think that such activities are wrong and not because I personally or morally object to the idea of young hotshots making millions of dollars but rather

9. For the agriculturally naive, see John Barth's *Giles Goat-Boy* (New York: Fawcett, 1974), esp. p. 235. Hint: "There is no term for 'service' that is not obscene, clinical, legalistic, ironic, euphemistic or periphrastic."

10. Anthony Flew, "The Profit Motive," *Ethics* 86 (1976): 312–22. See also Denis Collins, "Aristotle and Business," *Journal of Business Ethics* 6 (1987): 567–72.

because the promotion of the trading floor scenario and its even more luxurious counterparts in the plush offices of world financiers as *the* paradigm of business seems to me to betray just the sort of conceptual drift that has infected the business world in recent decades. It is betrayed in the idea that business is a game, a kind of gambling in which ruthlessness, "guts," and risk are primary virtues, in which "making money" is the one important virtue. It is betrayed in the amused (as opposed to outraged or disgusted) tones of voice in which a few amoral monsters are portrayed as some sort of corporate heroes. It is betrayed in the inhuman theoretical invention of *Homo economicus,* the economist's notion of a "person" who has no attribute other than "financial utility maximization," that is, making money as an end in itself. It is betrayed in the paradigm of the voracious trader, alone with his or her telephones, a voice devoid of personality and full of (shall we call it) salesmanship—pushing the product, skimming off the commission, making money in volumes. It is betrayed in the equally amoral and inhuman image of the giant, impersonal corporation, whose only purpose in its purely legal existence is to enrich its stockholders (who are, in turn, nothing other than *Homini economici*). It is betrayed in a world in which the virtues have lost their place, in which the sense of community has been sacrificed to the scramble for self-interest, in which the old ideal of doing good for others and getting rewarded in return has been replaced by the con job, the hope for something for nothing, the parasite.

The making of money pure and simple is not the culmination of business life, much less the fulfillment of one's social responsibilities. The very way we *think* about business has somehow gone very wrong, not just in its details but at its very conception. The trading floor may provide an extreme case, but it is the kind extremity that appears when an already distorted perspective is forced to face up to itself. This book, accordingly, is a battle in the war against those myths and metaphors and other forms of conceptual isolationism that lead us to think about business as a game—or worse, as a jungle or a war for survival—and neglect or abandon those virtues and that sense of shared community without which business would not be possible. Some of the metaphors I want to explode are extremely sophisticated and much in vogue—for instance, the recent rush to "social choice" and "game theory" as the key to economics and business practice, the presumption of acquisitive individualism and the fashionable notion of a "social contract" that tentatively binds all of us individuals together.[11] This takes us to the very heart of American thinking, of course, as Alexis de Toqueville pointed

11. A few recent examples: Michael Keeley, *A Social Contract Theory of Organizations* (Notre Dame: University of Notre Dame Press, 1988); Tom Donaldson, *International Business Theory* (New York: Oxford University Press, 1990); Thomas Dunfee, "Business Ethics and Extant Social Contracts," *Business Ethics Quarterly* (Jan. 1991)

out over a century and a half ago, and it has manifestations that are extremely sophisticated and beneficial. But it also implies an economic conception of mutual competition and self-interest in life that runs directly against the bonds of community and the notion of the public interest, except as an abstract afterthought or a purely theoretical promise. Of course, when competition gets rough, there is an all-too-familiar tendency for us to lose our sense of purpose and perspective, and then primitive competitive metaphors become almost unavoidable. But, contrary to the rhetoric of "competitiveness" such situations and circumstances are not the basis of the business world and do not provide the paradigm of business thinking. Business is defined first of all by its own sense of community and purpose, and that purpose is the satisfaction of public demand, the introduction of innovative, more efficient, more cost-effective products to fill a need and the optimal, ongoing relation between producer and consumer. Competition is a secondary relation, effective in assuring an optimal market, to be sure, but is not what business itself is about. So, too, commodity trading has proved to be a brilliant scheme for making money, but it should not be conflated with the serious business of raising capital for investment or protecting the hard-earned savings and retirement accounts of America's productive workers. A business becomes unethical not just when it violates the law or the public trust but also when it forgets its point and purpose.

The practical aim of this book is not to attack business or corporate life or to promote radical reforms that would undermine rather than improve the free enterprise system. Its aim is to reemphasize some very old ways of thinking that have gotten all but lost in the contemporary corporate world and provide a conceptual antidote to the self-destructive thinking and behavior of some of our best corporations. No change in markets or circumstances can explain what corporate America is putting itself through these days, but an examination of the myths and metaphors that guide so much of our behavior can do so. In place of the brutally competitive and disruptive imagery and narrowly "bottom line"–oriented thinking that is so pervasive these days, I want to underline the supreme importance of stability in the organization, to encourage a sense of community, which the best corporations already recognize (at least in their public relations), and to reinforce the importance of integrity in the individual. The concept of ethics and excellence is an attempt to put these virtues of cooperation and integrity together again, as Aristotle did so many years ago: a good, stable, harmonious, and successful corporation with good, secure, happy, and satisfied people working together. I agree that it sounds like a Mary Poppins as well as an Aristotelean vision of a rough-and-tumble world of corporate business, but it is certainly a promising alternative to the bloodletting images that we are now turning into self-fulfilling prophecies.[12] Don't we deserve—and certainly want—something better?

My uncompromising thesis is that business ethics, rightly conceived, is just good business. This does not mean that virtue always prospers, but it does mean that the integrity of the corporation and of the individual within the corporation is the essential ingredient in the overall viability and vitality of the business world. What we call "success" demands both ethics and excellence, not simply good fortune in the pursuit of wealth. It is important for business to encourage integrity, and "selling out"—a now archaic term that may just be coming back into style—marks the boundaries of that integrity. I do not want to idealize the free enterprise system but rather defend its values and virtues against its self-misunderstanding and self-abuse. I want to distinguish the point and purpose of our economic system from what it merely permits, and I want to resurrect old Adam Smith and the classic economists with no nonsense about "greed is good" and no pretense about economic life in an ethical vacuum. It sounds trite, but it is time to remind ourselves that prosperity for all and not just for a few really is the purpose and the justification of business life and that there is an assumption of shared public life and the social virtues without which business would still be— as it was for thousands of years in Western civilization—a marginal and largely contemptible set of activities confined, for the most part, to the outskirts of proper society.

2

Macho Myths and Metaphors

Our concepts structure what we perceive, how we get around the
world, and how we relate to other people. . . . If we are right in
suggesting that our conceptual system is largely metaphorical, then
the way we think, what we experience, and what we do every day
is very much a matter of metaphor.

GEORGE LAKOFF AND MARK JOHNSON,
Metaphors We Live By

Every discipline or profession has its own self-glorifying vocabulary.
Politicians bask in the concept of "public service" even while they pursue personal power and exploit the fears and prejudices of their constituents; lawyers defend our "rights" on a handsome contingency basis
as they lead us through a thicket of regulations and liabilities of their
own making; professors describe what they do in the noble language
of "truth and knowledge" even if they spend most of their time and
energy battling each other for status in exquisitely vicious campus politics. But in the case of business the self-glorifying language is notoriously unflattering. What we often hear is a confusion of wealth with
success, an obsession with "the bottom line" and "the profit motive,"
and a sequence of bloody metaphors invoking images of Darwinian
jungles and guerrilla warfare. If one listened only to the supposedly
self-glorifying rhetoric, one might well come away with the idea that
business life is a brutal battle for survival, devoid of rules, trust, or
courtesies in which mercy and mutual consideration (not to mention
altruism and concern for the public good) are sheer folly, Or, at best,
one might come to think that the aim of business life is to join an exciting game, take risks and be challenged, get there ahead of the other
guy, and, above all, "have fun." (It is worth nothing that the Japanese
don't have an exact translation for our notion of "having fun," and
after adolescence one supposedly learns that risks and challenges can
be foolish as well as invigorating, wasteful as well as productive.) Or,
more cynically, business life presents itself as a grueling necessity, without ultimate point or purpose ("Well, I've gotta make a living some-

how."). What is striking is the lack of vision, the failure to see the "big picture"—except of course in flights of rhetoric about "the magic of the market" and "the blessings of free enterprise" that have very little to do with the actual on-the-job experience of most corporate executives and employees. In the many such descriptions of business life, we hear surprisingly little reference to products or services or prosperity. We read and hear about deadlines, office politics, moral mazes, "tough" and sadistic managers, carrot versus stick theories of motivation, market pressures and keeping ahead of the competition, threatened layoffs, avoiding pink slips, possible promotions, getting ahead, arranging one's furniture for power and dressing for success, one-minute managing, and, of course, the omnipresent bottom line. It sometimes seems as if productivity and general prosperity have been reduced to mere means to profitability, rather than the other way around. And as the larger vision gets lost from view, people in business become so entrenched in their individual and increasingly isolated positions and ambitions that they lose sight of both the purpose of the organizations they work for and their own purposes in working for them. Needless to say, this is neither healthy and conducive to happiness and fulfillment for them, nor is it healthy and conducive to cooperation and efficiency in the corporation.[1]

The first line of attack in any concern about ethics in business must be against those images and metaphors that blind and govern so much of our thinking. Metaphors are not just, as one of our more popular publications puts it, "more picturesque speech." We live by and through metaphors. To repeat Lakoff and Johnson's view, "Our concepts structure what we perceive, how we get around the world, and how we relate to other people. . . . The way we think, what we experience, and what we do every day is very much a matter of metaphor." But if this is so, we should be horrified by the metaphors that are the currency of everyday business conversation. Immediately following the stunning 1991 military success in Kuwait, no one was surprised that *within hours* the ever-fluid jargon of business shifted into unabashed wartime rhetoric ("mass and surprise," "taking by storm').[2] We hear again and again about business as a "jungle," as a fight for "survival," a "dog-eat-dog world," a game defined by its "winners and losers." A casual glance during

1. Cf. Andrew Carnegie, writing in 1889: "The poor enjoy what the rich could not before afford. What were the luxuries have now become the necessities of life. The laborer has now more comforts than the farmer had a few generations ago. The farmer has more luxuries than the landlord had, and is more richly clad and better housed. The landlord has books and pictures rarer, and appointments more artistic, than the King could then obtain" ("Wealth," *North American Review,* June 1889). One might question some of Carnegie's generalities, and one should certainly challenge his defense of today's enormous inequalities between rich and poor, but the basic claim is that prosperity is the goal of the free enterprise system. Business at its best is also philanthropy writ large.

2. "The Gulf School of Management," *Newsweek,* Apr. 1, 1991, pp. 34–35.

takeoff through the executive-oriented advertisements in any airline or business magazine should be enough to convince anyone how pervasive these images and metaphors are. The concept of competition is used to assault, to terrify, and, of course, to sell products. One recent advertisement (for a telephone beeper) portrays the shadows of a wolf and a rabbit on the wall behind two executives (the executive who didn't buy the beeper is the rabbit). Indeed, if one believed these self-descriptions of business activity as Darwinian survivalism and jungle warfare one would be quite properly justified in outlawing all business activity as brutal and uncivilized behavior that no society should have to tolerate. (It is, of course, just such descriptions of business that the most hostile enemies of business have utilized so effectively, throughout much of Western history, to ban or regulate business activity.) I have often marveled at the abyss I observe in so much of the corporate world, between the polite, friendly faces and proud, cooperative conversations that I see and hear whenever I enter the offices of a successful corporation and the truly frightening images that get thrown around once the conversation gets more free-floating and abstract. "It's a jungle out there" I hear all the time, and "It's kill or be killed." Of course, none of this is to deny the sometimes vicious political in-fighting that goes on in almost every organization, nor is it to deny that in the business world not every company survives. But bankruptcy today is rarely fatal, and however horrible six months of unemployment may be it hardly compares with the war victim or refugee images invoked on its behalf.

How we look at what we do has a lot to do with how we do, and I would argue that much of the infighting within corporations and many of the casualties of corporate competition can be laid at the feet of the malevolent images that we impose on business and on ourselves. The word "ethics" refers somewhat ambiguously to both a set of theories and reflections about our behavior and to that behavior as such. Needless to say, the one influences the other, and as our theories and reflections try to be true to our actual intentions and activities, our intentions and activities themselves are shaped and given direction by what we think about them, what we think we are doing, what we think we ought to be doing, and what we would like to think we are doing. How a person thinks about business—as a ruthless competition for profits or a cooperative enterprise the aim of which is the prosperity of the community—preshapes much of his or her behavior and attitudes toward fellow employees or executives, competitors, customers, and the surrounding community. Thus, it is not as if business life and business talk are devoid of philosophy, whether or not this philosophy is articulated as such ("Well, let me tell you my philosophy . . ."), nor is business devoid of any conception of ethics and the virtues. But as has so often been commented and criticized, the philosophy that makes its rounds over business lunches and onto the business pages of many local papers is appalling. The virtues most often celebrated as business virtues too typically belong in a locker room if not in a treatise on Darwinism. Twenty years ago, Alfred Carr made his name once and for all in business ethics circles when he published one of the two most often refuted articles in the field (the other being Milton Friedman's infamous and more sophisticated "Social Responsibility" essay), arguing at length that business is a lot like poker and (therefore) does not follow the rules of ordinary morality.[3] But as the infuriated comments poured into the *Harvard Business Review*, it became apparent that the object of indignation was not Carr's game analogy but rather his choice of games. Poker is viewed as disreputable and primarily a vehicle for gambling. Had Carr chosen football, he probably would have won unanimity (though he would have failed to create such a controversy, obviously his intent). Indeed, one would almost surmise that the competition for the best business metaphors is akin to a barroom contest to find the least flattering, most offensive, and unethical image for business life and the business world. As Karl Marx might have said to the corporate world of today, "With friends like that, who needs Marxists?"

In the first third of this book, I want to examine and reject those metaphors that cast business in such a bad light and encourage such hostile, uncaring, and ultimately destructive behavior. Some of these are quite crude and explode as soon as they are seen for what they are, but others are much more sophisticated and built into the very fabric of our current theorizing. Some (such as "the profit motive") can be summarized in a slogan; others don't even have names—for instance, that obscure but effective form of self-defeating motivation that I call "abstract greed." Some seem not to be metaphors at all, notably our uncompromising emphasis on the importance of competition (which in turn gets captured in some of our most vulgar self-images) and some seem to lie at the very basis of our conception of ourselves as individuals, as if any alternative notion would have to be anti-individualistic, authoritarian, or worse. One metaphor in particular—what I will call the game metaphor—forms the basis of almost all economic and business thinking today, and accordingly I will devote considerable time to putting it in its place and, where necessary, abusing it. But the point of all this, throughout this discussion, will be my intention to shift the focus, from business as a ruthlessly selfish and greedy enterprise to business as a healthy aspect of a prosperous community. These terms may seem overstated, but I hope the following reflections on our current self-conceptions will make them seem, if anything, embarrassingly accurate.

3. Alfred Carr, "Is Business Bluffing Ethical?" *Harvard Business Review* (Jan.–Feb. 1968).

"IT'S A JUNGLE OUT THERE!"

Among the most damaging myths and metaphors in business talk are those macho Darwinian concepts of "survival of the fittest" and "it's a jungle out there." The underlying idea, of course, is that life in business is competitive, and it isn't always fair. But that obvious pair of points is very different from the "dog-eat-dog" and "every [man] for [him]self" imagery that is routine in the business world. It is true that business is and must be competitive, but it is not true that it need be cutthroat or cannabalistic or that "one has to do whatever it takes to survive." Of course, some of the animal metaphors are charming—an occasional boss is a "teddy bear" and a tough negotiator is a "tiger"— but most of them are demeaning. Employees, executives, and competitors are described as snakes-in-the-grass, rats, and a wide variety of rodents. Corporations in turn are modeled as fishtanks, snakepits, and catfights, and sometimes it is the botanical image of the jungle itself that gets invoked. But besides being bad biology and undoubtedly unfair to the animals, the jungle metaphors are particularly bad for business, which is (or should be) anything but uncivilized, devoid of rules, and ruled by the killer instinct. However competitive a particular industry may be, it always rests on a foundation of shared interests and mutually agreed-upon rules of conduct, and the competition takes place not in a jungle but in a society that it presumably both serves and depends upon. Business life, unlike life in the mythological jungle, is first of all fundamentally *cooperative*. It is only with the bounds of mutually shared concerns that competition is possible. And quite the contrary to the "everyone for himself" metaphor, business almost always involves large cooperative and mutually trusting groups, not only corporations themselves but networks of suppliers, service people, customers, and investors. And as for the view that the office itself is a jungle (in other words, it's a jungle *in here,* not out there), that state of affairs is virtually always the mark of the very worst kind of manager (typically characterized as a "beast" or a "bitch") and the worst kind of organization (or the lack of it). Such animal taskmasters may boast (usually falsely) of their efficiency, but much more likely their departments are poisoned by fear and resentment and stagnant from the resulting excess of caution and hostility. (That, at least, is a quite natural reaction.)

Competition is essential to capitalism, but to misunderstand this as unbridled competition is to undermine ethics and misunderstand the nature of competition too. Indeed, it is not only to misunderstand business but it is probably to misunderstand Darwin and jungles as well. However red in tooth and claw the steppes of Asia or the plains of Africa or the small mammalian communities in our own backyards may be, one of the primary principles of evolution seems to be cooperation, from the simplest multicelled organisms to the seemingly ineradicable colonies of ants, termites, and bees, the efficient packs and herds of carnivores and their prey, and, not to be left out of this impressive sociobiological portrait, ourselves. It is a point often made by both poets and biologists: a *Homo sapiens* deprived of a community and a culture is a pathetic, virtually helpless animal.[4] That comparatively gigantic brain is of relatively little value without the hand-me-downs of successive generations and the ability to cooperate and organize through language. It would be odd indeed if one of the most dramatic contributions to human evolution was a business miniworld in which the accumulated benefits of 10 million years (the reader will pardon this anthropocentric view of evolution) have been set aside in favor of a self-destructive intraspecies competition that most of the animal world has more wisely set aside.

"THE BRUTAL BATTLES OF BUSINESS"

Similar to the Darwinian metaphor but even more macho and more in tune with the collective nature of most human aggression and competition is the familiar "war" metaphor that one hears in so many corporate boardrooms. It has often been pointed out that the hierarchical structure of most corporations not only resembles but is modeled after a military chain of command. Military ethicist Anthony Hartle suggests that the military perspective and consequently military metaphors are intrinsically nationalistic, alarmist, pessimistic, conservative, and authoritarian.[5] In corporate America, company chauvinism replaces nationalism, but the employees are often referred to as "troops" in managerial meetings and competitors become "the enemy." Obedience is often rewarded in spite of its stupidity. Courses of action are typically called "plans of attack," "battle strategies," and "compaigns." Cash reserves become "war chests" and, in the current climate of "hostile takeovers," such reserves (and much more besides) are deflected from production and operations into the metaphorical "battle" for retention of the company. (Unfortunately, metaphorical battles can be very expensive, with a great many casualties outside of the inner circle of corporate raiders and golden parachutists.) But doing business is not a "battle," and business competition, even when the survival of the company is at stake, should not be confused with the mutual destructiveness of war. The object of business competition is to produce the best and (usually) the least expensive products and services. The point is not to

4. E.g., the anthropologist Clifford Geertz, *The Interpretation of Cultures* (New York: Basic Books, 1975).

5. Anthony E. Hartle, *Moral Issues in Military Decision-Making* (Lawrence: University Press of Kansas, 1989) with reference to Bengt Abrahamsson, *Military Professionalism and Political Power* (Beverly Hills, Calif.: Sage, 1972).

wipe out one's competitors. For business competition to make sense, the larger interests of the consumer and the society must be kept in mind. They and not the battleground or the war room are the test and determinant of success. Granted, it is hard to think quite so holistically when one's job is on the line and one's future is uncertain, but the difference between keeping (however faintly) the larger picture in mind and not doing so may well be the difference between, on the one hand, experiencing the rigors of competition and the time and energy it requires as part and parcel of one's proper productive role in the world and, on the other, finding the whole enterprise to be meaningless and being tempted by one of those all-too-readily-available illegalities. After all, isn't all fair in love and war? But the answer to this rhetorical question is an emphatic No, and since ancient times war has been limited by chivalric canons and other codes of honor.[6] If doing business does on occasion seem like going to war, even in the height of battle business presupposes a certain amount of mutual trust and cooperation, the honoring of contracts, respect for law and the rules of fair competition, no matter how vigorous the competition may be. (One might note that, when we really believe in what we are doing, business is a lot more like love than war.) But the virtues of business are not military virtues, despite the importance of obedience and the onset of occasional hostility.

"THE GREAT MACHINE OF CAPITALISM"

The machine metaphor is left over from the eighteenth century, when Adam Smith wrote his great treatise on economics and virtually every theorist in every discipline was still under the spell of the genius Isaac Newton, whose theories in physics had revolutionized modern thinking only a century before. Philosophers were trying to develop models of society that resembled the mechanisms of Newton's theories. Adam Smith's best friend David Hume tried to develop a theory of human nature according to the same mechanical model that explained the motions of the stars and the machinery of nature. Of course, it was also about this time that the industrial revolution was beginning in Britain, and machines were quite properly perceived as man-made miracles. The famous theologian William Paley proved the existence of God by drawing the analogy between the wondrous design of nature and the carefully designed machinery of a watch, arguing that just as we would assume that such a wondrous mechanism discovered on a deserted beach must be the product of some inventor, so too must we conclude that the wonders of nature presuppose a divine designer. But, theology and

6. E.g., among the ancient Greeks, the early Hebrew tribes, in ancient China and in the Hindu *Book of Manu*, in the teachings of Augustine and later Aquinas, Grotius, and Suarez. See Hartle, *Moral Issues in Military Decision Making*, pp. 57ff.

analogy aside, the impact of the argument wholly turned on the fascination with machinery, and so too the dream of the social philosophers and our first modern economists was to design a society that operated with order and efficiency. Adam Smith's economy, so considered, was a giant mechanism—the mechanism of the market—in which all of the component parts (individual producers and consumers doing deals and making exchanges on a voluntary basis) fit together in a most efficient and productive way, whether or not the "parts" themselves had any idea of their role or function.

Adam Smith hardly concerned himself about corporations ("joint-stock companies"), but it is easy to see how the machine metaphor would still appeal to corporate planners and managers, even two centuries after the metaphor has lost its caché in virtually every other line of thinking. (Indeed, even in physics and mechanics the machine metaphor has been replaced by more organic and holistic metaphors.) Corporations are supposed to "run smoothly." The parts are all supposed to work together, with the "gears well-oiled." Creaks and breakdowns are to be avoided, and the question of "fuel" is all important. The ideal is "efficiency," a notion borrowed for business directly from Newtonian physics. Employees (whether they know it or not) are cogs in a great machine, just as all of us and every corporation too are cogs in an even greater machine, the national (and now international) economy, the efficiency and operation of which can be measured by those mind-boggling numbers released every month by this or that government bureau or department. Thus managers speak quite freely (and without any sense that they are perpetrating dangerous poetry) about "greasing the wheel," and employees and managers become "human resources"—along with raw materials and fuel for the machine.

Today, of course, our favorite machine images and consequently our favorite metaphors tend to involve computers and software rather than the mechanisms of the industrial age. "Input" replaces knowledge and conversation, and all plans become "programs." Every human relation becomes an "interface," and we begin to describe the workings of our own minds in the computer language of memory banks, downtime, glitches, data searches, and so on. Computers, of course, have special utility and fascination as management tools, but what was once true of the old machines continues to be true (at least for the foreseeable future) of computers: they do only what we tell them to do: "garbage in, garbage out." That is not the way to think about business, as easy and refreshing as it may sometimes be to do so. After all, the nice thing about machines is that (when they work) they just do what they are supposed to. They don't complain. They don't get bored. They don't have frustrated ambitions. They don't get hurt. They can always be repaired or replaced. They don't have to be talked to or, worse, listened to with sympathy. They aren't, in other words, human, which is just what managers, employees, customers, and even corporations assuredly are.

The tempting virtue of efficiency and the appeal of the machine metaphor are thus limited and eliminated by what they leave out of the picture. Efficiency, it has often been pointed out (for example, by Peter Drucker), is not the same as *effectiveness,* and the latter, unlike the former, presupposes complex goals and purposes rather than simple measurable functions.[7] Before we praise a machine, we want to know what it does. (One can imagine some "Rube Goldberg" contraption with an enormously high efficiency rating but an utterly pointless product.) And of course machines can produce only what they are designed to produce, and as such the corporation is in the odd metaphorical position (much beloved by metaphysicians and theologians) of being its own designer. Innovation is left out of the machine metaphor. Adjustment and adaption to new circumstances, too, are beyond the range of most machines. A speedboat on the beach is nothing but a potential litter basket, and a car underwater is a deathtrap, not transportation. The inner workings of most corporations and of the business world as such are far more flexible and organic than the machine metaphor would suggest and such organic metaphors replaced most mechanism metaphors in the past century. Indeed, the forgotten virtue of the modern bureaucracy (itself a metaphor) is that it recognizes not only the function but the humanity of the individuals who make up our institutions. The worst single feature of the machinelike "cog" and "efficiency" metaphors is that they are obviously inhuman and offensive. Employees are not replaceable or intersubstitutable parts (an image of labor that Adam Smith sometimes took too seriously). People do not just serve purposes; they also *have* purposes of their own.

Corporations are far less like machines and far more like communities (one of our very oldest metaphors) than much business thinking would suggest. Indeed, we are just starting to realize that efficiency is often purchased at the expense of innovation, and a mechanical way of thinking about organizations is a sure route to stagnation and poor employee relations. One does not consult a cog or a gear wheel in deciding what it should do or how it should be treated, a sure cause of resentment of the part of employees. Management involves negotiation and understanding, not just manipulation and adjustment. Besides, it is only possible to conceive of a machine by *not* being part of it, and those who think of business or businesses in this way are inevitably outside of the very mechanisms they seek to understand and control. As tempting as it may be to think of other people or institutions as machines, it is virtually impossible to conceive of oneself as a machine or as part of a machine. We are, first and always, people, and business

7. Peter Drucker, *Management* (New York: Harper and Row, 1974).

if it deserves to be taken seriously at all is not just a machine or a mechanism or even an "instrument" but rather a system of activities designed and practiced by human beings who have much to gain (and much to lose).

THE GAME OF BUSINESS

Wars are brutal and jungles are uncivilized. Machines are inhuman and, besides, has everyone forgotten that business, above all, can be *fun?* Business competition leads quite naturally to an emphasis on "winning," but we've gotten more civilized in our competitive imagery and we now realize (how did we ever fail to realize) that people don't function mechanically as cogwheels but pursue their own goals—which good managers try to align with company goals—through challenges and incentives. Perhaps no insight has been more important to modern management than the seemingly obvious one, that people work best and most productively when they are in some (limited) sense working for themselves, responding to a challenge, and not merely doing their duty. So far, so good. But this rather benign imagery too readily falls into another metaphor, one particularly popular in sports-loving modern society. Business becomes a *game.* It thus takes on a welcome amount of human gusto and enjoyment. Given that business is above all a social *practice*—and games are practices too—doesn't it seem to follow (though fallaciously) that business is above all a game?

One wins (or loses) wars, but one also wins (or loses) games, and games are a lot more fun than wars. Thus, the game metaphor came to the fore in the Sixties (when life itself was commonly viewed as a game). Business was no longer described so bloodthirstily as a life-and-death endeavor but as something voluntary, thrilling, challenging—thus the sports and team imagery of much recent business talk, similar in some senses to military imagery but without the violence and much more aware of underlying mutual interests and rules of "fair play." The obvious problem with the sports metaphor, however, is that it makes business too self-enclosed, too merely coincidentally connected with productivity, service, and prosperity. When Michael Maccoby introduced his theory of "the gamesman" (in a book with that title) several years ago, he made no attempt to hide the somewhat pathological character of this new business paragon, pointing out that the heart of the gamesman was always in his or her own ambition and advancement and (only when convenient) in the interests of the business he or she was supposedly running.[8] But business for most people is not a game, to be played voluntarily for the challenge and the excitement. The

8. Michael Maccoby, *The Gamesman* (New York: Pocket Books, 1975).

business world encompasses and affects everyone, including customers and members of the community who cannot afford to "play." At least some of the horrors of recent years might well be blamed on the game mentality that wholly focuses executives on "winning" and blinds them to the impact they have on others outside the game. The Ford strategists who figured that it would be cheaper to settle the lawsuits stemming from the fatalities rather than to recall and fix the ill-fated Pinto were, in effect, playing a game, and they thus remained oblivious to the horror and suffering their game entailed. Had they shared in the horrors instead of remaining isolated in their corporate playing fields, their behavior might have been much different.[9]

Of course, most people in business don't see it as a game at all but rather as a way to make a living. Most people in business are not driven by overwhelming ambition, do not see business as a challenge or the corporation as a playground, are not interested in (and are put off by) what is now called "fast-tracking" and the "high-rolling" ways of success. Nevertheless, our idea of success remains too tied to the ideal of having fun and winning a game, to a notion of social irresponsibility that is protected and reinforced by the game metaphor. It is this metaphor that explains and justifies the behavior described by Michael Lewis on the trading floor, and is the same metaphor that has placed the financial community so safely beyond the reach of the demand of production and general prosperity. The metaphor of the game, however, is so pervasive in our society that it is by no means just a fun-loving interpretation of the give-and-take rumble-tumble of business life. It has become the dominant model—no longer just metaphor—for understanding the whole of economics if not all of human life. Indeed, its presuppositions, seemingly so obvious that they do not have to be discussed or even mentioned, have come to define our contemporary understanding of "rationality" and, in a few prominent authors, all of ethics as well.[10] Not all bad philosophy and dangerous metaphors are violent, vulgar, or naive, and much of business ethics, I will argue, has been hampered by some remarkably sophisticated, sometimes even brilliant theorizing, which, however it may keep improving itself, begins with a set of assumptions that do indeed make much of business into a game. Business becomes a game when it loses its essential aim, not just to make money but to provide essential goods and services and bring about a general and not a selfish prosperity. Business becomes a game when it takes on make-believe goals and purposes and when it pretends that it is an activity undertaken solely for its own sake ("business is business"). But before we examine the more sophisticated versions of these pervasive delusions, it might be instructive to take note

9. Art Wolfe, "Game Metaphors," *Business Horizons* (1989).

10. Notably David Gautier, following Thomas Hobbes (see the section on game theory, pp. 52–54).

of the familiar, mundane, naive, and sometimes downright disgusting comments that we suppress in ourselves but all-too-often hear unabashed from undergraduate business students and see just how far we have wandered from the Aristotelean sense of community and intelligent purposefulness that I want to defend here.

3

Abstract Greed

You can't ever get enough of what you didn't really want in the first place.

SAM KEEN

The increasing abstraction and separation of business language from questions of concrete human interests and production and prosperity take their toll not only on the vision of business as such but on the individuals who are trying to make their lives in a business society. In 1989 I asked my business ethics students, rather casually, how much money they thought that they could reasonably expect to be earning ten years from now. An economics major asked how she was supposed to know about ten years of potential inflation, so I assured them that 1989 dollars would do. A few thoughtful students confessed that, as they had no idea what they wanted to do for a career or a living yet, they could hardly estimate any expected income. But I told them that at the moment I was more interested in their expectations than I was in their career choices, and I asked for a few volunteers.

"Thirty-five thousand dollars," offered one student in the middle of class. The rest of the class, almost as one, chortled and guffawed.

"Too high or too low?" I asked, tongue in cheek, the answer being obvious.

"You can't even live on thirty-five thousand dollars a year," insisted one perturbed student, "even without a family."

"Well," I needled them, "how much would it take to live on?"

"A hundred grand," shouted a student at the back of the class, and almost everyone nodded or muttered in agreement.

"And do you think that you will make that much?" I asked.

"Sure," answered the same student, with more cockiness than confidence."

"How?" I asked

"Oh, I haven't the slightest idea. Probably in investments," he answered, with a nervous giggle.

Everyone laughed. I then asked the class (there were about a hundred of them) to write down the figure they "reasonably expected" to be earning in a decade, adjusted for inflation, etc. The class average was well over $75,000 a year, not counting a few visionary millionaires-to-be who were not counted in the averages.[1]

I often do that experiment, and I used to get much the same result and discussion, with almost every one of my classes. I'm happy to say that, with the turn into the 1990s, the figures are more modest and the ambitions more along the lines of "doing something worthwhile with my life." But whether this is because of a new social consciousness or because of economic despair foreshadowed by the Wall Street scandals and sackings and an economy deeply damaged by federal deficits I cannot yet say—though, of course, it may be both, just as the idealism of the Sixties was fueled by an affluent confidence mixed with fear and anger about the Vietnam War. These 1989 students were the last students of the Reagan years, filled with the promises of quick wealth and unhampered (unregulated) power that defined business thinking in those days. Everyone knew about the twenty-five-year-olds making their fortunes on Wall Street, and with that in mind, who wanted to go into teaching or social work or (even worse) manufacturing These students had enormous expectations, stoked everyday by the media, and very little sense of what to do with their lives—except, of course, for that relatively small number of elite students who managed the Prestige University M.B.A.–Wall Street route before burning out at twenty-eight or so.

What struck me then—and now—was not so much the enormous sums of money these students seemed to think that they wanted, deserved, and needed to live on but their utter naiveté about how to get it and their remarkable lack of sense about what to do with it. It is the money—no, not even the money but the sheer numbers themselves—that counted. Of course, there are always enough luxuries to covet and to buy, but there was very little desire for such things themselves, only an abstract desire for the ability to buy them. These business students also displayed almost total ignorance of what business life for most people (certainly most of them) actually involves, despite their three or four years of study of the subject. Somehow they thought that they would get a job (they were anxious about that) and then the money would flow in. There was very little thought or speculation about the social relations that actually define most business communities, little thought about what they would actually do to *earn* the money they made and

1. Adapted from my *Passion for Justice* (Reading, Mass.: Addison-Wesley, 1990).

virtually no thought whatever (for most of them) about what product or service the company they would work for would actually produce.[2] Once employed, they would do the tricks they learned in business school, suck up to an executive to two, and then climb the corporate ladder with the money too. All anxiety was focused on getting that first job and starting down the path to wealth promoted on all of those Sunday night television shows and Financial News Network interview-advertise-ments. The questions about Why? What? and Who? would just have to wait their turn.

I have called this phenomenon, this greed without desire, *abstract greed*. It is, in a bad phrase, greed without lust, greed learned but not com-prehended. Indeed, there isn't even any real desire, just the brain-washed sense that this is what one *ought* to want. (Needless to say, most students would forget about it after a few years of meaningful employ-ment and mortgage payments.) It is obvious that if most of these stu-dents actually had the desire and expectation for such fantastic amounts of money, they would be doomed to a life of frustration and a sense of failure, even if, without that desire and those expectations, they might be perfectly well off and quite happy. (As the Talmud says, "The rich man is he who is satisfied with what he has.") In abstract greed it is money, pure wealth, that is wanted, not to obtain anything or even to prove anything but wealth as a goal given and unquestioned, like honor, faith, or patriotism in some other societies. It is, to hear us talk, the ultimate good, more important than personal dignity and happiness. Indeed, it *is* our personal dignity and happiness.

Where does this peculiar attitude come from? It is not a "natural" desire. Indeed, it is spectacular just in the fact that it is so cut off from any natural desire, our need for other people and for self-respect, our need for relaxation and social harmony, even our need for stimulation and challenge. The much-touted "challenge" of business is, outside of Wall Street, almost always a challenge of creativity, of hard work and perseverance, of organization and cooperation, of good ideas and keen sensitivity to public needs and moods. It is not the challenge of "mak-ing money." Abstract greed isn't even greed. It isn't desire. And it plays only an artificial and distracting and destructive role in our ambitions. This is just what I want to argue, of course, about the myth that stands behind abstract greed, the myth of "the profit motive"—the idea that we are all ("naturally") motivated by the desire for (more) money. The very idea that money in itself is desirable and readily convertible into power and prestige is an idea that, in most ages and most cultures, has been condemned as a curse (that of King Midas, notably) or a sin (of "avarice"). And it has been condemned as a curse and a sin just because

2. For an interesting discussion of this familiar form of "alienation" or "fetishism," see Peter Hadreas, "Money: A Speech Act Analysis," *Journal of Social Philosophy* 20 (Winter 1989): 115–29.

it is so cut off from other essential motives and interests—in the well-being of others, in the good of the community, in the well-being of one's own soul. But, of course, no motive floats alone, without anchorage in our deepest needs and desires, and my students' abstract greed is obviously tied to all sorts of natural desires, especially the desire for the approval of their peers, the desire (if it is conscious enough to become a desire) to fit in with the times and to please their parents who too often give ill-considered advice based on their own frustrations. They want to fit the images provided by the media, and these are too often dressed in the glamour of wealth. (How could a Miami detective afford a ninety-thousand-dollar sports car?) It is the desire to achieve those dubious virtues that too many business executives, unthinkingly parroting the conventional "wisdom" of the times and their speech-writers, declare again and again to be the driving forces of American society—the pursuit of wealth, the importance of unfettered competition, the ruthlessness of the marketplace, the need to be an "individual" and to "rise above" everyone else (while maintaining that we are all equal, of course). Ivan Boesky's "greed is good" speech, paraphrased by Gordon Gekko in *Wall Street,* was only a slight exaggeration.

What gets left out are all of those virtues and values that those successful executives themselves obviously recognize and probably practice: the importance of patience, the fact that money ought to be earned and not merely coveted, the need for cooperation and mutual respect, the purpose of the marketplace not just to test the macho mettle of its participants but to supply everyone with jobs and inexpensive quality products and services. Again, it is good to see that the language is changing, but we probably have the Japanese and the Germans to thank for that. Competition can indeed be a moral force, prompting us to be honest with ourselves and not just more profitable.

These are the myths that give rise to those unreasonable and unjust desires and expectations that make people not more productive or competitive but unhappy and often vicious.[3] These are the myths that spawn empty ambitions and send people scrambling into careers that they don't really want and will never enjoy, sidetracking talents, interests, and concerns that might really make a difference. But what is especially upsetting about "abstract greed" is just what is so innocent about it, that it has nothing to do with real wants, real needs, or real expectations, and in fact militates against them, making the workplace not a joint venture defined at its best by the gamelike virtues of good

3. Consider, for instance, a recent essay by Michael Korda called "Seize the Moment," published, not insignificantly, by *Penthouse* (Apr. 1990) as an illustration of just such a goad to corporate in-fighting. His previous best sellers, *Power* and *Success,* exhorted a similar message, providing tactics for intimidating and defeating one's rivals within the corporation.

sportsmanship, team spirit, and mutual fun but, at its worst, a cut-throat, competitive nightmare. It is a set of myths that allows and encourages the vices to parade as virtues, selfishness to overwhelm mutual goals and fellow feeling, mutually destructive competition to win out over cooperation and real efficiency. To rethink business life is not to idealize or to romanticize it so much as it is to undo the false and damaging myths and metaphors through which we already define and misunderstand what we do.

4

The Myth of the Profit Motive

> The root of the confusion is the mistaken belief that the motive of
> a person—the so-called profit motive of the businessman—is an ex-
> planation of his behavior or his guide to right action. Whether there
> is such a thing as the profit motive at all is highly doubtful . . .
> [The concept of the profit motive] is a major cause for the misun-
> derstanding of the nature of profit in our society and for the deep-
> seated hostility to profit which are among the most dangerous dis-
> eases of industrial society. . . . And it is in large part responsible
> for the prevailing belief that there is an inherent contradiction be-
> tween profit and a company's ability to make a social contribution.
>
> PETER DRUCKER, *Management*

Abstract greed is already a falsification of and an abstraction from our
actual motives, but the abstracted form of abstract greed is what business theorists since the nineteenth century have often called "the profit
motive." It is the familiar almost trite view that what drives the free
enterprise system, and so too each one of us, is a built-in behavioral
mechanism, the desire for profit. But what is "profit," and what kind
of "motive" is this? "Profit" is a specialized term. It is not merely an
increase in wealth. The profit motive is not merely the desire for money,
and profit is not the satisfaction of any such desire. Profit is not as such
what one earns when one works for a living. It is not what one receives
for a good day's work or in return for something one has done or
made (a distinction meticulously defended by Aristotle and medieval
economists like Saint Thomas Aquinas). Profit, essentially, is the outcome of a monetary transaction, an "investment," what is left over after
all expenses are paid, subject, of course, to considerable creative fina-
gling over what is to count as an "expense" and, accordingly, what is
"left over."[1] Profit is part and parcel of a certain kind of economic
system that encourages certain kinds of complex, forward-looking
transactions (as opposed, say, to a barter system, in which the results

1. Eddie Murphy's *Coming to America*, a top box office success, reportedly "lost" 300
million dollars when author Art Buchwald sued for rights and a share of the profits.

are immediate and taking a profit is proof of unfair dealing and counts as theft). We talk loosely of profit as "what is left over" but, precisely speaking, much or most of "what is left over"—say, when a craftsman sells an object he or she has made—is really compensation for work well done, and thus not profit at all. Profits are over and above "fair exchange," including compensation for work and skill and a "fair wage." (The missing ingredient here, of course, is "risk," but more on that later.) At full fruition, this system of investment for profit is "capitalism," but there are more elementary systems of exchange that allow for and even encourage profit taking. Ancient and medieval markets were profit-oriented—and therefore viewed with suspicion or condemnation by respectable civic leaders. Indeed, any economy that employs money as an exchange medium at least opens the possibility of profit and, when such behavior is not only tolerated but encouraged, profit seeking becomes part of the social scenery. But does this indicate a "profit motive"?

One might loosely talk about the intention of making a profit as having "the profit motive." But such intentions are entirely a cultural phenomenon, specific to certain kinds of economy, and hardly a candidate for a natural passion or universal motive. Intending to make a profit in such an economy hardly satisfies the glorified ontology of "the profit motive" as it is defended by theoretical enthusiasts. Any intended outcome is motivated and has a motive, but we are hardly justified in thus describing human nature in such terms. Anthony Flew, defending profits but attacking the idea of a "profit motive," rightly asks whether we should also talk about a "wage motive," a "rent motive," and an "interest motive."[2] This little reductio ad absurdum quickly demolishes its target. Of course, people work for profits, in a system that encourages profit making. But it does not follow that there is a profit motive, or that such a system is justified, or that making profits is legitimate or desirable. So, too, we could speak of a "theft motive" or a "murder motive," but no one would thereby conclude that the actions that follow such motives are thereby justified or even excusable ("I'm sorry, Your Honor, I just had this overwhelming murder motive").

Profit is the outcome of monetary transaction, but the basis of the transaction is not specified. The profit motive, as a motive, has one aim only, and that is the purely monetary making of a profit. Any other aim or interest is distinct from and potentially at odds with it. And if there were such a motive, *how* one makes a profit would be, at most, of secondary importance. As some birds instinctually build their nests out of whatever materials they happen to find, so too we would build our fortunes from whatever opportunities come our way. But it is the fortune that is first and foremost; the "opportunity" is merely a means. (It

2. Anthony Flew, "The Profit Motive" *Ethics,* 86 (July 1976): 312–22.

is worth reminding ourselves, however, that the word "fortune" originally meant "luck," not "wealth.") In our day and age (now that the pillaging and looting of surrounding towns has fallen into disfavor), profits are the proper means to build a fortune. As one of my entrepreneurial friends once said to me—before he lost a fortune on an unfortunate investment—"You'll never get rich working for a living." Profit is, so considered, a return on an investment. It is not a reward for good ideas or hard work nor is it aimed at public prosperity or even self-satisfaction. It is a technical economic term, not a social or psychological concept. There are no built-in moral parameters (though defenders of the profit motive will always insist that these are "implied"), and the heady combination of "the profit motive" and available "opportunity" too readily gives rise to what Richard De George has called "the Myth of Amoral Business."[3] That is to say, the idea that business is its own motivation. It exists quite independently of any practical results, social concerns, or interpersonal considerations. The nature of the transaction is incidental (though for other reasons, including prudence and the promise of future profit, it ought to be legal and socially acceptable). The profit motive is said to be like the sex drive (an analogy often pursued by more informal business speakers—and not always as an analogy). It is always there, stronger in some people than in others. It may be unsociable, even antisocial, single-minded, and ruthless in its pursuit of its goal and ungenerous in its success, but it is nevertheless applauded and encouraged. It is said to influence if not determine all of our behavior and forces us to cast at least a jaded (that is to say, green) eye toward the bottom line of whatever it is we are doing. It should be easy to see why we ought to reject such a view of human nature.

The profit motive is often attacked as (and confused with) a form of selfishness. There is, however, no reason to accept this critique. Whether or not there is a profit motive, there is no reason to suppose that the pursuit of profit is essentially self-interested. Indeed, it could be as detached and impersonal as any other bureaucratic or self-assigned task or obligation. ("Well, I've got to go to the office and earn some money.") Of course, the pursuit of profits for one's own account is typically self-interested, but it need not be (acting to one's own advantage is not necessarily self-interested) and one need not pursue profits for oneself. Corporate managers typically pursue profits not for themselves but for others, the owners or the shareholders of the company. And although they may be well rewarded for doing their jobs or lose their jobs if they fail, it does not follow that they are being selfish. Self-interest is not selfishness. Anthony Flew makes the point rather nicely. Like most ethicists, he carefully distinguishes pursuing one's interest and selfish-

3. Richard De George, *Business Ethics* (New York: Macmillan, 1982).

ness. He considers as an example his daughters' eating their dinners; "but it would be monstrous to denounce them as selfish hussies, simply on that account." Flew adds that "the time for denunciation could come only after one of them had, for instance, eaten someone else's dinner too."[4] The question that critics of capitalism would raise is whether eating one's own dinner is indeed analogous to so innocently making a profit. They would argue that making a profit violates fair exchange and that "eating one's dinner"—to follow the analogy—is in fact eating (at least part of) someone else's dinner, a zero-sum view that may be true of some dinners but not necessarily of profits.

The missing ingredient in the standard critical accounts of profit making, we noted briefly, is risk. It is the taking of risks that justifies the making of profits, for who but a philanthropist or a (very) good friend would invest if he or she did not have the possibility of substantial gain? Indeed, would it not count as a gift rather than an investment if there were not such hope of return? Of course, there is the always difficult question, How much reward or compensation for how much risk? And the answers vary from the utilitarian "incentive" (just as much reward as it takes to get people to invest willingly) to the libertarian "whatever."[5] Friedrich von Hayek, for instance, argues at length that any effort to make reward commensurate with "merit"—for example, by estimating risk and calculating how much a person deserves in return—invites intolerable intrusion by the state into what ought to be wholly free human choices and transactions.[6] But on any such account, risk only justifies the making of profits. The notion of risk is not built into the notion of profit, and it is not presupposed (or even supposed) by "the profit motive." While we might *justify* profits on the basis of exposure to risk (and as a reward for innovation and successful marketing), we cannot explain the pursuit of profits by an appeal to compensation for risks. To raise the need for "incentives" is to get the explanation backward.[7]

Who is supposed to have the so-called profit motive? It is not enough to say, without further specificity, that our entire economic system operates on "the profit motive." Presumably it is first of all individuals

4. Flew, "The Profit Motive," p. 314.

5. During the energy crisis in the mid-1970s, Mobile Oil Company spokesman Herb Schmertz often defended his company's windfall profits by insisting that he "had never seen an obscene profit." It seemed as if profits, like Aristotelean virtues, could never be excessive.

6. Friedrich von Hayek, *Mirage of Social Justice* (London: Routledge and Kegan Paul, 1976).

7. Cf. Drucker, *Management*, p. 60: "Profit and profitability are . . . crucial—for society even more than for the individual business. Yet profitability is not the purpose of but a limiting factor on business enterprise and business activity. Profit is not the explanation, cause or rationale of business behavior and business decisions, but the test of their validity."

who are thus motivated, not businesses and corporations. True, the pursuit of profits is typically written into a corporation's charter, but this hardly constitutes a motive. Would it make sense to say that profit is the aim of the system as a whole?[8] But in this case profit would seem to be not a motive but rather an abstraction superimposed by speculative business theorists. But even individuals do not obviously have a profit motive. Employees don't have it: they have salaries to earn and jobs to do. Managers don't have it: they have obligations. Even top executives work for salaries and bonuses and not for profits as such (except insofar as they happen to be shareholders of the company as well). It is only the investors, the "owners," who hope for (hardly "work for") profits, and if anyone has the profit motive, presumably it is they. It is on their behalf, accordingly, that the entire system functions. But doesn't this seem a perverse and backward way of looking at the system? And how much does it leave out even about the stockholders themselves, now defined solely in terms of their economic risk and expectations with no reference whatever to their citizenship, personalities, or cares and activities in life?

Among its many faults, such talk of "the profit motive" makes any mention of "virtue" or "integrity" sound merely quaint and naively idealistic. It is worth noting that the phrase was invented by nineteenth-century socialists as an *attack* on business and its narrow-minded pursuit of the dollar, the mark, and the pound to the exclusion of all other considerations and obligations. The idea was to criticize and lampoon the vulgar focus and sometimes vicious lack of sensitivity and public spirit of certain ludicrous entrepreneurs. But the entrepreneurs, unfortunately, took the attack instead as a compliment and as a convenient way not only to describe but also to justify their myopia. Behavior that was merely greedy and selfish could now be defined and defended in terms of an abstract and honorable motive. Antisocial behavior could now be justified, in terms that would have horrified Adam Smith, as an essential (and even commendable) aspect of human nature.

To be sure, people in business do aim to make a profit and to stay in business most of them *have* to make a profit, but it is worth taking a moment to ask how and why they do so.[9] Businesses and business people make a profit, usually, by supplying quality goods and services, by providing jobs, and by "fitting into" the community. This would include, presumably, financial services and investment consultation, but it would exclude "parasitic" profits gained only by skimming without providing a service in return. (The distinction between "salesmanship"

8. Ibid.: "Profit and profitability are . . . crucial—for society even more than for the individual business."

9. Ibid.: "If archangels instead of businessmen sat in directors' chairs, they would still have to be concerned with profitability, despite their total lack of personal interests in making profits."

and "service" is, admittedly, sometimes hard to draw.) Moreover, profits are not as such the end or goal of business activity: profits are distributed and reinvested.[10] Profits are a *means* to building the business
and rewarding employees, executives, and investors. For some people,
profits may be a means of "keeping score," but even for those degenerate cases, it is the status and satisfaction of "winning" that is the goal,
not profits as such. It was for good reason, whatever else we might
think of his prejudices, that Aristotle scorned the notion of profit for
its own sake, and even Adam Smith was clear that it was prosperity,
not profits, that constituted the goal of the free market system, whether
or not the individual businessman or woman had this in mind. But to
single out profits rather than productivity or public service as the central aim of business activity is a falsification of most people's motives,
and just asking for trouble as well. Indeed, Norman Bowie has recently
argued that profits, like happiness, are best obtained if not pursued as
such. If you want to be happy, you need to pursue not happiness but
other goals, such as quality and dependability, and conscientiously at-
tend to them. So, too, "the more a business consciously seeks to obtain
profits, the less likely they are to achieve them." Bowie aptly calls this
"the profit-seeking paradox."[11] One might think of it as an astringent
conceptual antidote to the mythical profit motive.

A more sophisticated version of the myth of the profit motive avoids
the extravagant generalizations regarding human nature and more
modestly interprets the motive as a matter of contractual obligation,
not natural necessity. It states that the managers of a business are bound
above all by one and only one obligation, to maximize the profits for
their stockholders. "The social responsibility of business," writes Milton
Friedman in a famous polemical article, "is to increase profits." He does
not include the word "only," but it is clearly implied and argued for in
what follows. (Friedman's polemical penchant for extreme and exclusive views is evident in his other work as well, for example, his well-
taken emphasis on the impact of the money supply, which becomes
"monetarism," the absurd idea that money supply is the *sole* determinant of an economy.) Friedman argues that the managers of a company have a "fiduciary responsibility" to the owners (in a publicly held
company the stockholders), which is certainly true. But then he goes
on to argue that this is the *only* social responsibility of management,
and any use of corporate money for extraneous good causes—for ex-

10. Ibid., 60–61: "The first test of any business is not the maximization of profit but
the achievement of sufficient profit to cover the risks of economic activity and thus to
avoid loss. . . . To put it crudely, a bankrupt company is not likely to be a good company
to work for, or likely to be a good neighbor and a desirable member of the community.
. . . There is only one valid definition of business purpose: *to create a customer.*"
  11. Norman Bowie, "The Profit Seeking Paradox," in *Ethics of Administration*, ed. N.
Dale Wright (Provo, Utah: Brigham Young University Press, 1988).

ample, charity, general education, community development—is in effect "theft" from the rightful owners, money stolen (albeit in the name
of a good cause). We need not inquire whether this is the actual motive
behind most upper-management decisions in order to point out that,
while managers do recognize that their own business roles are defined
primarily by obligations rather than the "profit motive," that unflattering image of *Homo economicus* has simply been transferred to the stockholders (that is, the owners). But is it true that investors or owners care
only about the maximization of their profits? Do they not think that
there are all sorts of values and virtues to be considered along the road
to dividends and share value increases? And if some four-month "in
and out" investor does indeed care only about increasing his investment by 30 percent or so, why should the managers of the firm have
any obligation to him, other than to avoid intentionally frittering away
or wasting that money?

There is much more to say about Friedman's argument, of course,
from its nonsensically one-sided assumption of responsibility to his pathetic understanding of stockholder personality as *Homo economicus*, but
this is not the place for such an exploration.[12] My argument here is
simply that such talk about the primacy of profits and the obligation to
provide them is not only vacuous and misleading, it eclipses the larger
picture and all those other purposes that business is designed and managers are hired to serve. It neglects all those other constituencies—the
stakeholders—other than the stockholders and pretends that business and
the corporation are one-dimensional, purely profit-seeking entities. And
to give profits this sort of status is not only foolish in theory but cruel
and dangerous in practice. To take but one example, it is obvious to
anyone who has ever run or looked at the books of a business that
employees are, typically, the most expensive and demanding single cost,
in terms not only of salaries, cost-of-living increases, and expectations
based on merit and seniority, but secondary insurance and benefits
packages that may raise the average cost by an additional 30 to 50 percent.

Employees are, from a pure profit perspective, the most expendable
cost to a business, and here two quite different purposes and conceptions of business—as well as two often divergent interest groups—come
into focus. On the first, profits are the end and employees are the means,
and when one can improve the means (by cutting costs) for the sake of
the end, one should and is justified in doing so. But on the second
view, the employees are part of the "team" that is making the operation
possible, and whether or not one wants to describe the operation as
essentially profit-seeking, the primary entity is the team, not the profits.

---

12. See our arguments in Robert C. Solomon and K. Hanson, *Above the Bottom Line*
(New York: Harcourt Brace Jovanovich, 1983).

In the name of profits, employee rights will inevitably conflict with the bottom line. "Monopoly mentality—a board game way of thinking devoid of employees and consumers—will inevitably rule one's thinking.[13]

So, too, our understanding of consumers. Drucker writes, "[T]here is only one valid definition of business purpose: *to create a customer.*"[14] As so often in the hype-prone business-writing market, the claim is hyperbolic, and clearly contradicts other claims Drucker makes in the same book. But like so many other overstated claims, this one too contains a gem of insight. Drucker has just spent a few paragraphs dismantling talk and thinking in terms of "the profit motive," and now he presents us with one clear alternative as an end. But customers, one might well argue, are a (or *the*) means to profits. One seeks to expand one's list of consumers in order to make more, perhaps then to expand and decrease costs, only to make even more profits from further expanded sales. But it should be obvious that here again we have a kind of chicken-and-egg problem, though with a strong bias toward the chicken. One could look at the matter either way, but, as every salesperson knows, if a sensitive customer gets even a whiff of the sense that he or she is being "used" to make a commission or a sale, he or she will quickly run away. Customers are necessary to make profits, but it does not follow that customers are a means to profit making. Here again is Bowie's paradox. Companies that treat customers as ends in themselves, seemingly oblivious to their own costs, ultimately attract and keep more customers and win out on the bottom line as well.[15]

The most dangerous metaphors are those that present themselves not as metaphors but as straight matter-of-fact description about the ways of the world. Foremost among these is the idea that business at its very essence is defined by and driven by a basic human urge called "the profit motive." It is such talk of the profit motive, I suggest, that causes more damage to the virtues—and more emphasis on the wrong virtues—than any amount of sleaziness or dishonest dealings on the part of the business community. It is the narrow-minded language of the profit motive that gives rise to public suspicion and many of the dubious practices that are the object of that suspicion. The "myth of amoral business" persists not only among the suspicious public and some socialist-minded philosophers but among many business people themselves. That myth together with what I have called "abstract greed" are

13. That game itself is perhaps the most illuminating single exercise in business ethics, especially for those who are not in business or claim to have no sympathies for business. Where else can one experience all of the symptoms of antisocial pathology, run roughshod over thousands of imaginary people, and treat the world, if only for a few hours, as nothing but the unfeeling raw material for one's own ego esteem? And the dollars, after all, are utterly worthless, mere "monopoly money."

14. Drucker, *Management*, p. 61.

15. Tom Peters has been touting this theme as one of his keys to "excellence" since his *In Search of Excellence* (New York: Harper and Row, 1982) and before.

a vicious pair indeed, and though I wouldn't expect anyone involved in business ethics to buy either of them, an occasional letter to the editor from some assistant professor of management has a way of showing me how wrong I can be about this. The first task of business ethics is to clear the way through some similarly incriminating and dangerous myths and metaphors, which obscure rather than clarify the underlying *ethos* that makes business possible and make any talk of "virtue" sound merely quaint and naively idealistic.

This is how we misunderstand business and lose our sense of cooperation, community, and integrity: we adopt a too-narrow vision of what business is—for example, the pursuit of profits—and then derive unethical and divisive conclusions. It is this inexcusably limited focus on the "rights of the stockholders," for instance, that has been used to defend some of the very destructive and certainly unproductive "hostile takeovers" of major corporations in the past few years. To say this is not to deny the rights of stockholders to a fair return, of course, nor is it to deny the "fiduciary responsibility" of the managers of a company. It is only to say that these rights and responsibilities make sense only in a larger social context and that the very idea of "the profit motive" as an end in itself—as opposed to profits as a means of encouraging and rewarding hard work and investment, building a better business, and serving society better—is a serious obstacle to understanding the rich tapestry of motives and activities that make up the business world.[16]

16. This is one of many places that the current language of the "stakeholder" becomes a memorable summation of the breadth of corporate social responsibility, in place of the narrow view of profit seeking and "the profit motive." One way to think about the "stakeholder" as opposed to the "stockholder" is to think of obligation and interpersonal responsibility as a primary instead of one-dimensional, merely "fiduciary" responsibility.

5

Game Theory as a Model for Business and Business Ethics

We should not ask for more precision than a subject is capable of giving us.

ARISTOTLE, *Nicomachean Ethics*

The problem with ethics is that it is so—sloppy ("subjective" to those who confuse imprecision and controversy with indeterminacy and merely personal taste). But business, at least in theory, is so neat, so exact, so precise. As one of my businessman friends once told me (at the end of a conversation on the difficulty of measuring productivity and success in academia), "in business you always know how well you are doing. You just have to put your hand in your pocket." (I did not pursue the ambiguity of the suggestion.) Perhaps, one might think, if only ethics could be made more precise, more like business, then business ethics would be more palatable and we could dispense with metaphors altogether.

For instance, what if the reciprocal negotiations and agreements of the free market were themselves adequate to explain not only business but ethics as well? What if, without committing ourselves to the perhaps overly playful (and, some might argue, overcompetitive) metaphorical view that business is nothing but a game, it were nevertheless demonstrable that business could be literally understood as something very much like a game, an activity made up of goals and strategies and rules of fair play? This is the promise of "game theory," a system of mathematical models ideally suited to bargaining strategy and competitive ploys. Game theory was first conceived by John von Neumann in the early years of World War II, and from the very first it was seized upon by economists as a mathematical model for economic activity.[1] Even as originally conceived, game theory was not restricted to "games" as such.

1. John von Neumann and Oscar Morgenstern, *Theory of Games and Economic Behavior* (Princeton: Princeton University Press, 1944).

It applied to virtually all situations in which individual interests were causally and strategically interconnected, including public issues of governance and welfare and private competitions and exchanges. With the expansion of the theory as "decision theory," "social choice theory," and "rationality modeling," game-theoretic models of competition and cooperation came to be applied to such various social and political issues as voting behavior, theories of justice, and nuclear deterrence, to name but a few. But nowhere has game theory and its applications been more enthusiastically endorsed than in economics and general business theory.

Business is, to be sure, not just a game. But the rules and strategies and consequently the ethics of business would seem to be amenable to precise formulation under the auspices of the mathematical theory of games. There need be no presumption that business is "fun" (as in "fun and games"), nor need it be supposed that the various "players" (or "parties") are involved voluntarily. A "game," so considered, is any interaction between agents who have preferences and goals. It is not necessary that one of those goals be "to win." Not all games have winners and losers, and it is only necessary that one can be shown to be doing well or badly according to his or her own goals, and not necessarily in contrast or in opposition with others. It is not to be assumed that the activities in question are competitive. The appealing notion of a "cooperative game" opens the possibility of cooperative strategies and mutually satisfying ("win-win") outcomes. Indeed, at its most optimistic, game theory might be thought to give us an ideal "ethics" in which everything is fair and everyone is (more or less) satisfied even without any of those social constraints called "morality" that would seem to form the core of an ethics.[2]

The appeal of this model is obvious. If, in the simplest imaginable market situation Adam has an orange but wants an apple and Abraham has an apple but wants an orange and, after a very short discussion, they decide to trade, everyone is satisfied. It is an "optimal" outcome; everyone has his first preference and no one is disappointed. But it is not just the optimal outcome that pleases us. It is the procedure, the *reciprocity* of the market that makes it so appealing, the fact that (after knowing not only their own interests but the interests of others) both parties agree to the outcome that each desires. No outside authority has to issue instructions or impose sanctions. So long as there is informed agreement and mutual satisfaction there need be no additional call for "morals." (The assumption here is that "morals" are constraints on self-interest.) The picture does not change significantly if we add more people and introduce money as a mediating currency or add production to this overly simple picture of pure exchange; the basic prin-

2. David Gautier, *Morals by Agreement* (New York: Oxford University Press, 1986).

ciple of reciprocity and self-satisfaction through mutual satisfaction remains the same. Aristotle was just plain wrong if he thought that all trade is theft and exploitation. Trade based on reciprocal agreements would seem to be a paradigm of mutually satisfying civilized behavior.

But is this agreeable paradigm an adequate conception of business? Is it an adequate conception of games and bargaining situations? Is morality (or what could happily take its place) nothing but rational self-interested cooperation? The answer to all three questions is clearly No. Business is (obviously) not always the mutually satisfying and agreeable exchange (mediated by money) that the previous example represents. Business is not only competitive but sometimes exploitative as well. The world of business is pervaded by the Hobbesian distortions of "Force and Fraud."[3] Indeed, the idea of the game as a model for business is revealing in that it is not so much the exchange that seems central but rather competition and rivalry. Moreover, most games and some standard business negotiations presuppose ignorance rather than mutual knowledge. Few bargaining situations are as mutually well informed as a simple trade. Games (and game theory) involve strategies as well as goals, and strategies (usually) suggest not only competition but a certain secrecy. Acting in the face of uncertainty (at least, the uncertainty of the market) is par for the course. Market competition (as opposed, for instance, to one's bargaining with a supplier or customer) is not reciprocal and is partly based on mutual ignorance. Knowing what your competitor is doing but not letting him know what you are doing is an enormous advantage. And unlike the willing exchange example, business competition does not always work for optimal and mutually satisfying outcomes. Accordingly, the focus of most game theoretical debate these days is a particularly gloomy paradigm of a noncooperative game in which virtually everyone loses.

That paradigm is the so-called prisoner's dilemma, a competitive, non-zero-sum played by at least two persons.[4] (Credit for its formulation is

3. Hobbes, *Leviathan,* discussed as distortions of the perfect market by Gautier, ibid., ch. 4.

4. I am assuming that the reader is familiar with the simple basics of game theory and I will not go into any of the details, technically fascinating as they may be. The primary concepts are well known and have become virtually catchphrases in the business world (e.g., Lester Thurow's best selling polemic, *The Zero-Sum Society* [New York: Basic Books, 1980]). Even more familiar is the distinction between *competitive* versus *cooperative* games, although the distinction, even in games, is not always obvious. Are children's imaginative games, such as "cops and robbers," competitive, or cooperative? The entire game depends, like a Monty Python housing project, on the shared fantasies of all participants. *Zero-sum* games, of course, are those games that involve "a fixed pot" and winners and losers whose winnings and losings add up to zero (that is, no one can win more than others have lost). Poker is the usual example, for obvious reasons, but the purely monetary nature of that game is too easily taken as a paradigm of all games, including all business games. (Even in poker, if the players are playing primarily "for fun," is the

usually given to A. W. Tucker, a Princeton mathematician.) The prisoner's dilemma is best illustrated by the story that gives the example its name. Two men (Joe and Moe) are arrested and immediately separated by the district attorney. She instructs each of them that if he confesses (and the other does not) he will receive a greatly reduced term (one year) while the other will get the maximum (ten years). If they both confess, the D.A. will be able to convict them both (five years). What she does not tell them (but is plainly evident) is that if neither confesses, she won't have a case but can convict them on a lesser charge (2 years). What should (rationally) each do? The optimal outcome (that is, the least amount of time in prison for both of them) would result if neither confessed, but Joe figures that if Moe confesses and he doesn't, he's in for the long haul. Moe figures much the same way. So both confess, and what is rational is less than optimal.

It is easy to imagine any number of business situations that fit the same model. The most obvious is two competing businessmen that must set their prices in competition with one another without knowing what the other is going to do. Each will be cautious and set a price lower than he would if he were confident that the other would set a suitably higher price. In such cases, business competition (or, more accurately, noncooperation) is mutually disadvantageous, though it should be pointed out that this is usually to the advantage of the customer. (Thus we can understand consumer enthusiasm whenever there are price wars

---

enjoyment of the winners and losers so easily measured? Indeed, need there be "winners and losers" and is the game really competitive? Thus a problem: where are the boundaries of the game, within the game narrowly defined or circumscribing not only the game but a particular playing of the game, including the intentions and aspirations of particular players.)

Most games, even those in which there are clearly winners and losers, are not "zero-sum" games in such an obvious sense. A game of baseball has its winners and losers (unless it's a tie), but if we look at the *content* of the game, it is clear that the scoring is not zero-sum. A run for one team is not subtracted from the other. One could, however, take the "Peter Potter" view of gamesmanship: "He who is not one up, is one down," but even this is not clearly zero-sum, depending on the scoring of the game. A losing team can do impressively well (even win a "moral victory"). It can also utterly humiliate itself. *Non-zero-sum* games are those whose outcomes do not add up to zero, in which value can be increased or decreased in the playing of the game itself. This, I want to argue, is the nature of most business games, excepting only those that tend to get so much attention because of head-to-head competition, such as the famous business battles between Cornelius Vanderbilt and Jay Gould. (See Robert C. Solomon and K. Hanson, *Above the Bottom Line* [New York: Harcourt Brace Jovanovich, 1983], p. 118.) The complexities of almost all games increase as more people join in the game, and the simplest two-party bargaining situation (as in a marriage) can be thrown into confusion when a third party enters the picture. Matters are also complicated when it is the nature of the game that the best strategy for each individual player results in a less than optimal outcome. This is the nature of the prisoner's dilemma, and it is, as it stands, a convincing argument against the free market.

and, on the business side, the need for laws against collusion and price fixing.) But is this an adequate model of business? Is business made up of (in game theoretical terms) "utility maximizing" rather than "optimizing" decisions? That is, is it true that the typical business negotiation and the free market in general puts all parties in a worse-off position? A socialist would, of course, say Yes. But in defense of the market, the prisoner's dilemma might be taken as an atypical "worse case scenario." Or it might be denied to be a market model at all.[5] The obvious truth, I would argue, is that the business world involves a great many different sorts of activities and forms of interaction, some of which might be imperfectly captured in game theoretical models, including the "prisoner's dilemma." But the ill-fated attempt to capture all of business and economics (and the misleadingly singular "the market") in a single, mathematically precise model needs to deny this obvious truth.

Nevertheless, many philosophers and social theorists have tried to amend and adapt game theory to provide a normative theory of rationality and morality as well as a descriptive model of game playing behavior. The philosophical backdrop of such efforts can be found in the ethical philosophy of utilitarianism, the view that, starting with the premise that everyone wants to maximize his or her own pleasure and minimize his or her own pain, everyone ought to maximize the good for all.[6] (We will talk about this philosophy in more detail later in this section.) But the validity of that argument has been notoriously difficult to make out, and it has often been pointed out (for example, by German moral philosophers before and after Mill who found the utilitarian position just plain "vulgar"[7]) that one can obtain the position of social solidarity only by presupposing it, not by demonstrating it on the basis of individual self interest.[8] Moreover, pleasure and pain are hard

5. Gautier, *Morals by Agreement*, ch. 4, in which he argues that the market "is the very antithesis of the Prisoner's Dilemma" (p. 83). Of course, this applies only to the "perfect" market, which, as far as I can tell, has no relation whatever to the business world. An "ideal market situation" is not at all, as economists like to argue, an analogy of, say, an "ideal gas" or "mass" in physics, a projection of predictable behavior minus distorting factors such as friction and atmospheric gravity. As Lester Thurow has often said, when the heavens do not conform to an astronomer's predictions, no one goes around talking about "irrationalities" or "distortions." The theory is just wrong.

6. Mill: "only evidence that something is desirable is the fact that it is desired" (*Utilitarianism*, Indianapolis: Hackett, 1981, ch 4). Gautier: *Morals by Agreement*, (p. 59) "Value, then, we take to be a measure of individual preference—subjective because it is a measure of preference and relative because it is a measure of individual preference. What is good is good ultimately because it is preferred, and it is good from the standpoint of those and only those who prefer it" (*Morals by Agreement*, p. 59).

7. E.g., Kant in *The Philosophy of Law* (Edinburgh: Clark, 1889 (Hegel in his *The Phenomenology of Spirit* (Oxford: Oxford University Press, 1977), and Nietzsche in *Beyond Good and Evil* (New York: Random House, 1967).

8. Nietzsche, unlike Kant and Hegel, made this argument only as a criticism of social solidarity ("herd morality"). But, like them, he insisted that social consciousness was a

to quantify and, for more sensitive theorists such as Mill, too vulgarly hedonistic to qualify as ultimate ends of human behavior. Aristotle argued, notably, that pleasure in particular was never the goal of an activity but rather its welcome "accompaniment" when the activity was successful and well-done. Accordingly, contemporary game theorists reject any such hedonism and talk more generally about "utility maximization." This in turn becomes the working definition of "rationality" and the burning question for every theorist is whether there is or could be a rational solution to the most troublesome noncooperative games.

The most troublesome game, of course, is the prisoner's dilemma, and so long as one even suspects that it lies at the heart of business and that morality and business ethics are some sort of antidote or corrective, any adequate conception of either business or business ethics will be impossible. My argument here (as it has been all along) is that it is a mistake to begin with the supposition that business and ethics are in any sense opposed, and the game theoretical model is, in almost all of its versions, just a very subtle and sophisticated way of sneaking in that antagonism. Gautier tells us (in one of many such passages):

> The argument that the *laissez faire* economists would advance for an end to political constraints is clearly also an argument for an end to moral constraints. If each is not morally free to pursue her own gain, then some must benefit at the expense of others. Where earlier thinkers saw in unbridled pursuit of individual utility the ultimate source of conflict in human affairs, the defenders of the market see in it rather the basic of the true harmony resulting from the fullest compossible fulfilment of the preferences which utility measures. The traditional moralist is told that his services are not wanted. . . . The argument of the advocates of *laissez faire* may then seem to require the claim that where choice is both utility-maximizing and optimizing, it must also be morally right. But a more profound interpretation of their argument, which we endorse, is that it rests on the claim that morality has no application to market interaction under the conditions for perfect competition.[9]

Gautier distances himself from the laissez faire theorists, but his sympathies obviously override his disagreements. He would restrict the free market, but only because it is not in practice suitably "free," not "perfect competition."[10] His separation of morality and the market, how-

---

fundamental form of consciousness (even "rationality") *as well as* a calculated strategy of self-interest (by those who are too impotent to get what they want in any other way).

9. Gautier, *Morals by Agreement*, pp. 92, 93.

10. Gautier, ibid., 84: "One of the clauses in the agreement that gives rise to a rational morality provides for the choice of a perfectly competitive market, or a near approximation, as a social institution in those circumstances in which such a market is a practable alternative. . . . The world might be a better place if it were, as the enthusiasts of *laissez faire* economics have believed it to be, a perfectly competitive market. But it is not. . . . Because the world is not a market, morality is a necessary constraint on the interaction

ever, is just as insidious as the laissez faire theorists equation of the two. For the market construed (as we began by doing) as mutually satisfying exchange is not at all the same thing as the market construed essentially as competition (granted that it is competition in terms of exchange), and it is this perspective, this way of viewing the market that forces the separation of business and ethics, or what is wrongly interpreted as self-interest ("maximizing individual utility") and morality (as constraint). But the business world and the economic theories that describe it depend first of all not on mutual advantage and calculation but on trust and an *uncalculating* assumption of shared interest.[11]

This brings us back to the question of morality and business ethics, construed as constraints on individual self-interest. Is morality, we asked, nothing but rational self-interested cooperation? Or could a perfect market (at least in theory) dispense with morality, that is, dispense with those constraints that require us (on occasion) not to act in our own self-interest? Is the point and purpose of morality to insure (or, at least, make more probable) our long-term interests, a point that is already satisfied by the (perfect) market? That is, I believe, a thoroughgoing misunderstanding of morality, which is not concerned with individual interests, short or long term—which is not, emphatically, to say that it is *opposed* to our individual interests. Morality has to do with culture and tradition, shared rules and mores in living together. It is not, primarily, a matter of constraints, although it obviously includes a great many constraints, and many of those constraints (such as "taboos") can only with some ingenuity be argued to serve individual long-term interests. Moreover, morality insofar as it is concerned with individual interests is concerned not only with the satisfaction of the various parties but with the process and concerns according to which they become satisfied, including the fairness of the procedures as well as the fairness of outcomes (even if, for example, due to the desperation or stupidity of one party, both parties are satisfied). All of this (and more) makes the reduction of morality to the market or its replacement implausible.

This is not yet an argument against the use of game theory as a substitute for business ethics. Suppose we shift our emphasis from the outcome to the procedures and then try to formulate business ethics as a precise set of rules of "fair play." Could we then not salvage our optimism with the addition of an account of "fair competition," according to which some or even all parties may lose and thus be dissatisfied but, because they accepted the competitive and uncertain nature of market activity to begin with, they thus knew and agreed from the start

---

of rational persons. . . . The perfect market, were it realized, would constitute a morally free zone, a zone within which the constraints of morality would have no place."

11. See also David Copp, "Morality, Reason and Management Science: The Rationale of Cost-Benefit Analysis," *Ethics and Economics, Social Philosophy and Policy* 2 (Spring 1985).

that they could lose as well as win. And if it is known and agreed from the start that the competition in some particular industry is ruthless and involves a certain amount of deception, then the activities of the competitors in that industry would seem to be just and fair, even if observers on the outside find them morally repugnant. Game theory can present us with a precise model of such situations, whether or not we are willing to call the various results "morality." Such relativism has its virtues, but the eclipse of morality (say, in an illegal, disreputable, or otherwise antisocial industry) is not one of them.[12]

The trump card of the game theoretical notion of rationality is the threat that, if one is not maximizing utility, one will surely be taken advantage of by others who are. The ultimate paranoid notion here is the notion of the "Dutch bookie," a theoretical Donald Trump, who lies in wait for such nonmaximizers and pounces on them—a scenario made all too attractive by current obviously self-destructive business practices. But if we presumed and prepared for such a prisoner's dilemma scenario, would or could there be any business? Would you deposit part of your hard-earned salary in a money market account while harboring even the least suspicion that your money manager might be motivated to steal you blind if only he or she wouldn't get caught? Would you long tolerate a "buyer beware" atmosphere in which it was generally known that all merchants were out to cheat you? (That familiar discomfort in tourist markets might serve as a phenomenological example.)

My main objection to game theory is that it has become much more than the theory of (some) games and strategies and more than just a set of models (sometimes) applicable to business and economics. It claims to tell us all about "rationality." If game theory were to stop there, presenting us with a series of models of narrowly defined situations with unusually competitive, specific, and self-interested goals, it would not deserve attention in a book on business ethics (and at most a minor technical section in a book on business). But even when it is competitive

---

12. Morality has been explained according to game theory by Gautier (in, *Morals by Agreement*), who, on the one hand, explicitly contrasts morals and the market but, on the other, makes it very clear that morality, like market behavior, is ultimately determined only according to our negotiated preferences in what is essentially still a market situation—originally competitive negotiation in favor of long-term utilities. But he notes (p. 319 that "The underlying idea of the market is not that of a game. The market is the framework of an asocial rather than of opposed interaction; it is an optimal environment for those who must [!] engage in mutually instrumental interaction." Elsewhere (p. 59), Gautier states that "Value, then, we take to be a measure of individual preference—subjective because it is a measure of preference and relative because it is a measure of individual preference. What is good is good ultimately because it is preferred, and it is good from the standpoint of those and only those who prefer it." See also Jules Coleman, "Market Contractarianism and the Unanimity Rule," (*Ethics and Economics, Social Philosophy and Policy* 2 (Spring 1985).

and self-interested, business bargaining has a lot more to do with some shared sense of social psychology than with mathematics, and ethics has a lot more to do with cooperation and community than with coordinated self-interest. If you think that poker is a game of odds, you had better stay away from the table, and if you think that running a business is a study in applied finance, you had better stay in the seminar room. And if you think that the point of either activity is to "maximize your expected utility" then perhaps you need a psychiatrist or a philosopher to tell you something about the meaning(s) of life.

The use of game models in business is too often degrading to business rather than revealing. For example, the prisoner's dilemma model is often used to plot and account for business strategies in a "one-shot" situation, in which we find the depressing consequences of the model, that two rational players must forgo benefits that would be available to them if they were to cooperate. But, what sort of business would this be? It's one that we would call "fly-by-night." There is no repeat business. There is consequently no role for any of the Aristotelean or standard business virtues, which presuppose a continuing community and an ongoing practice, which depend on a "sense of honor" not just as an extraordinary but not-to-be-expected virtue but as a running assumption, a part of a person's or a business's character or reputation. Recent theory has improved this abysmal implicit portrait of business: at least it is generally agreed that business involves repeating games and is not "fly by night," and the strategy of repeated and continuing prisoner's dilemma type games has become a topic of considerable research.[13] The idea that business can be cooperative (without being collusive) is gaining acceptance and the overly narrow conceptions of the goal of the games (pure and preordained self-interest) is giving rise to a much more flexible picture of the goal orientation of business players. (We might, perhaps, distinguish between what one could call *unrefined* game theoretical models, the sort routinely and uncritically adopted by many economists, and *refined* models, the sort that have recently been recommended by justice-minded social planners and philosophers. The former assumes unembellished self-interest and more or less unbridled competition while the latter presumes mutual concern, cooperation, and, where need be, arbitration.) But it is the basic frame and perspective of game theory that I want to challenge, and not just

13. Notably, by Robert Axelrod in his book, *The Evolution of Cooperation* (New York: Basic Books, 1984). The best strategy in such situations turns out to be return trust and cooperation with trust and cooperation, breaches of trust and betrayal with breach of trust and betrayal as punishment, or "tit for tat." It is a result with obvious practical implications and enormous theoretical promise (e.g., in the evolution of punishment and revenge as well as cooperation), but the basic assumptions of the problem—utility maximization and the noncooperative stance—pertain to such sophisticated models as well as the more vulgar models, even when their conclusion is (qualified) cooperation.

its (frequent) lack of refinement. Indeed, as game theory gets more sophisticated, we tend to lose sight of the problem rather than solve it. And that problem, as I see it, is how to get people to think about business and about themselves in an Aristotelean rather than a neo-Hobbesian (or even a Rawlsian) way, which the game theoretical models simply presuppose.

RATIONALITY AND PRUDENCE

Game theory too readily equates "rationality" with prudential self-interest in the face of competition and conflict. Of course, not all games are played "against" anything (including "nature"), and, so too, not all (or even most) business activities are competitive. But though all game theorists allude to the possibility of cooperative games, it is illustrative that the game type that dominates discussion and is most often chosen as a model for business is the prisoner's dilemma, an uncompromisingly competitive and even vicious game. The paradigm here is insidious. The "rational" approach to a problem turns out to be self-interested and paranoid and the solution is the "safe" one—better not trust the other player because he or she might not trust you. But if games (in general) are so conceived, cooperative games turn out to be preferable only because they are the safest games; they do not eliminate selfishness or distrust but only emphasize strategies that assure mutually satisfying as well as optimal outcomes. (Thus the Hobbesian conception of society by contract, as the best solution to mutual hostility and fear.)[14] What is entirely missing is any sense of shared (as opposed to merely mutual) interests and dedication to anything larger or more meaningful than one's own interests.

I think that Nick Rescher gets it right when he accuses traditional game theory of begging two questions: whether rationality demands this prudential, safety-first approach and, much more important, whether rationality demands the cultivation of personal advantage to the exclusion of the interests of others.[15] Game theorists have taken it as "paradoxical" that rational participants in a prisoner's dilemma fail to reach their mutually preferred result. (According to Anatole Rapaport, "the paradox is that if both players make the rational choice, . . . both lose.")[16] Rescher denies the paradox: "There is in fact nothing paradoxical about

14. Here I have benefited from T. C. Schelling, *The Strategy of Conflict* (Cambridge: Harvard University Press, 1960); Edward F. McClennen, "Morality as a Public Good," a manuscript read at the Society for Business Ethics meeting in Washington, D.C. December 1988; Bernard Suits, *The Grasshopper* (Toronto: University of Toronto Press, 1978).

15. Nicholas Rescher, *Unselfishness* (Pittsburgh: University of Pittsburgh Press, 1975) pp. 38–39.

16. "Escape from Paradox, *Scientific American* 217 (1967): 51.

this. It shows merely that the realization of a generally advantageous result may require the running of individual risks, and that the pursuit of other disinterested prudence may produce a situation in which the general interest of the community is impaired."[17] But he adds, "for these lessons we did not need to await modern game theory; the moralists of classical antiquity told us as much many years ago."[18] Indeed, they did, but why should we choose as a model for business (much less for society) a situation so intrinsically antagonistic?

MOTIVATION AND SELF-INTEREST

Game theory begins with the assumption that each player is trying to satisfy his or her own interests. Even where the assumption is so weak and so abstemious about human nature to insist only on the "interests" (not "self-interest") of the players, the notion of competitive self-interest inevitably sneaks back in. (This is just as true of cooperative games as competitive games: a game becomes cooperative because this is the "rational" strategy for all parties to satisfy their interests.) Of course, refined game theorists insist that the notion of "interest" or "preference" here is not necessarily selfish; indeed it might include all sorts of altruistic desires—wanting to feed one's family or have money to give to the poor or to political candidates. But the slippage between this noncommittal sense of "interest" and self-interest is fast and furious. One can see it in John Rawls's characterization of "mutually disinterested rationality," for example:

> The assumption of mutually disinterested rationality, then, comes to this: the persons in the original position try to acknowledge principles which advance their system of ends as far as possible, They do this by attempting to win for themselves the highest index of primary social goods, since this enables them to promote their conception of the good most effectively whatever it turns out to be. The parties do not seek to confer benefits or to impose injuries on one another; they are not moved by affection or rancor. Nor do they try to gain relative to one another; they are not envious or vain. But in terms of a game, we might say: they strive for as high an absolute score as possible.[19]

I have always found it curious, at least, that in the "original position" people do not even know their own sex or ambitions but do know so much about game theory and the social sciences. They don't feel envy, affection, or competition but nevertheless pursue a very well-defined strategy for satisfying their (potential) desires. According to Rawls, those in the original position

17. Rescher, *Unselfishness*, p. 35.
18. Ibid.
19. Rawls, *A Theory of Justice*, p. 144.

do not know their conception of the good. This means that while they know that they have some rational plan of life, they do not know the details of this plan, the particular ends and interests which it is calculated to promote. How then can they decide which conceptions of justice are most to their advantage? . . . [T]hey assume that they would prefer more primary social goods rather than less. . . . [F]rom the standpoint of the original position, it is rational for the parties to suppose that they do want a larger share, since in any case they are not compelled to accept more if they do not wish to.[20]

In other words, get the goods first and you can decide what to do with them afterward. There may be no theory of human nature embedded here, but there certainly is a very strong *prudential* theory and it looks an awful lot like what I called "abstract greed."

MONEY AND MEASUREMENT

In most games, we like to keep score. (I don't take this as an essential feature of games, but it does seem to be one of the most durable features of game theory.) The best way to keep score is to have a dependable point system, a definite unit of worth. Not surprisingly, game theorists modeling society end up talking a great deal about money. Of course, here too the proper excuses are made, "money isn't the only or even the primary social good," "money is only a means and not an end," and so forth. But though the conversation may begin with talk about primary social goods, I find that soon we have yet another example involving money. Economists, of course, do not apologize for this. Money talk is their game, though they will admit, if pressed, that people do (at least occasionally) want things that money can't buy. (These are the various x factors hidden behind the asterisk that indicates the margin of error.) But social theorists in general like to talk about money, because money is a readily measurable utility, a readily comparable measure, an apparently clear basis for comparison. Of course, even some unrefined theorists recognize that equal amounts of money do not have equal significance for different people, and so the inescapable qualifications of marginal utility and the "utility of money" are (hesitantly) entered into the equation. But then the calculation proceeds as if all of this has been deftly settled with the simple declaration that we should "assume that these are the same." And when it's over, we can shift back to that very general talk about "primary social goods"—including such intangibles as health, freedom, self-esteem, and peace of mind, as if the quantification of one carefully defined domain of the theory will extend *ipso pipso* to the rest.

But various ends are hard to compare (one person wants to win a

20. Ibid., p. 142.

downhill ski race, another wants to sleep in a hammock) and so success and "maximum utility" may be hard to measure. If we were to assign every end a monetary value, however, and rate various preferences according to their exchange value on the market, we would indeed have a single scale on which to compare and evaluate ends and means and determine maximum utility. Thus the victory of the economists; and the rise of what Karl Marx called "fetishism."

THE ANOMALY OF ALTRUISM

Even where self-interest is not assumed as the basis of the game and the goal of each and every player, altruism gets treated as an anomaly, at best a fringe benefit not to be taken for granted but at worst an intolerable interference with the workings of the game. Imagine an extremely generous poker player, or one who did not want to take advantage of his unusually good hands, and you get the idea. And so we assume self-interest if not selfishness, or, worse, the unrefined game theorist promotes an extreme dichotomy between self-interest and altruism, to the great disadvantage of the latter (shades of Ayn Rand rather than Nietzsche). For example here is Moritz Schlick:

> The unrestrained development of such [altruistic] inclinations . . . can certainly not lead to the valuable, and will, in fact, be considered moral. To respect every desire of one's neighbor, to give in to every sympathetic impulse results, finally, neither in the highest measure of joy for the individual himself, nor indeed for the others; in such a case one no longer speaks of kindness, but of *weakness*.[21]

Rescher (who quotes Schlick with some sympathy) attacks this vision of presupposed selfishness throughout his book, insisting that it is a gross mistake to conceive of rationality in such a way that it conflicts with morality and the social good and to think of ethics in terms of "intelligent selfishness." He rejects the "prudentially safety-first-minded pursuit of personal advantage" that defines most game theory in favor of a theory of the "vicarious" sympathetic emotions. We obtain "utility" through our sympathy with others, experiencing joy at their successes, for instances, and not just from our own success. But even Rescher seems trapped in the old paradigm, which I take as a sign of its enduring strength. He distinguishes between "first order utility," the satisfaction of one's own desires, and "second order utility, one's satisfaction as the result of the satisfaction of another. But the very act of ordering (and the use of the word "vicarious") shows that Rescher too can't quite take seriously the idea of truly shared—not "vicarious"—satisfaction.

21. Moritz Schlick, *Problems of Ethics*, trans. D. Rynin (New York, 1939) pp. 202–3.

So, too, even cooperative games seem to me to presuppose just that notion of primary individual self-interest that I want to reject, whether or not supplemented or made possible by simultaneously satisfying the interests of others. The concept of the virtues—that is, as opposed to the skills required to play the game—gets lost here. I take it that this is what Rescher is aiming at when he attacks utilitarianism on the grounds that it insists that "everyone counts for one and only for one," which leaves no room, according to Rescher, for relationships, kinship, and other forms of affection and association. Of course, a flexible utilitarian can readily incorporate the "vicarious" sentiments and second-order utility into the "happiness calculus," but Rescher denies that the utilitarian can be so flexible. (For my dissent on the behalf of one of them, see my discussion of Mill at the end of Part I.) But my point is that the alternative to self-interested games is not altruism, much less self-sacrifice or even vicarious satisfaction. It is the very notion of discrete "players" with discrete interests that I want to throw into question.

GOODS AND GOALS

Even the "modest" assumption that our behavior is "goal-oriented" is, I think, inaccurate and prejudicial. Ned McClennen, for instance, insists that he can "avoid making any essentialist assumptions about human nature" and requires only the modest assumption that people are goal-oriented.[22] This is not to say anything about *what* goals they pursue, of course, or is it even to suggest a more general Rawlsian consensus on fundamental goals. But though one can hardly deny that we do have many goals in life, from, wanting to get to the garbage can before the dog does to wanting to win a Nobel Prize, I think that the view that our activities are essentially goal-oriented is mistaken and, sometimes, tragic. "But certainly," someone is sure to protest, "nothing is more central to an Aristotelean approach than the notion of teleology." And, indeed, that's so. But I think that what Aristotle had in mind by "teleology" was quite different from what we mean (and game theorists in particular mean) by "goal-oriented." For one thing, the satisfaction of desire, while certainly not irrelevant to Aristotle's teleology, is not at all what he has in mind. But a more basic concern is that when you look at Aristotle's conception of the ingredients of the good life, the virtues, and our various activities, it is evident that while these involve certain standards ("the mean between the extremes" and all that) it is not the satisfaction of those standards that motivates us, and one would be hard pressed to identify the "goals" that define most of those virtues. Our activities are not necessarily goal-oriented either. True, Aristotle begins

22. Edward McClennen, "Foundational Explorations for a Normative Theory of Political Economy,"

by insisting that "every art and science has its end," but if we look at one of those activities that Aristotle praised and prized above all others, namely friendship, it becomes clear that "goal orientation" has no proper application. What is the goal of friendship? Mutual pursuit of goals as the basis of friendship, concretely defined, would indicate something less than ideal friendship. So despite all of the celebrated talk about teleology, I want to suggest that the game-theoretical assumption of goal orientation is in fact un-Aristotelean— and misleading as a way of thinking about most human activities, including business.[23]

THE OPEN-ENDED PLAYING FIELD

As argued earlier, games and the contexts of decision making are too contained. It is with good reason that game theorists refer to "externalities," for it is self-containment that defines most games. The football field has carefully drawn lines around it, and only a specified number of players are allowed on the field. Poker gets played with a conscientiously nonpersonalized deck of cards, and every player is "in" or "out." There is no waiting on the fringe to "see how the hand goes" before joining in. Life, on the other hand, is always open ended. There need be no fixed number of players in most business deals, and business ethics has been conscientious in its insistence that the "playing field" of corporate business is not just the boardroom but the employees and customers and entire community, "stakeholders" and not necessarily insiders. Games are closed; the market is by its very nature open. Simply adding "players" to the game won't work, not because the complications are infinite (though sometimes it seems that way) but because human contexts change as we play with them, unlike the neatly painted board on which many games are played. There are never just fifty-two cards in the deck and never just n alternatives or players in the market, and the notion of "playing" a game radically changes when not only the spectators but a multitude of mere passers-by wander onto the playing field and have their lives greatly affected by the game.

THE ROLE OF THE RULES

Games, as we generally conceive of them (even Wittgenstein fell for this one), are thought to be rule-defined.[24] But business as a practice is much larger than that. The rules come after. Business ethics involves

23. For an excellent discussion of this non-goal-oriented concept of teleology in Aristotle, see Michael Stocker in *Essays on Aristotle's Ethics*, ed. Amelie Rorty (Berkeley: University of California Press, 1980).

24. Ludwig Wittgenstein, *Philosophical Investigations*. See also Suits, *The Grasshopper*.

phronesis, sensitivity and imagination, not just obeying the rules. Of course there are rules (especially laws) and it is both unethical and imprudent to disobey them. But I think that it is essential to see business and business life first of all as a *practice,* not a game (which is a very specific and narrow kind of practice), in which general expectations and mutual agreements are established before there are any rules, much less laws. As so often, I think that we get taken in by "social contract"–type thinking, when in fact it is the established practice that makes contracts possible—and rules sometimes necessary. But business has a lot longer history than business law, and rules, regulations, and laws are formulated not before but after business practices are established and, paradoxically, after the transgressions that they are designed to prohibit.

Let me end this discussion by insisting that game theory is not just a *model* for business. Game theory is *ideology.* It is instructive. It provides the frame within which participants in the practice are encouraged to operate, the lenses through which they should see what they are doing: "One should think of it this way." "This is how one should behave." "One should expect that this is what will happen." On a microlevel, imagine a salesman and his customer and the very different situations in which they would find themselves depending on whether they see the transaction as primarily competitive and perhaps as a prisoner's dilemma or rather as a joint effort to get mutual satisfaction. Of course, as in all microtransactions, the situation is largely determined by the context—for example, consider the difference between a visit to a used-car dealer and a trip to your contact lens specialist. But buying a used car, we might note, is by now established as a kind of medium-risk competitive game whereas buying a pair of contact lenses is, in any sense that concerns us here, not a game at all. In short, thinking about business and business ethics through game theory is not just a tool for understanding; it is a prescription, and one that, in many cases, we would be wise not to follow.

Many of the recent wrinkles in game theory do indeed blunt the objections that I suggest.[25] But this is not entirely fortunate, for the game theory metaphor, like so many systematically misleading metaphors in philosophy, needs not improvement but dismantling (as a model for business practices and, especially, for morality and business ethics; I certainly have no objection to the theory for its own sake, or as a powerful model *for games*). But game theory has now become the preferred way of doing both ethics and economics, and that is a very different matter. In the name of "rationality," we begin with a set of dubious, anti-Aristotelean presuppositions about business and human

25. Ned McClennen has done some of the wrinkling and I have learned much about the subject from him; e.g., Edward McClennen, "Prisoner's Dilemma and Resolute Choice" (Paradoxes of Rationality and Cooperation) and "Justice and the Problem of Stability," *Philosophy and Public Affairs* (1988).

decision making and then proceed, often with brilliance, to work out a detailed mathematical strategy. But however enticing the paradoxes of formalism (and they are indeed captivating), it is a mistake to think that by solving technical problems in a theory that is already off the mark we will thereby resolve the criticism that it is indeed off the mark.[26]

26. Jon Elster in many books, including *Solomonic Judgments* (Cambridge: Cambridge University Press, 1990), and *Ulysses and the Sirens: Studies in Rationality and Irrationality* (Cambridge: Cambridge University Press, 1989), keeps probing the breakdown of rationality, but, nevertheless, he won't give it up.

6

The End of Cowboy Capitalism

Competition consists in trying to do things better than someone else; that is, making or selling a better article at a lesser cost, or otherwise giving better service. It is not a competition to resort to methods of the prize ring, and simply "knock the other man out." That is killing a competitor.

JUSTICE LOUIS BRANDEIS, "Competition"

What America needs is not to be more competitive, but more co-operative.

ED FREEMAN, *Ethics Digest*

Competition is said to be the backbone of business, the engine that makes it move, the mechanism that makes the great machine of capitalism go, the "magic" in the magic of the market. Much of this, of course, is sheer demagoguery, an excuse for or a polemic against this or that government program, and much of it too is self-congratulation, proclaimed by spokesmen for giant companies who have indeed won the field or, more likely, have accumulated such a monopoly that they themselves have ended the competition—and would like to keep it that way. Most of it, of course, is just one more macho metaphor, the self-gratifying male image of the lone Wild West champion taking on all comers and "proving" himself against every challenger. It is what Ed Freeman has recently called "cowboy capitalism,"[1] without, I hope, thereby meaning to question the integrity of those few rough and un-derpaid herd tenders who have enough to cope with without having to live up to a cinematic myth as well. It is simply untrue that American business loves competition. No one would pretend that Hertz was de-lighted when "number two" Avis rose in the market from one more "other" car company to a true competitor, and no one should think that "Big Blue" was thrilled by the rapid success of Apple and a half dozen other computer companies which now challenge IBM's one-time domination of the information market. The rise of foreign competition

1. R. Edward Freeman, *Ethics Digest* 1 (1989).

is even more spectacular. What passed for "competition" between American automakers in the Fifties and Sixties was, in retrospect, a friendly games of cards in the cozy living room of an exclusive club. None of the players welcomed the competition from Japan (though they had long been upset by the growing market shares in Germany). A rather awkward but obvious analogy to this example of American lack of enthusiasm for competition other than just among ourselves occurs each year, when the (by far) largest audience in the world gathers around television sets to watch the playoffs and finals of the most popular and competitive sport in the world. It was not (what we presumptuously call) the World Series or the Superbowl. Notoriously, our Big Three sports, our three "national pastimes," are almost exclusively ours. Except for a few novice leagues around the world, no one else plays much baseball or basketball or (what we call) football. And so when we call it "the World Series" and declare our teams "world champions" there is a bit of irony if not hypocrisy in the embarrassing fact that nobody else is competing for the title. And yet in soccer, the one team sport where the competition is truly international, we prefer to remain at home. Do we Americans love "the competitive spirit"? Or do we rather prefer the comfort of old established rivalries within a carefully protected arena? Competition is not the be-all and end-all of business, but neither is it an attitude that we ourselves so happily embrace as we think we do.

Young upstart entrepreneurs, of course, dream the dreams of competition, but, most of the time, competition isn't the spur to action; it is just one of the possible obstacles to be faced. Much of the time, it isn't an obstacle at all, if only because the most insightful entrepreneurs (Jobs and Wozniak at Apple) don't enter a market that is already crowded with competitors but rather find or invent an entirely new one. They are moved by the excitement of their ideas, by the challenge of the project, by the promise of success, but not, particularly, by competition. This is not to say, of course, that competition has no place or is ultimately not very important for business. Anyone can think of industries that have grown lazy and incompetent because of lack of competition, especially in cases where an industry is protected from competition by the government. (Or, alternatively, where the industry in question is actually run by the government.) The Canadian wine industry, for example, has been in operation for almost as long as its competitor in California, longer than those in Washington state, and much longer than in Texas, which began development only a decade ago and put bottles on the shelves only in the past couple of years. It shares the geological good fortunes of these others, but—with apologies to my northern neighbors—the wine it produces is almost undrinkable. (The reds *are* undrinkable.) The Canadian government protected the industry. They had a virtually captive clientele, and there was no reason to be self-critical, to experiment, and to improve. Once that protection ended, the industry was on the brink of failure, kept afloat only by chauvinism and already-ruined palates. But the good news is that, with international competition, the industry is starting to show some sense of quality, as American car manufacturers learned for themselves after two decades of uneven competition with the Japanese and the Germans.

We all know of dozens of similar examples, if we can remember back before the products in question disappeared from the market. There can be no doubt about the value of competition, but it is a corrective and a constraint, not the carrot but, perhaps, more the stick that serves as a constant warning: nothing here is guaranteed or assured, there are no ultimate monopolies and business (your business) exists only because it succeeds in serving a purpose, in satisfying consumers, and if it fails to do so, or someone else can do it better or with more appeal, then the stick finds its mark and measures out its punishment. But, of course, competition isn't the only source of sanctions in the business world, nor should it be. Companies that unknowingly manufacture deadly products but then refuse to take them off the market immediately—for example, the makers of flammable children's clothing back in the 1970s—require a quicker hand than Adam Smith's "invisible" one. The public doesn't always pay attention, and, often, it is just the most vulnerable segment of the population that is the least informed. Government regulation, itself not known for its speediness or its immunity from public ignorance, is certainly not the best of the options, but until others (industrywide self-regulation and policing, for example) are willing to develop themselves, then competition will have to be coupled with government regulation in lieu of supposed consumer sovereignty.

The problem is to put competition in its proper place, to understand how it works, and why (and when) it is beneficial. The metaphors "mechanism" and "magic" may be edifying or exciting but they are hardly enlightening. Competition is a matter of motivation and social interaction, not machinery, and magic suggests, whatever else, the inexplicable, the mysterious. But there is nothing mysterious about competition or its effects, only a concept clouded by myths and metaphors. Most important of all, competition has an *ethical* quality (as magic may but mechanisms do not). Indeed, some societies see capitalism and business competition as "black magic," destroying age-old social structures at the first introduction of competition and consumerism. There is "healthy" competition and there is sick, debilitating, and depraved competition. There is fair competition and there is underhanded competition. There is constructive, positive, even inspiring competition, and there is mutually destructive, negative, inhibiting competition.[2] War and jungle metaphors give us the latter, along with all zero-sum games the point of which is to punch out your opponent, debilitate the competition, and win at his or her expense. Justice Arthur Goldberg once argued, "our devotion to free-wheeling industrial competition must not force us into accepting the law of the jungle as the standard of morality expected in our commercial relations."[3]

Business competition by contrast offers us the best examples of the former, in which competition serves as a spur to one's own excellence, an incentive to improve—even new heroes, ideals, and examples to follow. Of course, the line between constructive and destructive competition is rarely all that precise: a boxer improves his skills by routinely maiming his opponents, and most confrontational zero-sum ("win or lose") sports simultaneously involve the demonstration of one's own ability and the attempt to unseat, demolish, or conquer the competition. (The number of war metaphors in sports writing, of course, is utterly staggering.) And most businesses "in the heat of battle" will give way to the temptation to hurt the competition even as they try to improve themselves. But the nature and intent of the distinction is obvious, to separate those practices in which the primary goal is to promote excellence and those in which it is simply to prevail, preferably by undermining the opposition. We have little trouble distinguishing between the runner who wins the race by running faster and the runner who wins by tripping up his competitor. We had little trouble watching the chariot race in *Ben Hur* and recognizing that the good guy was the one who *wasn't* trying to demolish the chariot wheels or blind his opponent. Competition has ethical constraints, and foremost among these in business is the demand that competition be healthy, fair, and positive, encouraging excellence, innovation, efficiency, and productivity, and not merely keeping ahead of (or eliminating) the competition.

In today's business world, physical sabotage is relatively rare and in any case a criminal offense. But there are subtler forms of sabotage, and every business struggles with these. Perhaps nowhere is this more troublesome than in the "information industry," in which the distinction between "finding out for oneself" and sheer theft or plagiarism may seem clear enough, but the rules constituting both theft and plagiarism get ever more problematic. A notorious kind of example is the practice of hiring people away from one's competitors, often luring them

---

2. Lynne Sharpe Paine, "Ideals of Competition and Today's Marketplace," in *Enriching Business Ethics*, ed. Clarence Walton (New York: Plenum, 1990).

3. Justice Arthur Goldberg in *DuPont Nemours v. Christopher*, (Fifth Circuit Court, 1971), 400 U.S. 1024. Purely destructive competition, in which the sole aim of business is to hurt a competitor, is illegal. Cf. *Tuttle v. Buck*, in which a banker set up a barber shop for the sole purpose of putting a personal enemy out of business. The court ruled against the banker.

with offers that substantially exceed the usual package for that position. As the practice becomes more common, the salaries tend to rise accordingly even as the standards for fair competition evaporate. This is sabotage (or espionage) of a subtle sort, for in one sense one does not "take" information away from the competitor (as one would take a television set or a computer, for example) and neither does one destroy it (as one could destroy a television or a computer.) Indeed, that sort of sabotage and the actual destruction of information, while not unknown, is not the usual concern. ("Hackers" have bypassed security systems and erased or altered massive chunks of sensitive information.) The problem is that the *value* of the information is thereby destroyed, not the information itself, and one can see in the information industry, where new and exclusive information is the whole product, how "pure" competition can become—that is, it is not the having of the information oneself but having it exclusively that is the measure of excellence. Making the matter more complicated, of course, is the fact that, until very recently, the laws governing ownership, copywriting, and patenting of ideas and information as such were wholly inadequate to the information revolution of the past few decades, and the older sense of business competition, which had mainly to do with making and selling material objects, now had to deal with an entirely new conception of "the product" and, consequently, with fair competition as well.

Computer software companies, of course, are nothing but part of the information industry and are particularly vulnerable to this new form of negative competition—that is, stealing instead of inventing. There have always been black markets for stolen goods, but there the criterion for stealing is rather straightforward. But almost all companies have information that needs to be kept exclusive, whether it is the secret formula for Coke (the "classic" kind) or the marketing strategy for northern New Jersey. In the Coke case, the theft of the information is virtually tantamount to the theft of the product itself (less only the ingredient and manufacturing costs). In the marketing strategy case, however, the nature of the offense is much less obvious. It is clearly unfair competition (tantamount to bugging the halfback's helmet before the huddle) but, if one assumes the means of access are not against the law (itself a shady area these days), the offense is ethical rather than legal and the fault is in the nature of the competition. It is negative rather than positive and, quite the contrary of encouraging excellence, it produces increased secrecy and defensiveness and discourages innovation. It is estimated that the proceeds for popular software are something less than 30 percent of the actual sales and transfers because of extensive pirating and (how to distinguish?) rather freewheeling copying from office to office and from friend to friend. (Similarly, one should mention that the annual returns to authors of books that sell after their first year are comparably low, because of the used book market.) To be sure, it does not now appear that there will be a dearth of eager and inventive computer programmers in the near future or a decline in the quality and speed of innovation, nor do we expect any decrease in the number of authors who will set pen to paper or fingertips to keyboard. But the fact rubs against our sense of fairness and fair return, and the competition in such cases (pirates and used-book dealers, respectively) does not strike us as healthy competition in the slightest.

Oddly enough, the ethics and impact of competition is left out of one of the most obvious areas in business ethics, where it clearly belongs. In the much practiced business of "stakeholder analysis," the usual list of stakeholders—stockholders, employees, customers, vendors, the community, and the larger society—typically omits the rest of the industry and, in particular, the competition. But one's competitors are often the most directly affected by the activities of a corporation, and competitive relationships are at least as concerned with ethical questions of merit and fairness, rights and obligations, as the more celebrated fiduciary relationships with stockholders and responsibilities to employees and customers. The assumption seems to be that competitors, because they are so opposed to one another, are not part of the same sort of ethical network that ties together a single corporation and its constituencies. But this represents an unwitting and unfortunate slip back into the old battlefield mentality: "You can do whatever you like to the enemy even if you take care not to harm any civilians." The ethics of competition is absolutely central to business ethics and the Aristotelean approach in particular. But competitors are fellow seekers after a common prize, not obstacles to one another.[4] What could be more damaging, then, than that vulgar piece of market wisdom that preaches, "The only good competitor is a dead competitor," or the advice to aspiring entrepreneurs in a widely used policy textbook: "The best battleground is the market segment or dimensions of strategy in which competitors are ill-prepared, least enthusiastic, or most uncomfortable."[5]

Competition is not primary in business. Competition is essential, but it is neither the end of business activity (to "prevail" or, in the more Darwinian mode, to "survive") nor is it the mechanism or means of success in business. Business competition is possible and makes sense only within a framework of mutual interest and cooperation, and competition in general (even in the jungle) is possible only within a system that can distinguish healthy from unhealthy, positive from merely negative competition. In business, this framework is the demand for prosperity and the various demands of justice. There is little doubt—except

4. Rudolf Callmann, *Unfair Competition, Trademarks and Monopolies*, 4th ed. (1981). Quoted in Paine, "Ideals of Competition," pp. 95, 109.

5. C. Roland Christensen and Kenneth R. Andrews, *Business Policy: Texts and Cases*, 6th ed. (Homewood, Ill.: Irwin, 1987) p. 239.

in the most extreme laissez faire theorists—that these are forms of competition that have the potential to be devastating not only to our economy but to our social and psychological well-being. The mutual sabotage and destruction of many recent and much-publicized business deals, no matter how exhilarating for the participants, inexpensive for consumers, or amusing for spectators, have far-reaching consequences that cannot be measured by the usual short-term standards. We cannot and never will allow "unbridled" competition, and even the most extreme "laissez faire" theorists defend the absolutely free competitive market because they believe that competition will in effect provide its own constraints through consumer activity (though this is hardly "sovereignty") and the law of supply and demand, coupled, one would hope, with some sense of consumer responsibility and sense of the public good as well. Competition is but one of several interlocking strategies for improving productivity, price, and quality, not the framework of business activity itself, and, as the Eastern Europeans have recently discovered (much to their distress), there are many necessary but customary restraints on a market system other than those specified by the law of supply and demand alone or those formulated into law by way of government control and regulation. The "conservativism" of business refers not just to its most common political preferences but to an essential if usually unacknowledged component of all business life, those forms of self-constraint and habitual integrity without which free enterprise would become an underworld of crime, extortion, and black marketeering.[6]

It might be argued that what distinguishes business competition is the fact that, as opposed to most other areas of legal activity, competitors are actually permitted, even "privileged," to harm one another.[7] Indeed, Paine even goes so far as to suggest that antitrust law, in particular, ensures that such harm actually occurs. Of course, whatever a firm does may, with or without intending to do so, hurt a competitor, whether it is hiring the best person for a position that both have open, luring away an outstanding employee from the other company, taking the lion's share of a limited market, or soaking up a substantial proportion of the limited equipment or capital (as the U.S. government regularly does with impunity). But notice that this view presumes a zero-sum situation in which markets are already limited and not created and there are too few outstanding people for a position. But many markets are discovered or invented, and the supply of qualified and even outstanding employees is not a factor that is wholly external to business. Entrepreneurs leap into markets that are not already established, perhaps nonexistent, and it is not clear that they are hurting their com-

6. Cf. David Gautier, *Morals by Agreement* (New York: Oxford University Press, 1986), esp. ch. 4 (we only need morals when market breaks down).
7. Paine, "Ideals of Competition."

petitors (if they have any) by doing so. Fast-growing businesses expand their markets and provide new resources and plenty of room for similar companies, and it is not as if the competition for either markets or resources is mutually harmful or destructive. Of course, if it weren't for the competition, one might be taking in an 80 percent market share instead of only 65 percent, but it is not as if keeping someone from increasing the profits 15 percent is exactly harming them. So, too, corporations train people; they do not just find them. (Which is one good argument why luring trained people away is sometimes akin to stealing.) But it is not as if training more good people is in any obvious sense keeping them away from a competitor and, thus, hurting them. To the contrary, it would seem as if the one is doing the other an enormous favor, which is to the detriment of neither.

Our celebration of competition is in fact one of those grand abstractions from an enormously complicated and largely unseen network of cooperative arrangements. The shared language we speak is essential to even the most primitive negotiations (excepting only, perhaps, the flash of a fist or a throaty growl) and even the most obvious offer presupposes some shared conventions and expectations. The most basic contract presupposes an ethical world of (qualified) mutual trust and dependable commitments. The most "ruthless" business competition assumes from the start that a standoff is better than mutual destruction. (There are occasions to the contrary, but these are exercises in vengeance, not business.) Even in zero-sum betting games, the win-or-lose competition presupposes a context of cooperation. And when we consider the many kinds of competition, between creative artists as well as nations and football teams, we begin to appreciate how one-sided is our usual view of head-to-head, all-or-nothing competition. Many forms of competition, Paine reminds us, "leave a great deal of room for individual differences and creativity." Many involve very little attention to one's rivals and have little to do with knocking them down or outwitting them. The best activities and practices aim to create a superior performance. In spite of our warlike, Darwinian, and competitive metaphors, business competition of this sort, where it is well done—a top-quality product at a reasonable price, the only entry in a hungry but wide-open market, an insight into opportunity before the market is saturated—may result in no competition at all. "Business more closely resembles the highly creative activities which . . . basically depend on the creativity of the participants to define their character."[8]

My point is to appreciate the place and purpose of competition, not to idolize it or celebrate its effects in isolation of the society in which it plays a central role. Is it in fact constructive or is it rather more de-

8. Paine, ibid., p. 95.

structive? Is an entry into the fray a display of what Paine calls "independent initiative" or is it just an attempt to rip off a few bucks after someone else's creative efforts?[9] Is a competitor acting on strength or taking advantage of another competitor's weaknesses? The purpose of competition, after all, is to inspire and reward innovation and effort.[10]

9. Paine, ibid., overstates the case: "At a minimum, one should not present another's work or creation as one's own." But this concerns cheating, not competition. If I plagiarize Shakespeare I am cheating, but I am hardly competing with him.

10. Paine rightly brings the argument home to academia as well: "At the logical extreme, such an inbred system would cease to innovate altogether. One can observe in certain academic fields a gradual narrowing of topics and approaches considered legitimate. Scholars define their problems in terms of those set for them in the literature. One cannot help but wonder whether less attention to the literature in the field and a more liberal attitude toward legitimacy might not lead more frequently to significant intellectual advances" (ibid., p. 98).

7

Atomic Myths and Metaphors: Individualism and "the Entrepeneur"

Nineteenth century America was individualistic compared with the peasant cultures of Asia or the villages of old Europe; but it was not individualistic as we understand the term today. Most people lived in communities of face-to-face relationships. For better or worse, you were stuck with your minister, your neighbor, your brothers and your sisters. . . . In the new industrial city [by contrast] the first loyalty was not to the community but to the self.

JAMES COLLIER, *The Rise of Selfishness in America*

The underlying metaphor of so much of our thinking—though again we rarely think of it as a metaphor—is our much-celebrated idea of "the individual" and, in business especially, "the self-made [man]." Never mind that the most often leveled criticism of most corporate cultures is that they suppress individuality and stifle individual expression and creativity. Never mind that today's self-made man or woman succeeded in part by "fitting in" and by becoming one with (and probably an indispensable part of) some organization. Even the garage workshop genius had to be thoroughly steeped in the culture that made his or her invention possible. The obvious exceptions to this rule, those precocious inventors who through their random tinkering create a product or prototype that will not find its market for years, even centuries, and then perhaps in some other culture, only underscore the point. The lesson of such inventiveness is not easily grasped by too many contemporary corporate managers, who understandably prefer predictable conformity, short term "results," and control to the eccentricity and patience from which new ideas emerge. By way of compensation, we are flooded with seminars and whole courses on "innovation," attempts to control the creative process—as corporate managers like to say, "like trying to nail Jello to the wall." But the mistake on the other side (often

74

defended by the same high-control managers) is to over-emphasize an utterly vacuous sense of the individual. The point is that we will never understand the world of business (or any other human world) unless we begin with human interrelations and how people "fit in" with organizations and institutions. It is not first of all individual motives and attributes that make the business world possible. It is an established set of *practices,* in which group organization and not individual personalities are the principle structure.

The continuing corporate obsession with the almost mythological character called "the entrepreneur" would be a kind of joke if it did not also display such fatal self-deception and even, in some cases, cruelty and hypocrisy. It is an illusion—shared by more than half of today's managers—that they "would start their own businesses if they could," as if the structure and security of corporate life were only a temporary deviation from an otherwise solo performance. I have attacked this celebrated notion at greater length elsewhere,[1] but here I want only to reiterate the utter inappropriateness of such a concept within the typical corporate setting. Entrepreneurs set up businesses, it is true, and it may even be that behind every successful business is some entrepreneur, that is, one of those relatively rare individuals who are both creative and business-minded, who are willing to take considerable risks and work single-mindedly to translate their dreams and ideas into marketable reality. But corporations, once formed, do not operate on the same risk-prone, creative principles that motivated the originator of the business, and the corporate world could not possibly function if, as we so often hear, everyone were to aspire to be an entrepreneur. True, large corporations tend to be somewhat like giant barges, slow-moving (even in a crisis), hard to turn around, with lots of momentum (or inertia) to continue in a manner now well established. Thus we have the almost continuous efforts to "shake up" the corporation and "give it some new blood"; pointless and usually destructive mass firings resulting, despite the flurry of internal activity, in an even more timid and slow-moving beast, and—more benign but equally pointless—frequent seminars (often side by side with "innovation'" and "entrepreneurship"), as if taking a course in the belly of a giant corporation would somehow teach an employee to act as if he or she were not in a corporation at all. The truth is rather that what makes corporations work and flourish are not the rapid turnaround and enormous risk undertaken by the entrepreneur but precisely that dependability and security that comes with being so established—and this is just as true of the sense of security of the employees in the corporation who trust its stability and fairness as it is of the consumers who trust the company

1. Robert C. Solomon with K. Hanson, *It's Good Business* (New York: Athenaeum, 1985), pt. 3, sec. 2, "A Hero for Our Times." The figure referred to above—actually 60 percent of executives interviewed—is from a Knight-Ridder poll, Sept. 1991.

for the established quality of its products and services. The key to success of most corporations is that unheralded hero who used to be called, with some disdain, "the company man" (now also "the company woman"). It is not just the rare, eccentric individual who makes a company successful. It is also all of those individuals who are perfectly content with submerging their personal identities into the organization and maintaining its structure as part of their own being.

We are all, of course, individuals, in a number of important (and not so important) senses. Except for the rare phenomenon of "Siamese" twins, we are each physically discrete entities. It is true (a minute of mathematics may cast some doubt on the claim) that each of us is unique in a number of ways: the number of hairs on our heads, the shape of our fingerprints, the precise contours (as opposed to some Freudian-like general outline) of our childhood experience. We each (in some sense that is surprisingly difficult to delineate accurately) feel only our own pains and emotions, and (in an even more debatable sense) have our own desires and interests. But such physical and circumstantial individuation too easily eclipses the fact that, except for sheer physical pain, we often share our feelings with others, and most of our desires and interests are not only shared with but created by and with other people, even (especially) those that seem selfish and in conflict with others. The desire for status, most notably, is almost always comparative and mutually created. The demand for most consumer goods, as every advertiser knows so well, is best stimulated by encouraging envy, an emotion distinctively appropriate for a consumer society.[2] Resentment, by contrast, is more appropriate to socialist societies—and to large organizations such as corporations. To understand human motivation, therefore, is not so much to have an account of human nature (except in terms of our one overwhelming feature as "social animals") but rather to understand how people are encouraged and made to desire in specific groups and social arrangements. Our personal identity, in turn, depends not so much on our discrete personal features or our individual thoughts and memories but on our parts and role(s) in various practices.

Business is such a practice or set of practices. No one should pretend that the exchange of weavings among the Trobriand Islanders is the same activity as trading futures in the Chicago commodities market, or that the archaic word "capitalism" has the same reference in Tokyo and New York. Even the most basic business transaction presupposes distinctive human arrangements in which individuals play their parts. There is no "invisible hand," or even a visible one. There is an organized culture, which includes the various practices of producing "commodities," drawing up contracts, making exchanges, and maintaining private

2. See Helmut Schoeck, *Envy* (New York: Harcourt Brace Jovanovich, 1970).

ownership, all of which are "designed" (though through human evolution and not necessarily by any particular individual) to produce just those results that Adam Smith found so remarkable.

Families and community life are practices too, we might add, even though they have an obvious biological basis. (We need not honor that much-celebrated but false distinction between "natural" groups or units and "conventional" or "contractual" organizations.) The shape and size of a family, nuclear or extended, authoritarian or egalitarian, patriarchal, matriarchal, or (typically) infantarchal, is the product of a certain culture. (Our current ideal of the "traditional family" and its values, as far as I can discern, is largely the product of 1950s television series such as *The Donna Reed Show* and *Leave It to Beaver.*) Communities, of course, are as varied as our symbols and cultures, though to be sure some form of the tribe or "extended" family has been biological since (and before) the first Neanderthals. I mention this only to offset the common belief that business activity, in particular the concepts of exchange, incentives, and personal gain (not quite the same as "the profit motive"), is built into our genes and therefore not dependent upon or part and parcel of any particular set of cultural practices. Even if there were such a genetic origin for basic business activities (which is at best highly controversial), this would not undermine the claim that business is, as such, a practice (or rather a set of practices). It presupposes human organization, not just in the obvious sense that it takes at least two people to carry out an exchange of any kind but in the deeper sense that the notion of exchange itself would be unintelligible without certain arrangements if not institutions.

It is this emphasis on the primacy of institutional arrangements that has become essential in combating what many philosophers have taken to calling "atomic individualism," the appealing and long-standing idea that we are each first of all individuals who then enter into various agreements with one another, whether wholly voluntary or under considerable duress.[3] Indeed, according to this tradition (which has had its heyday since the seventeenth century but has roots that reach back to ancient times), not only particular human agreements but the grandest of all possible arrangements—the formation of society itself—is the product of such a "social contract." It is an appealing idea insofar as it emphasizes the priority of individuals over societies and governments and thus became the backbone of that certainly welcome modern political movement called "liberalism," a word that has altered its meaning and in many ways degenerated over the years. (In the classical sense, however, Milton Friedman is just as much a liberal as John Kenneth Galbraith or Walter Mondale.) It is attractive too in its emphasis on

3. The term "atomic individualism" has become extremely common in social philosophy, but I take it here from Elizabeth Wolgast, *A Grammar of Justice* (Ithaca: Cornell University Press, 1988).

individual autonomy and responsibility and in its uncompromising humanism, the insistence that the satisfaction of individual human needs (including those concerning spirituality) must be the first priority of any government or ruling body.

This emphasis on the priority of individuals and their subsequent arrangements and agreements has always suggested a historical and anthropological absurdity—the primeval existence of isolated individuals who somehow and for some reason gather together and make various agreements—and the foremost defenders of the social contract (Thomas Hobbes, John Locke, Jean-Jacques Rousseau, and, today, John Rawls) have all insisted that their conception is an illuminating fiction rather than a historical claim. But even as fiction the idea of naturally autonomous and independent individuals contradicts the most obvious feature of human life, that each of us is born, quite helpless and dependent, into a family and a society of some sort, and we retain that dependency in a variety of ways throughout our lives. The often brilliant philosophers who have defended liberalism, of course, have not been blind to such obvious facts of human nature. They present the notions of autonomy and contractual agreement as ideals, and specifications of the social contract today typically have some such form as "what a fully rational adult *would* agree to if he or she had a choice of alternative social arrangements."[4]

It is easy to see how some such idea lies at the basis of most business thinking, for it is voluntary choice—in itself an undeniable political ideal—that stands at the foundation of all business activity. The mistake is thinking that the nature of such choices is "natural" and not structural in certain societies, and that social interference (for example, through regulation) in our independent choices is unwarranted and illegitimate. There is, for many "free market" thinkers, a quasi-evolutionary corollary to this claim: if everyone would be allowed to make his or her choices unencumbered, the overall good for the society and the species would be maximized. But what this presupposes—and the whole of evolutionary theory soundly refutes it—is that "natural" systems are as such never dysfunctional. Because corporations, in particular, are not natural but voluntary organizations, however, it does not follow that the model of the natural community is inappropriate, or that the idea of the corporation as an organism or being with purposes of its own is or should be subject to the sort of sarcastic abuse heaped upon it recently, for example, by Michael Keeley in his *Social Contract Theory of Organizations,* nor does it follow that the social contract analysis should be embraced with the enthusiasm of Tom Dunfee, for example.[5] Apart from the original founders of a company, the stage

4. Notably, John Rawls, *A Theory of Justice* (Cambridge; Harvard University Press, 1971).

5. See also Jules Coleman, "Market Contractarianism and the Unanimity Rule," *Ethics and Economics, Social Philosophy and Policy* 2 (Spring 1985).

is not "original" or primeval, and once a corporation has been operating for only a few years (or in a few cases, even a few weeks), a corporate culture is already in place, with established ways of doing things.

The concept of a *practice* is the key to a workable alternative to atomic individualism, which does not require us to give up our treasured notions of individual value or autonomy but rather situates these in a social context and particular activities. We are not first of all individuals who then enter into various agreements with one another but first of all members of families and groups in which we learn to identify ourselves in terms of our positions and our roles, in conjunction with and in comparison and contrast with others. Our roles allow us to make certain choices but not others, allow and encourage certain agreements and not others. The arrangements that are basic to business, in particular the possibility of exchange, are in fact quite specific. One is not allowed to trade just anything, and there are many aspects of family and community life where wheeling and dealing is bad taste or taboo. It is in very few societies that an entrepreneurial youngster who treats every childhood game as a business deal is encouraged rather than chastized or ridiculed. Indeed, even within the domain of proper exchange, every parent knows that children have to learn and usually must be taught to trade and trade fairly, to make promises and live up to them. What they learn, in other words, are the basic rules and expectations of the most rudimentary business practices, not first of all by way of making a profit but by way of fair exchange—not being cheated oneself as well as not cheating others.

What is missing in many of the most vulgar and destructive metaphors of business life is just this conception of business as a practice. Jungle and "survival" metaphors are particularly guilty of this obliviousness to or denial of the very civilized social arrangements that define all business activity, and so we are not at all surprised when an advocate of the jungle or survivalist mentality fails to honor the most basic rules and understandings (not keeping one's word or paying one's debts, treating a contract as a matter of legal enforcement rather than a mutual agreement). These rules and understandings are not arbitrary or an illegitimate imposition on some more "natural" way of doing business. They are the foundations of the practice, without which there could be no business. Imagine how complicated the simplest exchange would be if there was no implicit understanding about how such an exchange would take place. They would resemble those childhood transactions in which each playmate refuses to let go of the item to be traded until he or she has a firm grip on the item to be acquired. Or, in adult life, think of how basic and taken for granted the idea of "trust" has to be for any financial institution to exist. (Some of them put the very word in their name.) How little it takes to create a "bank scare" and close the doors in the face of panic. Business is first of all a practice, which means that not anything goes and there are strict limits to what individuals may or may not do, only some of which are canonized into law.

Some of the metaphors we have discussed, however, take the conception of a practice very seriously. Games, we noted are practices, indeed, perhaps the most obvious examples of human practices. Games have strict rules and shared goals, and though they are (usually) competitive they nevertheless presuppose mutual adherence to a complex set of understandings, the violation of which might well make one particular game easier to win but, as a result, would make any further pursuit of the game impossible. (Bobby Fisher used to play chess in such a way that he made further challenges notoriously uninviting.) But the positive point about games as examples of practices and as an analogy to business is that games make it very clear just what we mean when we idealize and celebrate individuals, not as independent entities but as *players,* usually as *members* of a team, whose identities are based on their positions or roles in the game, how well they play, and whatever idiosyncrasies they may have that contribute to the game. To insist on this is not to deny the "individuality" of the players. No one with any sense would insist that forcing the members of a team to wear matching uniforms is an offense to their individuality or human dignity, nor would it make much sense to say that team members display their individuality through small eccentricities not directly connected to the game itself. To be sure, athletes often bear some favorite identifying trademark, a colored headband or a peculiar hairdo, but this is not wherein their individuality lies. Indeed, we note these trademarks only because their bearers are exceptional players, and it is being so exceptional or at least good *at the game* that defines individual identities. (Of course, being exceptionally incompetent also establishes one's identity in the game, but this usually results in one's getting out the game and seeking a quite different identity.) Outside the game, it is not as if one's game-based identity evaporates. It forms part (sometimes a very large part) of one's conception of oneself and one's self-worth. We will play other roles, and at least some of these will be very different from game-based roles, but our composite identity is made up of all of these. There is no underlying self that is more basic to our various role-based identities or is necessary to somehow hold them together. (In moments of crisis— in the midst of divorce or after being fired from one's job—it is entirely tempting to seize on some other aspect of one's identity as the "true" one. Divorced men and women quite understandably become workaholics, and "out-placed" executives quite naturally find that they derive renewed satisfaction from spending time with their families.)

Most of business life consists of roles and responsibilities in cooperative enterprises, whether they be "Mom and Pop" stores or multinational corporations. Individualism continues to serve many valuable purposes in the business world, not least among them the constant reminder of the importance of individual employee rights and responsibilities and the recognition that individual initiatives are often more successful than overly organized group conferences, in which interpersonal relations distract from or wholly eclipse attention to the putative problem at hand. But atomistic individualism oversteps these important considerations to advocate not only an implausible theory of human nature but a largely destructive illusion of corporate organization. There is a sense in which virtually every employee of a corporation (even the boss's son-in-law) is there by virtue of his or her own individual voluntary choice. This is the most important aspect in which a corporation differs from a society as such. Most people are born into a society, and the option to leave is far easier to raise in a political argument—"America, love it or leave it"—than it is to translate into a real personal possibility. But it is a fatal mistake to think that a corporation is therefore to be thought of as nothing but a voluntary coming together of numerous individuals. This familiar image of corporations is as misleading, at least, as the equally false idea of the corporation as a legal fiction. A corporation is primarily a community, but communities are not just durable collections of individuals. Communities have *structures*. Communities are *organized* (even the most disorganized.) And community structures and organization exist quite independently of the particular individuals who are part of them (which is not to say that one could have a community with no members, as a mathematician might have a "null set" with no members). And to understand how even the smallest corporation operates, one has to understand the structure and organization, in which only exceptional cases are expressions of a single personality (for instance, an unusually dynamic and charismatic CEO, often the founder of the company as well). Indeed, reference to individual personalities in corporations more often than not takes the form of a *diagnosis*, the attempt to identify what has gone wrong with the organization and distorted the structure. This is not always fair or fruitful, for it may be the organization or the structure itself that is at fault. But even here, it is evident that the fact that certain individuals don't "fit in" the corporate structure is as much the property of the structure as the personality of the individual. And when a business has a structure such that virtually *no one* seems to fit into it, it is a fair bet that part of the reason is that it demands individual identities that are themselves distorted or degrading. (Such structural defects are often mistaken for mere personality "conflicts." A healthy part of the demand for "integrity" among prospective employees has to do not only with the question of whether they will "fit in" and be dependable but, much more important but harder to grasp, with the expectation that they will (on the basis of past experience and accumulated confidence) resist and perhaps straighten out structural distortions in the organization.

Business is a social practice, not the collective activity of isolated individuals. It is possible only because it takes place in a culture with an established set of procedures and expectations. Corporations are communities with a structure and an organization in which individuals find their roles and create their identities *in the terms of the organization*. But my aim in being so insistent on this point is not merely a matter of ethical theory; I have found that it is essential to business ethics in practice. The commonly held complaint that "pressure to conform to corporate goals" conflicts with an employee's "personal values," while we readily understand it, is doubly confused. There are no "personal values" in the sense literally intended, for one can have a value (as opposed to personal taste) only if the value in question is more than merely personal. Our personal values are themselves emblematic of our shared identities and our membership in various organizations (for example, religious or political), in families and communities, and, of course, in our careers and professions and the groups and organizations that make them possible. In any decent corporation, most of one's values coincide with the values of the corporations and one's personal goals fit into the larger goals of the corporation. The language of "personal values" emerges, I find, only when there is some perceived conflict, some pressure that is not just the pressure to do a good job and succeed (which presumably coincides with one's own values) but the pressure to do what one views as wrong or unethical *usually in the very terms of the values of the organization in question*. The conflict is not so much corporate values versus personal values as it is corporate values versus corporate values. The language individualism gets in the way of understanding rather than helps it along. The most personal ethical issue tends to be structural and organizational, even if it is the identity of the individual and his or her understandable discomfort that remain the focus of our Aristotelean concerns.

Corporate life is life and is not merely terms of a contract. I want to end this section with two metaphors, one of which may be outrageous and the other by now routine, but both of which I think suggest an approach to business and business ethics that is far healthier than the individualistic and overly competitive metaphors that now rule so much of business thinking. The first (the outrageous one) is that we should start to think (again) about what it means to join and be part of a corporation. It used to be the case, in many industries, that the relationship between employee and company was something like a family, and it was said of the most loyal and hard-working employees and executives that they were "married to the corporation." That phrase, I suggest, is a far healthier and more egalitarian image of the employer-employee relationship than the current emphasis on "contracts" and "organization by agreement."[6] Of course, one does *join* a company. One is not born into it, and one is, in any case, free to leave (with, perhaps, certain contractual conditions). But the "quid pro quo" emphasis on contracts misses the main point. Marriage is also a voluntary agreement, based on a (usually written but inadequately detailed) contract, but only a fool (or a survivor of a very bitter divorce) would maintain that marriage is *just* a contract. Marriage is, first of all, a relationship, and its multiple obligations and demands for mutual concern and respect are for the most part not spelled out in any contract, nor could they be. Those obligations and demands, which may be minimal at first, multiply with time, and when two people or an employee and an organization have been together for a long, long time, those obligations may even outweigh the benefits of the partnership. A spouse who abandons an aging husband or wife is viewed with considerable condemnation, and a company that fires its older workers after twenty or thirty years of service—sometimes, these days, just before their pensions are fully vested—deserves at least as harsh condemnation as the spouse. Cynics may point our that a marriage is easy to get out of these days, but the point is not that corporate loyalty, like some marriages, is necessarily forever. Indeed, it is easier to get a divorce (at least in some states) than it is to fire some employees, but the emphasis in either marriage or a career is not ease of exit (we will have more to say about this in Part III). It is the much-more-than-contractual nature of the relationship and its mutual obligations. An employee or executive who is always asking "What's in it for me?" doesn't belong in the organization. Psychologically and spiritually, he or she is not really a "member" anyway, whatever his or her contractual status.

The final metaphor is that of a corporation as citizen. Citizenship, like marriage, might be said to be based on a kind of contract, but to pursue this beyond the obvious is to misunderstand its primary nature as a relationship. Some duties may be more or less spelled out in advance (concerning payment of taxes and military service, for instance, or the maintenance of roads and protection against foreign enemies), but most mutual obligations and the demand for mutual respect are not and cannot be legislated or contracted (thus the unworkability of laws or constitutional amendments governing such matters as respect for the flag, but that is not for argument here). To be sure, one can be *born* into citizenship, but whether one is born a citizen or spends considerable efforts to become one, citizenship is first of all a relationship of shared identity and mutual concern. Although I will argue that corporations are citizens, I do not just mean, in the now familiar language of business ethics, that they have "social responsibilities." Indeed, if our

6. E.g., see Mark Pastin, *The Hard Problems of Management* (San Francisco: Jossey-Bass, 1986), esp. pp. 138–45.

conception of the corporation remains on the primitive level of "legal fictions" and "profit maximizing organizations," we will have considerable difficulty showing how or why social responsibility could pertain to corporations rather than just individual citizens. But if we think of the formation of a corporation as the creation of a new citizen, in which the relationship of shared identity and mutual concern with the larger society is central, then the demand for corporate social responsibility is no longer mysterious or controversial. Indeed, it becomes virtually trivial. The corporation does indeed receive benefits and privileges from the state of which it is a citizen, but it has duties and obligations in return. The Japanese corporation is perhaps exceptional in the extent to which this is so obvious, but it is only the degree of formal interlocking or "interface" between government and business, not the idea of corporate citizenship, that is unusual, much less unique. Corporations, like all of us, also have the right to pursue their own interests, which may among other things include profits rather than happiness, but this right has all sorts of preconditions and limitations that include but are not limited to the prohibition against harming others. The idea of citizenship, in other words, is not just a personification of the corporation (which has some justification) but an insistence on the larger moral framework within which all of business must be viewed and evaluated. "Business is business" perhaps, but business is also a social practice based on human relationships in which individuality and personal autonomy are by no means denied or compromised but rather given a context in which to be meaningful.

8

Beyond Selfishness: Adam Smith and the Limits of the Market

> How selfish soever man may be supposed, there are evidently some principles in his nature, which interest him in the fortune of others, and render their happiness necessary to him, though he derives nothing from it except the pleasure of seeing it. Of this kind is pity or compassion, the emotion which we feel for the misery of others. . . . The greatest ruffian, the most hardened violator of the laws of society, is not altogether without it.
>
> ADAM SMITH, *The Theory of the Moral Sentiments*

Adam Smith is typically cited as the "father of capitalism" and, consequently, of modern business and its underlying ideology. But the Adam Smith who is so cited is virtually the antithesis of the Aristotelean vision, wholly devoid of ethics, ruthlessly individualistic and almost Hobbesian, obsessively concerned with what Aristotle and Aquinas condemned as *chrematisike* and what later came to be called "the profit motive." Granted that this horror story of greed and amorality has a happy ending—the prosperity of all under the auspices of "the invisible hand"— but the vocabulary of the vision is so unflattering, and so false to its supposed author, and it could not but have had disastrous influence on thinking about business ethics. This is what Patricia Werhane, in her new book on Adam Smith, calls "the prevailing view."[1] The prevailing view is by now tediously familiar, often cited by defenders of the free market who have never even looked at Smith's actual work, and it is now promoted with a great many scholarly, polemical, and downright dishonest variations. But even in its traditional, run-of-the-classroom versions, the prevailing view of Adam Smith's philosophy renders him far more like Boesky and Gekko than even the most rabid reading allows. Most economists and free enterprise lobbyists refer only to *Wealth*

1. Patricia Werhane, *Ethics and Economics: The Legacy of Adam Smith for Modern Capitalism* (Oxford: Oxford University Press, 1991). My thanks too to Charles Griswold of Boston University, who is working on similar topics.

of Nations and ignore that book's place in the whole of Smith's philosophy. In particular, they utterly ignore *The Theory of the Moral Sentiments* and its central thesis—never abandoned in the economic theory of *Wealth of Nations*—that people are naturally cooperative and sympathetic, and that their self-interest naturally includes concern for others and their opinions. *Wealth of Nations* in turn is taken as an uncompromising defense of unfettered competition and the free enterprise system, not only in its proper province of production and exchange but as applicable to every aspect of human activity. Smith quite explicitly rejects this interpretation. But for our purposes here, I want to make three basic points, all of them grounded in the view that Smith was neither schizoid nor inconsistent, and retained essentially the same views between the time he wrote *The Theory of the Moral Sentiments* in 1759 and the completion of the much more famous *Wealth of Nations* in 1776. My argument, of course, is that Smith himself was much closer to the Aristotelean viewpoint (as we might expect from his friendship with Hume) than the Friedmanesque parodies and the prevailing view suggest.

First, There is nothing in Smith's work that would even for a moment suggest that "greed is good," and the "invisible hand" metaphor—upon which such an enormous weight has been placed despite the fact that Smith mentions it *only once* in *Wealth of Nations*—plays a much smaller role in Smith's view of the market and morality than is usually implied.

Second, Smith is no individualist in the Hobbesian mode, and he emphasizes the importance of institutions and of social and interpersonal relationships much more than he does our concern for individual self-interest, though he does not, of course, deny the latter.

Third, Smith's notion of "self-interest" is not at all the asocial or antisocial sentiment that it is usually made out to be. It is certainly not Hobbesian, nor even Rousseauian (that is, benign indifference rather than open hostility). It is already intrinsically social, and doing good is a matter of neither duty nor compulsion (whether by contract or force) but a genuine source of pleasure for its own sake.

Let's look at these briefly, one by one.

GREED IS *NOT* GOOD

It has often been pointed out—for example, by Thomas Sowell, who is no enemy of the free enterprise system—that Adam Smith does not have even a single kind sentence to say about the character or motivation of the ordinary businessman. I want to add to that the observation that Smith has nothing good to say about greed, even as a means much less as an end, nor would he recognize much less endorse the " greed is good" philosophy that has recently come to caricature the workings of the market and taken on all the attributes of a virtue. What Smith does defend is the idea that self-interest is not in itself either antisocial or destructive. In the context of his times—and in our eyes the intolerably oppressive piousness and self-denial of Presbyterian Edinburgh—Smith's defense of self-interest must have been a remarkably liberating thesis. In a "merchantile" world where governments and guilds offered horrible punishments to those who dared economic ambitions, where merchants and industrialists sometimes had to be virtually dragooned to spur productivity and innovation, a defense of the legitimacy and even the patriotism of self-interest played an important social role indeed. We can easily appreciate how unfettered enterprise would be a position well worth pushing against the dead weight of the traditions of the time. (I can't help but think of this as I read Alasdair MacIntyre's celebration of these same Scottish traditions, which were, he claims, philosophically "sold out" by Hume.)[2] But Smith certainly never meant to celebrate greed as such, and his defense of the pursuit of profits was *always* contained within the context of an established society and its traditions. The goal of the industrialist and the businessman was to be a *gentleman,* and not just wealthy. *The Theory of the Moral Sentiments* makes clear even if *Wealth of Nations* does not that self-interest must always be kept in balance with benevolence and the other moral sentiments. It is the prosperity of the nation that is the goal of Smith's vision, and the self-interest of the individual, we should note well, is defended for its role in that pursuit, not as an end to be celebrated in itself.

As for the "invisible hand," it should be obvious from what I've just said that there is much less work for it to do than the proponents of "personal greed and public prosperity" would suggest. The individual pursuing his own self-interest and profits is not so blind to virtue and the public good as Smith, at his most critical, allows, and the goal of the business enterprise (as of every other) was to establish oneself as a solid citizen, contributing to the good of society and establishing oneself (according, let's not forget, to the appropriately called "Protestant ethic") as a virtuous member of society.[3] The workings of the market are not so "invisible" to its participants as Smith's metaphor would suggest. (Much less is it therefore "fair"—an astoundingly bad leap in logic. Partiality may be a key ingredient in injustice, but it certainly does not follow that impartiality assures justice.) There have been attempts to identify the invisible hand with the ideal observer (or "impartial spec-

2. Alasdair MacIntyre, *Whose Justice? Which Rationality?* (Notre Dame, Ind.: University of Notre Dame, 1988).

3. Cf. even H. L. Mencken, "The character that actually marks off the American is not money-hunger at all; it is what might be called, at the risk of misunderstanding, social aspiration." Quoted by Gore Vidal, *The Impossible H. L. Mencken* (New York: Doubleday, 1991).

tator") of *The Theory of the Moral Sentiments,* in part to make just such a point. The ideal observer is "ideal" because he (or she) does not have any self-interest tied up in the situation or decision he is asked to approve. In that sense the ideal observer is impartial, But the ideal observer is of moral importance (though in fact I dispute just how much moral importance has been attributed to him in Smith's work) just because he *does* have all the right moral sentiments. He may be impartial but he is not at all *dispassionate* (as more recent incarnations of this weird character—for example, Roderick Firth—have become).[4] The vision of a free market unfettered not only by government regulation but by moral sentiment and public virtue is not at all what Smith had in mind, and the idea of an "impartial market" too is, as we have all long come to suspect, something of a mere myth and metaphor as well. As Werhane insists at one point, the market is only as "impartial" as the persons working on its behalf, and, I would add, only as humane and as ethical as its proponents and participants as well.

COMMUNITY BEFORE SELF-INTEREST

Adam Smith did not hold that radical individualist view to which so many of his colleagues in Great Britain and France subscribed. Hobbes's view of human nature—at least according to *that* prevailing view (which is also debatable)—was unflinchingly belligerent. People were "naturally" selfish and joined society only for their mutual protection and self-interest. For Smith as for Hume, people are naturally social and benevolent.[5] They seek one another's approval and by nature "desire of being what ought to be approved of, or of being what he himself approves of in other men." They sympathize with each other's interests and misfortunes and care about the prosperity of all. Indeed, Smith, even more than Hume (for whom it is a merely "artificial virtue") has a keen sense of and place for justice in his theory, both in a personal and an institutional sense, though both, it must be said, militate against the individualist viewpoint. Personally, the virtue of justice is mainly negative, as a natural aversion to harming our neighbors. But positively, it is also a sense of fair play, and, institutionally, justice is "the main pillar that upholds the whole edifice of society." It is justice, not greed or self-interest, that ties personal virtue to the institutional framework, and this "by nature" rather than by conventional agreement or a "social contract." Indeed, it is justice that upholds the legitimacy of contracts, and so it could hardly be (as in so many authors, up

4. Roderick Firth, "Ethical Absolutism and the Ideal Observer," *Philosophy and Phenomenological Research* 12 (1952); 317–45.

5. I think MacIntyre misrepresents them on this when he claims that they were essentially egoists hiding behind a facade of philosophically manufactured "sympathy."

to and including John Rawls) in any sense the result of such a contract. Contracts are agreements between individuals, but justice (and Smith's philosophy) is first of all concerned with interpersonal virtues and society, not the isolated individual out to make a buck and believing as his excuse that some invisible hand will make it come out alright.

SELF-INTEREST IS SOCIAL

Finally, Smith's notion of "self-interest" cannot be understood primarily in terms of competition but rather, first of all, in terms of social solidarity and cooperation. It may be true, as he himself argues, that self-interest is our strongest motivating principle, but what this means is not that we are "selfish" or in any way antagonistic to one another. Our self-interest is constituted within society and tied to that system of virtues that makes us good citizens and contributes to the well-being and happiness of others as well as to our own. I have already mentioned, but it is essential to mention again, that for Smith the primary ingredient in self-interest is not personal want but rather the desire for approval and the respect of our fellows. "Nature, when she formed man for society, endowed him with an original desire to please, and an original aversion to offend his brethren." A person's self-interest is thus not selfishness and it is not detached from the social virtues that gain us that approval—productivity and financial intelligence are certainly two of those virtues—much less antisocial. It is the importance of the personal virtues that lead Smith to make the very Aristotelean claim that acts of benevolence give us pleasure not because they serve our own interests but for their own sake, and it is the importance of these virtues that allows me to conclude that Adam Smith, whether or not we want to continue to celebrate him as the father of a capitalism morally run wild, certainly deserves a more prominent place in that long ethical tradition that runs back to Aristotle—and perhaps the central place in that much newer discipline called business ethics, a study not of the legitimacy and of the means of making profits but of the moral character of the people who make them.

9

Beyond Cost/Benefit Analysis: Utilitarianism Refined

> According to the greatest happiness principle, the ultimate end (for our own good or that of other people) . . . is an existence exempt as far as possible from pain, and as rich as possible in enjoyments, both in point of quantity and quality.
>
> JOHN STUART MILL, *Utilitarianism*

The accounting conception of ethics in business, "cost/benefit analysis," has rather recent roots. In a sense, of course, people have always "calculated" their advantage and weighed alternative ways of doing things, but the particular techniques of measuring and comparing alternative courses of action in more or less quantitative terms depend not only on modern business methods but also on the predominance of money and financial worth as broad-based measures of values. As an ethics, such quantitative methods date back to the eighteenth century, when they were considered rather revolutionary. Jeremy Bentham, an English legal and political reformer, developed a "calculus" for balancing crimes and punishments in law, and generalizing this, advocated a "happiness calculus" for making ethical decisions of every kind. What gets measured and weighed is pleasure (and pain), and the calculus is designed to maximize the amount of pleasure (and minimize the amount of pain). The result, called *utilitarianism,* soon became one of the dominant schools of ethics, particularly in England and America. Utilitarianism is the basis of social cost/benefit analysis, or, one might say, utilitarianism is cost/benefit analysis writ large. But utilitarianism need not be so identified, and an "enlightened" utilitarianism ought to jettison the obsession with quantification and calculation that still today defines that theory.[1] And yet, such an enlightened utilitarianism (and the rejection of cost/benefit

1. David Copp, "Morality, Reason and Management Science: The Rationale of Cost-Benefit Analysis," *Ethics and Economics, Social Philosophy and Policy* 2 (Spring 1985).

analysis) was defended well over a century ago, by one of the best-known defenders of the theory.

John Stuart Mill was not the father of utilitarianism, but he is, most ethicists would agree, by far the best (and best-known) expounder of the utilitarian doctrine. But his enlightened version of utilitarianism and his rejection of cost/benefit analysis have been largely ignored, or roundly criticized. John Rawls famously complains, for example, that utilitarianism doesn't adequately distinguish between persons, and so treats distributive justice between persons as if it were a matter of deliberation among the wants and needs of a single individual. This is true of some utilitarians, perhaps, but certainly not of Mill. So, too, it is argued (in virtually every sophomore ethics class in the country) that utilitarianism has nothing or at least too little to say against the sadist who succeeds in getting quantitatively more positive "hedons" (pleasure-units) from his sadism than the number of negative hedons suffered by his victim. So, too, it is argued that utilitarianism has no argument against the unscrupulous but ingenious rich who bilk the poor but make them suffer no more than they themselves gain. (In the words of a recent *New Yorker* cartoon, depicting two fat, rich men sitting around in their club: "I see that the poor are getting poorer, but the rich are getting richer, so it all evens out in the end.") Some utilitarians may think that way, perhaps, but not Mill. It is argued that utilitarianism has nothing to say about "rights," which founder Jeremy Bentham did call "nonsense on stilts," but this is certainly not true of Mill, who devoted a substantial chapter in *Utilitarianism* to questions of rights and justice. Bernard Williams points out, somewhat critically, that utilitarianism is attractive because it "provides a common *currency* of moral thought . . . different sorts of claims can be *cashed* in terms of happiness."[2] I want to suggest that these metaphors can be taken rather literally, that it was indeed the emergence of a "cash and carry" consumer society that gave particular impetus to this peculiarly quantitative view of ethics. But, again, not for John Stuart Mill. In his "proof" of utilitarianism, he takes special pains to emphasize the importance of the virtues and of quality, taste, and sophistication in the pursuit of happiness.[3]

Looked at from a large perspective, utilitarianism seems to be unchallengeable. It is the philosophy that says that what counts, first and foremost, is the overall well-being of society, conceived as a collection of many individuals with their own needs and interests. This does not mean that society consists just of individuals and not of families, groups, neighborhoods, associations, and all sorts of other interpersonal relationships, much less that society is constituted by individuals (rather

2. Bernard Williams, *Morality* (New York: Harper and Row, 1972), p. 92 (my emphasis).

3. John Stuart Mill, *Utilitarianism* (Indianapolis: Hackett, 1981), ch. 4.

than the other way around). Mill, like his predecessor Smith, is very clear about our essentially social being and our natural sympathies and sense of community. "The same superiority of intelligence, joined to the power of sympathizing with human beings generally, enables him to attach himself to the collective idea of his tribe, his country, or mankind in such a manner that any act hurtful to them raises his instinct of sympathy and urges him to resistance.[4] It does not claim that what people ultimately want is money or pleasure in the vulgar senses that Mill so roundly criticizes, nor does it contradict claims about individual rights, though it does suggest that, on occasion, society may need to compromise individual rights for the common good. It does not deny that what may be most essential to both the common good and the good of every individual are mutual respect and strict obedience, even reverence, for a certain moral code, nor does it deny that what is essential for the common good is a shared religion, or proper education and cultivation of the moral sentiments, or keen competition for luxuries to keep people working and productive as well as challenged. It simply says what no author I know (except for a few ascetic fanatics) denies: that it is the prosperity and well-being of society as a whole, and therefore the happiness of the largest possible number of its members, that is our ultimate concern in ethics. By way of a contrast, one might consider the infamous declaration of the late Ayatollah Khomeini, commenting on the protracted war with Iraq, that "it was good for the people who were martyred and good for those whose children were martyred."[5]

Of course, this intentionally vacuous account of utilitarianism isn't the subject of the ongoing and sometimes rude debate between utilitarians, Rawlsian liberals, Marxists, and libertarians. Everything depends on how the notion of the "common good" is quantified, what sort of measure we use for "hedons" and what we mean by "everyone is to count for one and only one." But here, I want to argue, is just where John Stuart steps back from the fray, insisting, as Aristotle did before him, that one should not ask for more precision from ethics than a subject can give you. It is this quantitative agnosticism that drives many contemporary utilitarians up the wall with Mill, struggling to correct his seemingly casual attitudes toward proof and calculation by deriving this or that new interpretation of his work, from the rather ingenious discovery of "rule-utilitarianism" by J. O. Urmson several decades ago to the remarkably sophisticated explorations of Richard Brandt and others in more recent years.[6] But I take Mill very seriously when he

4. Mill, *Utilitarianism*, p. 51.
5. *New York Times*, Nov. 20, 1988.
6. E.g., J. O. Urmson, "The Interpretation of the Moral Philosophy of J. S. Mill," in *Theories of Ethics*, ed. P. Foot (Oxford: Oxford University Press, 1967), pp. 128–36, and R. B. Brandt, *A Theory of the Good and the Right* (Oxford: Oxford University Press, 1979).

tries to abstain from "proving" the truth of the principle of utility; better for him that he didn't even try to couch his very commonsense argument in a form that professional philosophers so readily interpret as not a "proof" (in scare quotes) but as a famously bad argument. And I take him even more seriously when he struggles to free himself from the vulgarity of the Benthamite "happiness calculus," making it very clear that the problem he perceives isn't just the difficulties in measuring quanta or hedons of happiness and in calculating the potentially infinite consequences of any given action but the very idea of *quantity*—whether of pleasure or happiness or anything else. A standard objection against Mill—I confess I've often employed it myself—is that when he introduces the notion of "quality" of pleasures he undermines just the virtue that utilitarianism had to offer: the ability to figure out the correct answer to an ethical question. So long as the calculus operated along a single dimension (of pleasure or happiness or whatever), the comparison of quantities (however calculated) established the solution. The many varieties of decision theory today similarly presuppose some such dimension and outcome. But by adding a second dimension (at least) to the equation, Mill makes it impossible to carry out the comparison. It's like comparing the scores of a basketball team and a hockey team to see which is better. And, of course, Mill's own argument concerning the comparison and preferability of different qualities of pleasure is hopeless. It is better to be a Socrates dissatisfied than a pig or a fool satisfied, he tells us, because Socrates has tried both sorts of pleasure (which presumably the pig and the fool have not) and he prefers the Socratic pleasures, however incomplete, to the pig pleasures, however so satisfying (at least, for a pig.) Now, there are all sorts of problems with this, notably whether Socrates could experience pig pleasures in a properly piglike fashion and so do a fair comparison, but I think what Mill is getting at here—and, again, undermining himself with what looks too much like an argument—is an idea that he surely endorsed and had read about with considerable enthusiasm in his study of the great Greek philosophers. Its terms, however, are hardly utilitarian in the Benthamite sense, although the emphases on the common good and the importance of individual happiness (and the avoidance of suffering) were surely central to it. But the vocabulary of this older ideal consisted of terms like "excellence," "honor," "respect," "virtue," and "citizenship," even "duty" and "nobility." It would also include "friendship"—not in the utilitarian sense (which Aristotle explicitly rejects as one of the "lower" forms of friendship) but in the noble sense of mutual cultivation and inspiration. In *Utilitarianism*'s last chapter, where Mill launches into his discussion of rights and justice, he makes it quite clear that—contrary to the usual attack by Kantians and Rawlsians—he is not just trying to finagle his way out of an inadequacy in his theory but rather to give utilitarianism a very different sense of "the common good" and individual happiness. It is not a theory of collective pleasure but an Aristotelean conception of the virtues as part and parcel of both individual and general well-being. In Rawlsian terms, he really does try to give us a theory of the good that is one and the same with a conception of what is right, in which justice is not (as in Rawls) a set of constraints but part and parcel of the good life. And that means envisioning oneself not as an individual seeker after pleasure or any higher goals either but as a member of society whose happiness (and pleasures too) depend primarily on one's sense of honor and contribution to the community.

Utilitarianism is often taken to be *the* business philosophy, the only sensible answer to those nagging questions about "ethics," the hard-headed quantitative theory that captures and expands the insights of cost/benefit analysis. I have ended the first part of this book with a brief examination of John Stuart Mill because I want to suggest that even utilitarianism admits of an Aristotelean interpretation in which cost/benefit analysis drops out of the picture and an image of the good life emerges as primary. So, too, Adam Smith, the grandaddy of capitalism, did not (as one recent book has it) "discover economics and destroy morality" but rather saw an integrated vision of business and the virtues in a community of gentlemen with concern and prosperity for all. In this first third of the book, I have been mainly critical, especially of those models of business that reduce all of this rich social practice to a single-minded, one-dimensional pursuit of wealth or analyze it all in terms of competition and strategy and deny the importance of larger aims and social thinking. So, too, I hope to have created at least some embarrassment about the metaphors that run so rampant in business chit-chat. They are not just colorful forms of speech; they are degrading and destructive images that desensitize business dealings and eclipse the most basic ethical considerations. In the next part of the book, I want to consider a very different set of models and metaphors and a theoretical framework within which business emerges as an honorable and socially significant activity. By "theory" and "framework," however, I do not mean an overly formal and abstract system that in any way pretends or appears to be "scientific," for that too readily leads back into just those myths and metaphors we have just left behind. It is rather a theory that, as Aristotle tells us, tries to be appropriate to the rather free-wheeling practice of business it describes, and it is a framework that tries to display the same flexibility required of any dynamic, creative community.

II

AN ARISTOTELEAN APPROACH TO BUSINESS: FRAMEWORK AND THEORY

10

Business Ethics: "The Third Wave" and the Problem of Theory

> During the 70s and early 80s, at the beginning of the development of the field of business ethics, writers rushed to provide teaching materials to hungry classrooms. This was the first wave. But once textbooks were available, professors realized that in order to achieve credibility, the field demanded theoretical grounding. Since the only possible sources for this grounding were the already-defined disciplines, it was those disciplines—especially philosophy and the empirical disciplines—that were the forces used to create the second wave. . . . The third wave exhibits bipartisan awareness of ethical theory and business, while also referring to a recognized body of interdisciplinary literature.
>
> THOMAS DONALDSON, "The Third Wave"

We are gratefully past that embarrassing period when the very title of a book on "business ethics" invited—no, required—that malapert response: "must be a very short book." Today, business ethics is a recognized concern of many if not most leading business executives, and the number of major corporations that have at least a token program in ethics significantly outnumbers those that do not. Business ethics is recommended or required in most of the leading business schools in North America, and it is even catching on in Europe (one of the too rare instances of intellectual commerce in that direction). Studies in business ethics have now reached what Tom Donaldson has called "the third wave," beyond the hurried-together and overly philosophical introductory textbooks and collections of too-obvious concrete case studies, to serious engagement in the business world. Conferences filled half-and-half with business executives and academics are common, and in-depth studies based on immersion in the corporate world, such as Jackall's *Moral Mazes,* have replaced more simple-minded and detached glosses on "capitalism and social responsibility."[1] Business ethics has moved

1. Robert Jackall, *Moral Mazes* (New York: Oxford University Press, 1988).

beyond vulgar "business as poker" arguments to an arena where serious ethical theory is no longer out-of-place but seriously sought out
and much in demand.

The problem with business ethics now is not vulgar ignorance but a
far more sophisticated confusion concerning exactly what the subject is
supposed to do and how (to employ a much overworked contrast) the
theory applies to the practice of business. Indeed, a large part of the
problem is that it is by no means clear what a theory in business ethics
is supposed to look like or whether there is any such theoretical enterprise. It has been standard practice in many business ethics courses
and—whether cause or effect—most standard textbooks, to begin with
a survey of ethical theory.[2] This means, inevitably, a brief summary of
Kant and deontological ethics, a brief survey of utilitarianism with a
note or two about John Stuart Mill and a distinction or two between act
and rule, pleasure versus preference utilitarianism, and some replay of
the much-rehearsed contest between the two sorts of theories. Given
the business context, libertarianism or some form of contractualism is
often included as a third contender. "Justice" is a natural introductory
section, and John Locke on natural property rights is an appropriate
inclusion too. But is this the theory of business ethics? Not only is the
application to concrete business situations in question—and then the
message to students is too often an unabashed relativism ("if you are a
utilitarian, you'll do this, if you're a Kantian, you'll do that")—but it is
not even clear whether there is, then, anything distinctive about business ethics. There is just ethics, or rather ethical theory, whatever that
may be. Indeed, one is almost tempted to retreat to the tongue-in-cheek
advice of Robert Townsend, former CEO of Avis and author of *Up the
Organization*, that if a company needs a corporate code of ethics, it should
tack the Ten Commandments on its bulletin boards. And so with its
success assured, at least for the time being, business ethics faces both a
crisis of theory and a pragmatic challenge, that is, what is to count as a
theory in business ethics and how that theory applies and can be used
by flesh-and-blood managers in concrete, real-life, ethically charged situations.

One possibility is that the theory of business ethics is really the philosophy of economics, that is, economics as ethics: social-political philosophy with an emphasis on economic justice. Thus the theoretical
questions of business ethics are those raised by John Rawls in his *Theory
of Justice* in 1971 and by his colleague Robert Nozick in *Anarchy, State
and Utopia* in 1974.[3] The questions of business ethics are those posed

2. Among the best: Beauchamp and Bowie, *Ethical Theory and Business* (Prentice-Hall,
1983); Manuel G. Velasquez, *Business Ethics* (Englewood Cliffs, N.J.: Prentice-Hall, 1982);
Richard De George, *Business Ethics* (New York: Macmillan, 1982); T. Donaldson and P.
Werhane, *Ethical Issues in Business* (Englewood Cliffs, N.J.: 1979).

3. John Rawls, *A Theory of Justice* (Cambridge: Harvard University Press, 1971); Robert
Nozick, *Anarchy, State and Utopia* (New York: Basic Books, 1974).

repeatedly by Amartya Sen and Jon Elster in their various books and articles and in a more informal way by John Kenneth Galbraith and Lester Thurow in the pages of the *New York Review*. This, of course, is rich and promising territory. The theories are well developed and, though they may take Kant, Locke, and Mill as their precursors, they raise concerns that are particular to economic concerns and ask, with regard to the system as a whole as well as particular practices within it, whether the free market is indeed a just and fair mechanism for the distribution of goods in a grossly inegalitarian world. The theories here are well argued and impressively formalized—in the sophisticated techniques of game theory, social choice theory, and all of those other accoutrements that make theories look like theory—in other words, adequate for publication in the most serious professional journals and conducive to a positive tenure decision.

Such theorizing is, however, irrelevant to the workaday world of business and utterly inaccessible to the people for whom business ethics is not merely a subject of study but is (or will be) a way of life—students, executives, and corporations. Here, especially, the practical problem comes back to haunt us; how do these grand theories of property rights and distribution mechanisms, these visionary pronouncements on the current economy apply to people on the job? Of course, one could argue that this is the case in any science, and not just in the sciences either. The hard part of any academic teaching is taking very sophisticated theoretical material and watering it down for the *hoi poloi* or, more modestly, making it accessible in terminology that is not oversimplified. But quite apart from the offensive patronizing attitude presumed by this view, especially in the so-called liberal arts, it is inadequate for a more theoretical reason as well. The grand theories of the philosophy of economics, however intriguing they may be in their own right, are not adequate for business ethics, and for many of the same reasons that the classic theories of Kant, Locke, and Mill are inadequate. The theories themselves are incomplete, oblivious to the concrete business context and indifferent to the very particular roles that people play in business. Their inaccessibility or inapplicability to the ordinary manager in the office or on the shop floor is not just a pragmatic problem but a failure of theory as well. What we need in business ethics is a *theory of practice*,[4] an account of business as a fully human activity in which ethics provides not just an abstract set of principles or side-constraints or an occasional Sunday school reminder but the very framework of business activity. The heart of such a theory will not be a mathematical model but a down-to-earth, matter-of-fact account of the values that do and should govern business and business enterprises

---

4. Not to be confused with *praxis*, the abused Greek term for "practice" that has come to inspire long-winded theoretical exhortations and is easily confused with an Eastern European version of stuffed cabbage.

by way of motivating the people who actually live and work in business. But with all of the emphasis on macroeconomics, social science research, and abstract rules and codes of ethics, too many business ethicists (like some country folk singers searching for love) have been looking for theory in all the wrong places.

11

The Aristotelean Approach to Business Ethics

> "Money's easy to make if it's money you want. But with a few exceptions people don't want money. They want luxury and they want love and they want admiration."
>
> JOHN STEINBECK, *East of Eden*

I have called the theoretical framework developed here "an Aristotelean approach to business." As Aristotle is famous largely as the enemy of business, some justification of this approach would seem to be in order. True, he was the first economist. He had much to say about the ethics of exchange and so might well be called the first (known) business ethicist as well. But Aristotle distinguished two different senses of what we call economics, one of them *oecinomicus* or household trading, which he approved of and thought essential to the working of any even modestly complex society, and *chrematisike*, which is trade for profit. Aristotle declared the latter activity wholly devoid of virtue. Aristotle despised the financial community and, more generally, all of what we would call profit seeking. He argued that goods should be exchanged for their "real value," their costs, including a "fair wage" for those who produced them, but he then concluded, mistakenly, that any profit (that is, over and above costs) required some sort of theft (for where else would that "surplus value" come from). Consequently, he called those who engaged in commerce "parasites" and had special disdain for moneylenders and the illicit, unproductive practice of usury, which until only a few centuries ago was still a crime. ("Usury" did not originally mean excessive interest; it referred to any charge over and above cost.) Only outsiders at the fringe of society, not respectable citizens, engaged in such practices. (Shakespeare's Shylock, in *The Merchant of Venice*, was such an outsider and a usurer, though his idea of a forfeit was a bit unusual.) All trade, Aristotle believed, was a kind of exploitation. Such was his view of what we call "business." Aristotle's greatest medieval disciple, Saint Thomas Aquinas, shared the Philosopher's dis-

101

dain for commerce, even while he struggled to permit limited usury (never by that term, of course) among his business patrons. (A charge for "lost use" of loaned funds was not the same as charging interest, he argued.) Even Martin Luther, at the door to modern times, insisted that usury was a sin and a profitable business was (at best) suspicious. Aristotle's influence on business, it could be argued, has been long-lasting—and nothing less than disastrous.

In particular, it can be argued that Aristotle had too little sense of the importance of production and based his views wholly on the aristocratically proper urge for acquisition, thus introducing an unwarranted zero-sum thinking into his economics. It can be charged that Aristotle, like his teacher Plato, was too much the spokesman for the aristocratic class and quite unfair to the commerce and livelihoods of foreigners and commoners. It is Aristotle who initiates so much of the history of business ethics as the wholesale attack on business and its practices. Aristotelean prejudices underlie much of business criticism and the contempt for finances that preocupies so much of Christian ethics even to this day, avaricious evangelicals notwithstanding. Even defenders of business often end up presupposing Aristotelean prejudices in such Pyrrhonian arguments as "business is akin to poker and apart from the ethics of everyday life"[1] and "the [only] social responsibility of business is to increase its profits."[2] But if it is just this schism between business and the rest of life that so infuriated Aristotle, for whom life was supposed to fit together in a coherent whole, it is the same holistic idea—that business people and corporations are first of all part of a larger community—that drives business ethics today.

We can no longer accept the amoral idea that "business is business" (not really a tautology but an excuse for being socially irresponsible and personally insensitive). According to Aristotle, one has to think of oneself as a member of the larger community—the *polis* for him, the corporation, the neighborhood, the city or the country (and the world) for us—and strive to excel, to bring out what is best in ourselves and our shared enterprise. What is best in us involves our virtues, which are in turn defined by that larger community, and there is therefore no ultimate split or antagonism between individual self-interest and the greater public good. Of course, there were no corporations in those days, but Aristotle would certainly know what I mean when I say that most people in business now identify themselves, if tenuously, in terms of their companies, and corporate policies, much less corporate codes of ethics, are not by themselves enough to constitute an ethics. But corporations are not isolated city-states, not even the biggest and most powerful of the multinationals. "The sovereign state of ITT" may indicate power

1. Alfred Carr, "Is Business Bluffing Ethical?" *Harvard Business Review* (Jan.–Feb. 1968).
2. Milton Friedman, "The Social Responsibility of Business Is to Increase Its Profits," *New York Times*, Sept. 13, 1970.

and political autonomy, but it is, nevertheless, part and parcel of a larger global community. The people that work for them are thus citizens of (at least) two communities at once, and one might think of business ethics as getting straight about that dual citizenship. What we need to cultivate is a certain way of thinking about ourselves in and out of the corporate context, and this is the aim of ethical theory in business, as I understand it. It is not, let me insist, anti-individualistic in any sense of "individualism" that is worth defending. The Aristotelean approach to business ethics rather begins with the two-pronged idea that it is individual virtue and integrity that counts, but good corporate and social policies encourage and nourish individual virtue and integrity.

The Aristotelean approach, as I want to construe it here, begins by agreeing with Aristotle in his suspicion of purely financial thinking and dealing, what we call "the profit motive." Michael Lewis's traders seem to me to be the perfect equivalent of the sort of marginal characters that made respectable Athenians hide their wallets and their daughters at home. They too were not doing anything illegal, but their mercantile activities were (unlike the activities of Lewis's traders) not respectable. They did not seem to contribute anything to the society. The seemingly obvious place and purpose of "finance" in society needs to be reconsidered, and the problem is to define "finance" and "profits" in such a way that not all of business suffers from Aristotle's indictment.

Second, to call the approach "Aristotelean" is to emphasize the importance of community, the business community as such (I want to consider corporations as, first of all, communities) but also the larger community, even all of humanity and, perhaps, much of nature too. This emphasis on community, however, should not be taken to eclipse the importance of the individual and individual responsibility. In fact, the contrary is true; it is only within the context of community that individuality is developed and defined, and our all-important sense of individual integrity is dependent upon and not opposed to the community in which integrity gets both its meaning and its chance to prove itself.

One of the most important aspects of the "Aristotelean" approach is the emphasis on the purposiveness (or "teleology") that defines every human enterprise, including business. But that purposiveness transcends the realm of business and defines its place in the larger society, though the popular term "social responsibility" makes this sound too much like an extraneous concern rather than the purpose of business as such. On both an individual and the corporate level, the importance of the concept of *excellence* is intricately tied to this overall teleology, for what counts as excellence is defined both by its superiority in the practice and its role in serving larger social purposes. "Aristotelean" too is a strong emphasis on individual character and the virtues (where a "virtue" is all-round personal excellence), embedded in and in service to the larger community. It is the role of the individual in the corporation (and of the corporation in society) that concerns me, not the individual alone, not the structure of the corporation abstracted from the individuals that are its members (and not the nature of "capitalism," abstracted from the character of particular corporations and the communities they serve.) That is why the idea of business as a practice is absolutely central to this approach: it views business as a human institution in service to humans and not as a marvelous machine or in terms of the mysterious "magic" of the market.

Finally, it may be theoretically least interesting but it is perhaps nevertheless most important, but I prefer the name "Aristotelean" just because it makes no pretensions of presenting something very new, the latest "cutting-edge" theory or technique of management, but rather reminds us of something very old, a perspective and a debate that go all the way back to ancient times. What the Aristotelean approach promises is not something novel and scientific but an approach that is very staid and established and above all very human. The idea is not to infuse corporate life with one more excuse for brutal changes, a new wave of experts and seminars and yet another downsizing bloodbath. It is to emphasize the importance of continuity and stability, clearness of vision and constancy of purpose, corporate loyalty and individual integrity.

The bottom line of the Aristotelean approach to business ethics is that we have to get away from "bottom line" thinking and conceive of business as an essential part of the good life, living well, getting along with others, having a sense of self-respect, and being part of something one can be proud of. Aristotle argued that what I have called "abstract greed" ("the profit motive") was a kind of pathology, a defect of character, an "unnatural" and antisocial vice. Not that he was against wealth and comfort (no ascetics, those Athenians), but in the quest for the good life money wasn't worth worrying about. To which one might well reply, of course, that aristocrats in an aristocratic society (and their favorite philosophers) didn't have to worry about such merely material matters, but we do. But the point is not that we should stop thinking about money or trying to make a living or that we can or should discourage our students from their current career paths. It is a question of perspective, and a question of what that living, those career paths, amount to. Are they, in fact, just a means to make money? Or are they, as they should be, worthwhile activities that provide the meaningful substance of half of our adult waking lives, the source of our sense of self-worth and many of our friends? Is the company we work for a white-collar version of hell, or is it a community where (despite the early hour) we are glad to see our colleagues and get on with the work of the day? We talk about "making a living" as if it is primarily a matter of income, but the truth is that the living we make has as much to do with life and meaning as it does with paying the rent. Unhappy middle managers will testify that there seems to be nothing more demeaning and more contrary to the good life than giving years of your life to a company that ignores your every effort and continually reminds you of your expendability.[3] Students and job hoppers (and, let me say, even professors of the humanities) who accept a position on the basis of salary alone and then hate their job miss the obvious: what makes for happiness is not money to spend but a full and meaningful life and a decent and prosperous community.

Part of the problem is the way we tend to separate—or pretend to separate—our business from our personal lives, as if these were unrelated and independent, as if one "left one's values at the office door." But of course, not only do we spend an enormous amount of our waking lives "in the office"; our values are not divided up into two (or more) categories, like outfits in the closet separated into "business" and "leisure." With only small variations, the values we were raised with as children are the essential values of our professional as well as our personal lives. But this false separation of business and personal values has another, even more depressing consequence. Since we tend to identify the personal part of our lives as pleasurable (whether or not it is), we characterize the business part of our lives as "work," meaning not just effort and energy but a burden, defined by duties and obligations and responsibility. The very suggestion, therefore, is that business is distasteful, unpleasant, deleterious to one's own better self, and in one's interests only by virtue of its outcome: the salary or wealth that one manages to accumulate. There is too little sense of business as itself enjoyable (the main virtue of the "game" metaphor), that business is not a matter of vulgar self-interest but of vital community interest, that the virtues on which one prides oneself in "personal" life are essentially the same as those essential to good business—honesty, dependability, courage, loyalty, integrity. Aristotle's central ethical concept, accordingly, is a unified, all-embracing notion of "happiness" (or, more accurately, *eudaimonia,* perhaps better translated as "flourishing" or "doing well"). The point is to view one's life as a whole and not separate the personal and the public or professional, or duty and pleasure. The point is that doing what one ought—doing one's duty, fulfilling one's responsibilities and obligations—is not counter but conducive to the good life, to becoming the sort of person one wants to become. Conversely, becoming the sort of person one wants to become—which presumably includes to a very large extent what one does "for a living"—is what happiness is all about. Happiness is "flourishing," and this means fitting into a world of other people and sharing the good life, including "a good job," with them. A good job, accordingly, is not just one that pays well or is relatively easy but one that means something, one that has

3. E.g., Earl Shorris, *The Oppressed Middle* (New York: Doubleday, 1976).

(more or less) tangible and clearly beneficial results, one that (despite inevitable periods of frustration) one enjoys doing. Happiness (for us as well as for Aristotle) is an all-inclusive, holistic concept. It is ultimately one's character, one's integrity, that determines happiness, not the bottom line. And this is just as true of giant corporations as it is of the individuals who work for them.

There is no room in this picture for the false antagonism between "selfishness" on the one hand and what is called "altruism" on the other. For the properly constituted social self, the distinction between self-interest and social-mindedness is all but unintelligible, and what we call selfishness is guaranteed to be self-destructive as well. And "altruism" is too easily turned into self-sacrifice—for instance, by that self-appointed champion of selfishness, Ayn Rand. But altruism isn't self-sacrifice; it's just a more reasonable conception of self, as tied up intimately with community, with friends and family who may, indeed, count (even to us) more than we do. What the Aristotelean approach to business ethics demands isn't self-sacrifice or submerging oneself to the interests of the corporation, much less voluntary unhappiness. What it does demand is the recognition that the distinctions and oppositions between self and society that give rise to these wrongheaded conceptions are themselves the problem, and the cause of so much unhappiness and dissatisfaction. So, too, the most serious single problem in business ethics is the false antagonism between profits and social responsibility. There is an academic prejudice, for example, against clever profit-making solutions—the obviously optimal solution to "social responsibility" problems. It is as if moralists have a vested interest in the nobility of self-sacrifice (that is, self-sacrifice by others). This is the same problem, philosophy students will recognize, once raised by the theory of egoism in ethics, for example, in the famous exchange between Thomas Hobbes and Bishop Butler. According to all such views, either an action is selfish or it is selfless, and the Aristotelean synthesis of self-interested, noble behavior is eliminated from view. Once one introduces such artificial oppositions between self-interest and shared interest, between profits and social responsibility, the debate becomes a "lose-lose" proposition, either wealth and irresponsibility or integrity and failure. The Aristotelean approach is first of all a "win-win" proposition, a framework for mutually interested action.

The Aristotelean approach to business ethics begins with the concept of the individual embedded in the community and the ultimate importance of happiness as the sole criterion for success. But "happiness" is a large, ill-defined notion. What makes one person happy may not be the same as for another. One middle-aged manager will be content only when she finally makes senior vice-president and is happy to invest most of her time and energy to do so; another is perfectly happy with his middle-manager status, his congenial colleagues, and his comparatively ample time with his family. But this is not to say that any form of satisfaction or contentment counts as happiness. We have all seen friends who have just endured a traumatic separation go through periods of what is easily recognizable (to everyone but them) as "false happiness," a subjective sense of well-being that has far more to do with the repression and rationalization of awful thoughts than it does with contentment or a sense of well-being. The same sense of "false happiness" can occupy a major portion of a person's life, though only with difficulty and continuous psychological effort. It can more easily pervade an entire community's life, when people continuously encourage the wrong values and the wrong goals in one another (for example, promoting competitive, even ruthless behavior toward one another in pursuit of some merely emblematic prize, demeaning family life and treating all things domestic and affectionate as inferior). What is happening in contemporary society, it has often been argued, is very much a version of this "false happiness," when money becomes the emblematic prize and competition for money the test of "manhood" and when family life suffers from neglect, or worse.[4] Whatever happiness may be, and however it differs from person to person, there are certain essential if variable personal ingredients that are required. We can summarize them in a single word, in the concept of the *virtues.*

The concept of the virtues provides the conceptual linkage between the individual and his or her society. A virtue is a pervasive trait of character that allows one to "fit into" a particular society and to excel in it. Aristotle analyzed the virtues as the basic constituents of happiness, and these virtues included, we should add right away, not only such "moral" virtues as honesty but also many "nonmoral" virtues such as wittiness, generosity, and loyalty. (Aristotle, in fact, did not even bother distinguishing between what we would call the moral and the nonmoral virtues. He considered them all important.) The virtues were, on the one hand, essential aspects of the individual. On the other hand, they were precisely the "excellences" that a certain society required. The underlying assumption was that a person is who he or she is by virtue of his or her place and role in the community, by virtue of his or her actions and sense of judgment, by virtue of how his or her virtues all "hang together" to form what we might blandly call "a good person."

A virtue, to be very brief for now, is an excellent and admirable characteristic to have, not just in some narrowly defined context (as it is a virtue to be ugly in an "ugliest man contest") but in the larger social scheme as well. A virtue is a trait that helps one to fit into and contribute to society. Honesty is obviously a virtue. If everyone lied—to begin with one of the oldest and most evident philosophical insights—no one would believe anyone. There will always be liars, and there are prac-

4. See, for example, Philip Slater, *The Pursuit of Loneliness* (Boston: Beacon Press, 1970).

tices that encourage and even require less than forthright disclosure, but there could not be a society of liars, even in Hollywood or on Wall Street. Courage is a virtue. There will always be cowards but most of us at some time or other have to stand up for our convictions and our freedom. Otherwise, we have no convictions and there is no freedom. But in addition to these rather general virtues, there are also virtues specific to particular institutions, activities, and practices. Spontaneous creativity and unpredictable behavior may be applauded in an artist or an intellectual but it is (usually) disastrous in a linebacker. Loyalty is almost always a virtue within a relationship or an organization, but it is a virtue that has its obvious limits. ("My company, right or wrong," displays the importance of such limits, even in their denial.) Virtues may be specific to particular institutions, activities, and practices, but they will always be measured in a larger arena. A virtue is an individual excellence that is defined in part by its contribution to the public good, even or especially in those exceptional circumstances in which it seems to run counter to corporate or public policies. Extreme examples are provided by whistle-blowers and Henry-David Thoreau–type protesters, but every honest man or woman who is ready and willing to speak out against waste or corruption exemplifies such virtues as well.

In certain aspects of business (as in the military), what is called "ruthlessness" can be a virtue, but it would surely be a mistake to generalize this as an essential virtue for everyone in every circumstance and it is usually a mistake to give it much value even in the most "ruthless" business. It is all too evident that even in the appropriate context this virtue (like most virtues, even honesty and courage) can be excessive and turn into a vice. Thus the virtue of a virtue (a phrase I borrow from Nietzsche) always depends on some larger context, a context in which the practice itself (art, football, business) is evaluated for its social value. Many contextual virtues thus betray their limits and some supposed virtues turn out (from a larger perspective) not to be virtues at all. In the business world, in particular, we should be on the lookout for those macho, mock virtues that in any civilized context would and should be subject to ridicule and contempt. When Lewis describes the ideal of the trading floor as "that most revered of all species: a Big Swinging Dick," we have demeaned the very idea of the virtues in favor of an adolescent, unproductive, and indefensible conception of business.

What is worth defending in business is the sense of virtue that stresses cooperative joint effort and concern for consumers and colleagues alike. Aristotelean ethics is an ethics of virtue, an ethics in which personal and corporate integrity occupies the place of central concern and focus. But virtue and integrity are not to be found in a vacuum. They do not appear miraculously in the atomistic individual, they cannot be contracted or commissioned, nor are they the special province of saints.

They are not (except cynically) the result of a cost/benefit calculation of utility, and they cannot be dictated according to abstract rules or principles (thus the nagging vacuity of such principles as "Be courageous!" or "Be generous!"). A virtue has a place in a social context, in a human practice, and accordingly it is essentially part of a fabric that goes beyond the individual and binds him or her to a larger human network. Integrity—literally "wholeness"—also has to be understood (in part) in the context of a community and, in business life, the corporation. It consists not just of individual autonomy and "togetherness" but of such company virtues as loyalty and congeniality, cooperation and trustworthiness. Of course, this also means that the corporation itself must be viewed as a morally and socially responsible agent, a view that does not, however, compromise the ultimate importance of the responsibility and integrity of the individuals who work within it.[5] Nothing is more damaging to business ethics (or to ethics in business) than the glib dismissal of corporations as agents because they are "legal fictions" or the equally fatuous if familiar insistence that the sole purpose of corporations (and, therefore, the sole responsibility of their managers) is to turn a profit and fulfill their "fiduciary obligation to the stockholders."[6] The pursuit of integrity is determined from the start, I have argued, by such dangerous myths and metaphors about business, corporations, and the people who work for them. Corporations are neither legal fictions nor financial juggernauts but communities, people working together for common goals. That seemingly simple realization, which so much of corporate life has seemingly rejected in recent years, is the first principle of Aristotelean business ethics. And with that emphasis on integrity and community comes not only the fulfillment of obligations to stockholders (not all of them "fiduciary") but the production of quality and the earning of pride in one's products, providing good jobs and well-deserved rewards for employees, and the enrichment of a whole community and not just a select group of (possibly short-term) contracted "owners."[7]

5. This two-level view of the individual and the corporation, integrity and virtue *in* and *of* the corporation, has its classic analogue in the imagery of Plato's *Republic*, and many of my themes will echo where they do not repeat Plato's insistence on the importance of harmony and proper perspective in both the good society and the healthy individual soul. It is this presumption of essential participation and cooperation that is the heart of the Aristotelean perspective as well. Despite the cheerleading emphasis on "team work" in the modern corporation, however, it is just this sense of harmony and cooperation that gets systematically undermined.

6. Friedman, "The Social Responsibility of Business."

7. Alistair M. NacLeod, "Moral Philosophy and Business Ethics: The Priority of the Political," (unpublished manuscript) on the importance of institutional arrangements: "once institutions are seen, not as relatively unmalleable, quasi-organic structures which it would be perilous to try to modify, but as elaborate human artifacts serving a wide range of

The Aristotelean approach to business presupposes an ideal, an ultimate purpose, but the ideal of business in general is not, as my undergraduates so smartly insist, "to make money." It is to serve society's
demands and the public good and be rewarded for doing so. This ideal
in turn defines the mission of the corporation and provides the criteria
according to which corporations and everyone in business can be praised
or criticized. "Better living through chemistry," "Quality at a good price,"
"Productivity through people," "Progress is our most important product"—these are not mere advertising slogans but reasons for working
and for living. Without a mission, a company is just a bunch of people
organized to make money while making up something to do (for example, "beating the competition"). Such activities may, unintentionally,
contribute to the public good, but Adam Smith's "invisible hand" never
was a very reliable social strategy,[8] and the difference between intending to do good and doing good unintentionally is not just the special
sense of satisfaction that comes from the former. Contrary to the utterly irresponsible and obviously implausible argument that those ("do-
gooders") who try to do good in fact do more harm than good, the
simple, self-evident truth is that most of the good in this world comes
about through good intentions. Meaningful human activity is that which
intends the good rather than stumbling over it on the way to merely
competitive or selfish goals.

I once distinguished, in a book called *It's Good Business*, between
macro, molar, and micro ethics, and within this limited distinction it
should be evident that I am going to argue for the importance of micro
business ethics—the concepts and values that define individual responsibilities and role behavior as opposed to the already well-developed
theories of macro business ethics, the principles that govern or should
govern our overall system of (re)distribution and reward. (In ethics as
such, one might argue, the neglect has taken a different twist, ignoring
the larger social and anthropological setting in favor of individual autonomy and well-being.) The distinction between micro and macro is
borrowed from and intended to be parallel to a similar dichotomy in
economics. (I have elsewhere argued that economics is a branch of ethics, but that is another story.)[9] That distinction, however, is left over
from the ancient days of Lord Keynes and is also inadequate. The integral or "molar" unit of commerce today is neither the individual entrepreneur or consumer nor the all-embracing system that still goes by

human purposes, the question whether they ought to be preserved in something like
their present form or changed in some way—radically transformed, even, if they no
longer secure the interests, private or public, which provided their raison d'être is bound
to win an important place on the moral theorist's agenda."

8. See Patricia Werhane, *Ethics and Economics: The Legacy of Adam Smith for Modern
Capitalism* (Oxford: Oxford University Press, 1991).

9. Robert Solomon, "Economics and Ethics," *Business and Society Review* 46 (1983).

the antiquated nineteenth-century name "capitalism." It is the corporation, a type of entity barely mentioned by Adam Smith in a few dismissive sentences (and of minimal interest even to Keynes). While I will always hold that the existential unit of responsibility and concern is and remains the individual, the individual in today's business world does not operate in a social vacuum. He or she is more likely than not an employee—whether in the stockroom or as chief financial officer—and our basic unit of understanding has to be the company, or rather, the employee in a company, and, in particular, in a company whose perceived primary purpose is "to make money." Theory in business ethics thus becomes the theory—that is, description and contemplation about—individuals in (and out) of business roles as well as the role of business and businesses in society, *the-individual-in-the-organization*. People in business are ultimately responsible as individuals, but they are responsible as individuals in a corporate setting where their responsibilities are at least in part defined by their roles and duties in the company and, of course, by the bottom line. Businesses in turn are defined by their role(s) and responsibilities in the larger community, where the bottom line is only an internal concern (if the business is to stay in business and the shareholders are to hold onto their shares) but for everyone else may be a minimal consideration.

In terms of explicitly ethical thinking, too much of business ethics today is focused on questions of policy—those large questions about government regulation and the propriety of government intervention, such as in failing industries and affirmative action programs, and in very general business practices and problems, such as pollution control, opacity and lying in advertising, employee due process, and the social responsibilities of companies to their surrounding communities. All of this, of course, is perfectly proper for philosophers and other social observers who have the luxury of standing outside of the pressures of the business world to survey and possibly control through legislation the larger scenery. But what gets left out of these well-plumbed studies and arguments is an adequate sense of personal values and integrity. What is missing from much of business ethics is an adequate account of the personal dimension in ethics, the dimension of everyday individual decision making. Accordingly, I want to defend business ethics as a more personally oriented ethics rather than as public policy, "applied" abstract philosophy, or a by-product of the social sciences. But business ethics so conceived is not "personal" in the sense of "private" or "subjective"; it is rather social and institutional self-awareness, a sense of oneself as an intimate (but not inseparable) part of the business world with a keen sense of the virtues and values of that world. It is an Aristotelean approach to business ethics.

12

Alternative Approaches to Business Ethics

> There are certain virtues, both to the individuals and to the society at large, of encouraging people to act in socially appropriate ways because they believe it the "right thing" to do, rather than because (and thus, perhaps, only to the extent that) they are ordered to do so. . . . What seems needed as a "remedy" is some institutional analogue to the role that responsibility plays in the human being, guiding action toward certain values where the ordinary legislative prohibitors are unavailable or, on balance, unwise.
>
> CHRISTOPHER STONE, *Where the Law Ends*

With what is this Aristotelean approach to be contrasted? First of all, I want to contrast it with the emphasis on public policy that has preoccupied our subject. In many business schools, the very phrase "business ethics" was avoided like a bad smell for many years, and curriculum committees took delicate recourse to "public and social policy," so as not to offend or overly amuse the students. There is nothing wrong with policy studies, of course, and I don't for a moment suggest that they be replaced or discarded. But policy decisions aren't usually made by folks like us. We rarely even get to vote or speak for them. For the ordinary line manager or even most executives, policy questions are, for the most part, something to debate over lunch, usually by way of reaction to some fait accompli. And there is something missing from policy decisions that is absolutely central to ethics on virtually any account, namely, personal responsibility. The ethical problems that the average manager faces on the job are personnel and routine administrative decision-making problems, not policy problems. Some of those problems have to do with temptations—an attractive competing offer, a convenient kickback, personal relationship, or prejudice against an employee. Some have to do with conflicts of duties, mixed messages, crossed loyalties. Business ethics begins, for most of us, in some conflict of roles within an organization, implementing policies or decisions not of our own making and often against our better judgment. Whatever else business ethics may involve and however sophisticated its theories may become, it means knowing that even such decisions (and their consequences) are nevertheless one's own to live with. Ethics is not just a subject for executive boards, planning committees, and government overseers but for all of us, in the details as well as the larger dramas of our everyday lives.

The standard course or seminar in business ethics has, quite naturally, piggybacked on standard philosophical ethics courses. Until very recently, virtually every such course began with a more or less detailed survey of the two leading theories in modern ethics, "duty-defined" (or *deontological,* after the Greek word for duty, *deon)* and *utilitarian* theories. The former, best represented by the eighteenth-century German philosopher Immanuel Kant, stresses the centrality of very general rational principles (for example, "treat people as ends and never merely as means"). The latter, usually represented by John Stuart Mill (whom we briefly discussed in the preceding chapter), pays more businesslike attention to costs and benefits or, more accurately, the various interests and preferences of all concerned. These two theories are then typically "applied" to various ethically loaded case studies and problems. Sometimes, an additional theory, usually of the contractual variety, is added to this traditional duo, but what is worth noting here is how rarely the Aristotelean approach is ever even mentioned in this context, despite its evident applicability to any community of people working together for common ends. The problem is not Aristotle's own prejudice toward business, which is in any case secondary to the importance of his theories. The problem is very much like the preference for impersonal policy and the theorist's timidity with all considerations that even hint at the personal. Both deontological ethics and utilitarianism stress the importance of broad general principles, which can then be applied to particular cases. It is the nature of the Aristotelean approach, by contrast, to start with the particular community and context and understand cases (and abstract principles) within that community and context. The two traditional ethical approaches have often been criticized as clumsily irrelevant, or overly abstract for the particular situations faced by business managers, and for good reason. Whatever their other virtues, they simply are not the right kind of theory to provide the day-to-day understanding of business required by business ethics.

The Aristotelean approach is to be contrasted with that two-hundred-or-so-year-old obsession in ethics that takes everything of significance to be a matter of rational principles, "morality" as the strict Kantian sense of duty to the moral law. This is not to say, of course, that Aristotelean ethics dispenses with rationality or, for that matter, with principles or the notion of duty. But Aristotle is quite clear about the fact that it is cultivation of personal character that counts, long before we begin to rationalize our actions, and the formulation of general principles need not be an explicit step in correct and virtuous behavior as such but is more often a philosopher's formulation about what it means to act rationally.[1] Most important for our purposes here, duties too are defined by our roles in a community (for example, a corporation) and not by means of any abstract ratiocination, principle of contradiction, or a priori formulations of the categorical imperative. Kant, magnificent as he was as a thinker, has proved to be a kind of disease in ethics. It's all very elegant, even brilliant, until one walks into the seminar room with a dozen or so bright, restless corporate managers, waiting to hear what's new and what's relevant to them on the business ethics scene. And then they are told: "don't lie," "don't steal," "don't cheat"—elaborated and supported by the most Gothic non-econometric construction ever allowed in a company training center. But the problem is not just its impracticality and the fact that we don't actually do ethics that way: the Kantian approach shifts our attention away from what I would call the inspirational matters of business ethics (its incentives) and the emphasis on excellence (a buzzword for Aristotle as well as Tom Peters and his millions of readers). It shifts the critical focus from oneself as a full-blooded person occupying a significant role in a productive organization to an abstract role-transcendent morality that necessarily finds itself empty-handed when it comes to most of the matters and many of the motives that we hear so much about in any corporate setting.

The Aristotelean approach is also to be contrasted with the rival ethical theory of "utilitarianism." I have already raised certain questions about the vulgarization of utilitarianism and its humanistic focus in John Stuart Mill. But utilitarianism shares with Kant that special appeal to compulsives in its doting over principles and rationalization (in crass calculation) and its neglect of individual cultivation of character. But I can imagine a good existentialist complaining quite rightly that the point of all such "decision procedures" in ethics and appeals to policy and policy makers in business ethics is precisely to neutralize the annoyance of personal responsibility altogether, appealing every decision to "the procedure" rather than taking responsibility oneself. And then there are the standard problems of such intended calculation—how does one measure the harm or benefit of an action (if nothing so readily countable as money is involved) and how does one compare the needs and preferences of two different people or groups? I am not denying the importance of concern for the public good or the centrality of worrying, in any major policy decision, about the number of people helped and hurt. But I take very seriously the problems of measurement and

1. See, for example, John Cooper, *Reason and the Good in Aristotle* (Indianapolis: Hackett, 1986).

incommensurability that have been standard criticisms of utilitarianism ever since Jeremy Bentham (Mill's mentor and teacher), and there are considerations that often are more basic than public utility—if only because, in most of our actions, the impact on public utility is so small in contrast to the significance for our personal sense of integrity and "doing the right thing" that it becomes a negligible factor in our deliberations.[2]

What I am arguing, or about to argue, is a version of what has recently been called "virtue ethics," but I do want to distance myself from much of what has been defended in philosophy under that title. First of all, I want to reject those versions of ethics that view the virtues as no more than particular instantiations of the abstract principles of morality. This is an analysis that has been argued at some length, for instance, by William Frankena and Kurt Baier, both distinguished defenders of "the moral point of view."[3] But if, for example, being an honest man or woman is nothing other than obeying the general Kantian-type principle, "do not lie," if being respectful is a conscientious application of the "ends" formulation of the categorical imperative (not even Kant held this), if one's sense of public service is an expression of the utilitarian principle, then this is emphatically not what I have in mind, nor did Aristotle. To be witty or magnificent (two Aristotelean virtues not taken seriously enough by our contemporaries) is surely not to express or apply certain principles, but neither is courage, temperance, or even justice (contrary to many of our finest social thinkers today). To imagine our good existentialist here again, one can hear him saying, presumably in French, that one's personal judgments precede rather than follow one's abstract ethical pronouncements. Of course, this isn't exactly Aristotelean (Aristotle was no existentialist), but modified it makes a good Aristotelean point: choice and character are cultivated first, philosophical ethics—if one is lucky enough to study in the right academy—afterward. Theory in business ethics consists in part of just such reflection on the cultivation of the right virtues and their nature.

I also want to distance myself from some of the now-familiar features of what is being defended as virtue ethics, in particular the rather dangerous nostalgia for "tradition" and "community" that is expressed by Alasdair MacIntyre and Charles Taylor among others.[4] Of course, the Aristotelean approach does presuppose something of a sense of community (as both MacIntyre and Taylor point out at great length) and

2. See, for example, Bernard Williams, *Morality* (New York: Harper and Row, 1975).

3. William Frankena, *Ethics*, 8th ed. (Englewood Cliffs, N.J.: Prentice-Hall, 1981); Kurt Baier, "Radical Virtue Ethics," in *Ethical Theory; Character and Virtue*, ed. P. French et al., (Notre Dame, Ind.: University of Notre Dame Press, 1988).

4. Alasdair MacIntyre, *After Virtue* (Notre Dame, Ind.: University of Notre Dame Press, 1981); Charles Taylor, "The Nature and Scope of Distributive Justice," in *Justice and Equality*, ed. F. Lucasch (Ithaca: Cornell University Press, 1986).

in business ethics, it is this sense of community that I particularly want to emphasize. But there is a difference between the more or less singular, seemingly homogeneous, autonomous (and very elite) community that Aristotle simply took for granted and the nostalgic (I think purely imaginary) communities described or alluded to by recent virtue ethicists, often defined by a naive religious solidarity and unrealistic expectation of communal consensus. No adequate theory of ethics today can ignore or wish away the pluralistic and culturally diverse populations that make up almost every actual community. Even the smallest corporation will be rent by professional and role-related differences as well as divided by cultural and personal distinctions. Corporate cultures like the larger culture(s) are defined by their differences and disagreements as well as by any shared purpose or outside antagonist or competition, and no defense of the concept of corporate culture can or should forget that corporations are always part of a larger culture and not whole cultures themselves. And yet, in place of the abstract nostalgia that defines much of the current fascination with "communities," many modern corporations would seem to represent just such communities. They enjoy a shared sense of *telos* as many communities do not. They invoke an extraordinary, almost military emphasis on loyalty and, despite the competitive rhetoric, they first of all inspire and require teamwork and cooperation. Corporations are real communities, neither ideal nor idealized, and therefore the perfect place to start understanding the nature of the virtues.

There has been some suggestion in the literature that virtue ethics is a more "feminine" ethics than Kantian or utilitarian rule-bound ethics. I disagree. I thus want to distance myself from some recent feminist writings, including the work of one of my own best students, which have drawn a sharp contrast between the good, warm, feminine virtues of caring and concern and the oppressive, impersonal, war-mongering masculine principles of justice and duty.[5] I certainly agree with the shift in emphasis, from Kantian justice to compassion and caring, but it is not my intention to supply one more weapon in the perennial war between the sexes, and it seems to me that Aristotle—certainly no feminist—has much to say about the virtues that has little or nothing to do with the fact that one is a male or a female. It may be, as some writers have recently argued, that the increasing numbers of women in significant executive positions will change the dominant ethic of corporate America. I do not yet see much evidence for this promising proposition, but I think the importance of emphasizing the virtues (including the so-called feminine virtues) should not be held captive to gender distinctions.

5. Cheshire Calhoun, "Justice, Care and Gender Bias," *Journal of Philosophy* 83 (Sept. 1988).

Finally, I want to contrast the Aristotelean approach with what is now commonly called "the case study method." As Joanne Ciulla has argued in some detail, this supposedly new methodology goes back to ancient times, where it typically went under the controversial title of "casuistry."[6] The case study method begins with particular cases, whether real or imagined, and brings in abstract principles as needed to solve whatever problem(s) the case embodies. Casuistry was always opposed to the more philosophical "top-down" approach to problem solving, and it thus incurred the wrath of the philosophers, from Plato (who argued against the casuistry of the Sophists) to the current day, when "applied ethics" is viewed by more traditional professors as an affront to the discipline. But casuistry and today's case-study method still emphasize "the case" and the abstract principles that might be brought to bear on it too much to the exclusion of the larger context and the particular character of the parties and people involved. Thus it is often rightly a source of complaint that the Harvard case-study system, for example, feigns engagement but in fact encourages quick solutions-at-a-distance. Although the cases typically include a modicum of biography, the idea that management is mainly "people dealing with people"—rather than abstract problem solving—gets lost. The Aristotelean approach, by contrast, insists that people come first. Most real-life cases become cases not so much because of a dramatic convergence or clash of principles but because of the personalities involved. Real-life case studies are defined by character rather than by cases, and business life—as opposed to the studious preparation for it—is first of all a kind of social life, a submersion in a preeminently social, not case-study, world.

6. Joanne Ciulla, "Casuistry and the Case for Business Ethics," 1989 Ruffin Lectures, in *Business and the Humanities,* ed. E. Freeman (New York: Oxford University Press, 1991). See also S. Toulmin, *Casuistry and Cases.*

13

Business as a Practice

> Not essentials, not luxuries, but things that made ordinary life eas-
> ier. . . . To people looking for a large vessel that wouldn't taint
> water or food, and wouldn't leak, imagine what a blessing an enamel
> basin was.
>
> v. s. naipaul, *A Bend in the River*

I am often asked, What is business ethics? That is a secondary question
and a relatively easy one. The hard question, the one that so confuses
the proper characterization and understanding of "business ethics," is
the seemingly more straightforward and noncontroversial question, What
is business? It is not simply engaging in an activity with an eye to making money, for we do many things to make money that are not business, and we make money doing many things that are not primarily
money-making activities—for example, in most professions (teaching,
medicine, religion, art, music, and, I will argue, much of what we call
"business"). One can be "in business" and not make money, even for a
very long time. The idea of "nonprofit institutions" has become primarily a tax question, not a question of intent or success.[1] The purpose
of business is to promote prosperity, to provide essential and desirable
goods, to make life easier—the "blessing [of] an enamel basin" for poor
villagers in East Africa, pots and pans for the households of northern
Britain. Business is, if we look at the etymology, *busy/ness* (from the Old
English *bisignis*). It is, first of all, *activity*, being *occupied*, making
oneself busy rather than just making money as such. Making or taking
in money is secondary, the result or reward of activity. But "being busy"
alone is not yet business, for business is a quintessential *social* activity.
It involves trading partners and consumers, at the very least, and it
presupposes a network of implied and explicit understandings and
agreements, a shared set of rituals (how to bargain, how to pay), more

1. One could argue that the status of so-called nonprofit organizations ultimately amounts
to purely a tax question, not a question of intent or success. Compare, for example, the
operations of "commercial" and "academic" (nonprofit) publishers. My thanks to Tina
Hanna for her extensive research into this question.

than a modicum of mutual trust and some underlying system of evaluation, only the details of which are settled in actual bargaining and negotiation.

Business, in other words, is a *practice*. This may seem like an awfully tame insistence, until we consider almost the entire history of economics and business thinking. According to the standard microeconomic paradigm (and there are many who refuse to acknowledge the legitimacy of any other paradigm, except as government intrusion and interference) business is nothing but the isolated commercial transactions of autonomous rational agents devoid of moral constraints as well as external political rules and sanctions.[2] There need be no presuppositions, no prior agreements, no shared community or culture or system of evaluations. The market emerges, as if from nowhere (other than from the free will of the agents involved), and the result (if one assumes a perfect and "undistorted" market) is harmony and the mutual satisfaction of all. Even those who think larger and more systematically refuse to go beyond the fictitious notion of a "social contract"—between business and society, between business and business, within the corporation (indeed, the corporation as *nothing but* a contractual fiction). But this gigantic myth assumes an impossible model of autonomy and cooperation and a wholly implausible portrait of the market and of society in general.[3] Business competition and negotiation do not arise out of nowhere, without an already existing network of understanding and implicit agreements. To say that business is a practice is to insist that the market is not, in that radical (but nonsensical) sense, "free." It requires a complex ongoing system of (qualified) mutual trust and shared understanding, whether as part of a single culture or by way of the coordination of cultures (much easier if they are both already business cultures).

To say that business is a practice is to say that it is not only a social activity with (at least) several participants but that it has goals and rules and boundaries and a purpose. But the goals of a practice and the purpose of a practice, though necessarily connected, are not the same. The goal of a game of solitaire, for example, is to get all the cards faceup on the table, according to certain procedural rules and in a certain order. The purpose of the game, usually, is to "kill time." So, too, the immediate objective in a game of football is to carry the ball across your opponent's goal line, but the *purpose* of the game may be to enjoy a Sunday afternoon with one's buddies, to keep in shape, or, in the nonstandard case, to make some money. Goals, one might say, are internal to the practice. The purpose of the practice is the reason for

2. For the most sophisticated account of this "market without morals," see David Gautier, *Morals by Agreement* (New York: Oxford University Press, 1986), esp. ch. 4 (discussed in Part I here).

3. See my *Passion for Justice* (Reading, Mass.: Addison-Wesley, 1990), esp. ch. 3.

engaging in the practice. There may be any number of such purposes, obviously, and different participants may have different purposes, even in the same game. (Joe wants to "let out some aggression." Fred is trying to lose weight. Sam is reliving his high school glory days.) So, too, there are any number of goals in the game, but these, unlike the purpose(s) of the practice, are defined and structured by the practice itself. In football the goal is to carry the ball across a certain line, but one does that in order to score a touchdown, which one does to give one's team six more points, which one does in order to win the game. And in order to get into a position to carry the ball across the line, one pursues certain preliminary or subsidiary goals, trying to get a first down, trying to get an extra two yards on the play, trying to keep the defensive line from piling up on the quarterback. And, of course, one is trying to keep the ball away from the other team. The rules of football make it quite clear how these various goals are related to one another, and to play the game is to accept that hierarchy of goals and the rules that define them.

Games are paradigmatic practices, and by observing the structure of games we can learn a lot about practices in general. Business is not a game, of course; I hope I exhausted that metaphor in the preceding chapter. But business is a practice and, as such, has several gamelike features. Like competitive and team sports, it involves several or many people. It has rules, some of them (too many of them) encoded in law, but others internal to the practice, the product of shared agreement, and often unspoken. (The idea of spelling out all of the rules of any practice is a hopeless, infinitely regressive task.)[4] It has goals and purposes, boundaries, participants, coaches (consultants), and spectators. It is obvious that the goals of a game must be suitable to (though they are not definitive of) the purpose of playing the game. (One would not play solitaire as a way of keeping in shape, for example.) But especially here is the practice of business particularly troublesome, for goals and purposes tend to be indistinct if not identical, and therefore readily conflated and confused. Most important, the narrowly defined internal goal of "making a profit" is confused with the purpose of business. But the purpose of business is not to make a profit, and profit making is by no means the only goal internal to the practice. It can and has been argued that profit making is not even a goal of business, but rather a

4. I do not want to argue here for the implicitness of most "rules" in business, but it is important to insist, even in passing, that in even the most regulated or rule-governed game or practice there is always a web of underlying, often unstated presuppositions, expectations, and shared values, some (but not all) of which are specific to people's different roles and positions in the practice. As Robert Jackall says of what he calls, "rules-in-use": "these rules may vary sharply depending on various factors, such as proximity to the market, line or staff responsibilities, or one's position in a hierarchy. Actual organizational moralities are thus contextual, situational, highly specific, and, most often, unarticulated" (*Moral Mazes* [New York: Oxford University Press, 1988], p. 6).

condition of "staying in the game," a necessity and not an aspiration.[5] The goals internal to the practice might in general be summarized as "doing well," but "doing well" is by no means limited to making profits. Profits are not even an adequate way of "keeping score." In response to Milton Friedman's polemic that "the social responsibility of business is to increase its profits," one is tempted to suggest the equally pigheaded and one-sided view that "the social responsibility of business is to ignore profits." I think this is also obviously false, but it is probably much better for business.[6]

It also becomes evident that, even in the relatively simple paradigm of the game, the boundaries (that is, who is in and who is not) are not altogether clear. Certain people are designated "players," and they in turn are defined in terms of certain definitive roles or positions. But are only the players part of the game? How about the referee, the coach, the spectators? They affect the game and are affected by it as well. And if the line between "inside" and "outside" the game is none too clear, how, then, can we so neatly distinguish between goals and purposes of the game? Because we distinguish between "professional" and "amateur" sport, we tend to be pretty clear about the fact that monetary payment for games and rewards for winning are exterior to the game. "Enjoying the game," however, is not part of the game as such, but neither is a payment or reward. Is playing well an aspect of playing the game or something in addition to it? Is the good feeling of having played well part of the game or a reward for having done so? Are good sportsmanship and "being a good sport" an essential part of the game or are they virtues in their own right? We need not feel threatened by such muddles; they rather provide a moral: in any practice, purposes are more primary than goals and objectives, even if the latter are clear and precise while the former are variable and vague.

The neat separation of player and spectator in most games is not so readily available in business. In a rough-and-tumble football game, an occasional bystander on the sidelines may be knocked over, and in an Indianapolis 500 race, a few spectators may be killed, but these unfortunate victims are not thereby part of the game and, while there are all sorts of devices to protect them, their well-being and even their entertainment are not and cannot be the primary purpose of the game. The odd status of professional wrestling makes this quite clear. In few other sports would even a hint of "playing to the audience," rather than playing the game well, be tolerated.[7] In business, however, it is not at all

5. Peter Drucker, *Management* (New York: Harper and Row, 1974), p. 60.

6. Norman Bowie, however, has actually argued this thesis. See his "The Profit Seeking Paradox," in *Ethics of Administration,* ed. N. Dale Wright (Provo, Utah: Brigham Young University Press, 1988).

7. An occasional gesture, in between shots or to display great confidence, is acceptable. Magic Johnson could throw a wave to the audience and Ted Williams might spit at them,

clear who the "player" (and who the "spectator") might be. The world watched as Kravis and Johnson fought over the fate of RJR (described in exquisite, scandalous detail in *Barbarians at the Gate*)[8] but the appearance of a private game of high finance was misleading. Employees as well as ordinary stockholders, many communities as well as the small army of lawyers, bankers, and advisors were neither spectators nor disinterested bystanders, but had invested and were affected deeply. sometimes disastrously. Insofar as the purpose of business is to provide for the prosperity of the entire society, one might say that there are no mere spectators and the purpose of the practice is to provide for those who know very little about the practice or even that it exists. And then there is the consumer. On some accounts, the consumer is one of the key players; in others, the consumer is more like the referee.[9] But this rather odd debate about the status of the consumer only shows the inadequacy of the usual game model as an understanding of business. Business is a practice that is far more all-embracing and holistic than any game. There is no such protective self-enclosure as most games enjoy, and virtually everyone is affected. But if business isn't a game, it is nevertheless a practice, and "the market" must be understood not as an empty unstructured space in which free agents voluntarily test their skills against one another but as a preexisting community with a network of values and needs (only a few of them biological) and a system of rules that define and constrain the nature of negotiation and the sorts of things that can be negotiated.

In the business world—which is, essentially, our world—no one is outside of the practice, nor could they be, given the power of business and its pervasiveness in our society. The "impact" of business cannot be cordoned off like a football field or a raceway. Except for a few specialized markets, there can be no protective signs such as "Keep off the track" or "Players only." As we have seen quite clearly in recent years, a personal grudge match in the elite offices of a few high-flying financiers in New York or London can have far-reaching and sometimes disastrous consequences for secretaries, fieldworkers, housewives, and retirees in some small midwestern town or southern suburb. Business is not, in general, played for recreation (as most games are) whether

---

but their overall purpose is to win the game and prove themselves the best in the business, not to entertain the audience.

8. B. Burrough, *Barbarians at the Gate* (New York: Harper Collins, 1990).

9. Lynn Sharpe Paine ("Ideals of Competition") argues that the consumer is, in effect, the "judge' in business competition. It is the consumers, she says, "who decide not merely whether the rules have been followed but who make more highly discretionary judgments of quality." The problem with this analogy is that it is not permitted to bribe judges, but perfectly permissible to bribe consumers, for example, with rebates, giveaways, sweepstakes, and "an extra two ounces *for free!*" Consumers are part of the business context, not its overseers.

or not some or even many of the participants enjoy it, and even when it is played as a game by a powerful few, the impact is such that it cannot and should not be viewed as merely a game. Indeed, one might say that the impact of business *is* the practice. The practice of business is the effort to find or create and satisfy markets, to change the world or, at least, to be on the crest of change.[10] One gets a reward for doing well (having a positive impact, finding the right market) and a penalty (one is out of the game) for having no or a negative impact.

If business were a self-enclosed game, the point of which were to make a profit, there would indeed be a serious problem of what has come to be called "the social responsibility of business." But the business world is a practice with profound social impact, not a game. It is the world in which tens of millions of Americans earn their living and pay for the necessities and comforts of civilized life. It is the world in which houses are constructed and furnished, food is grown, shipped, sold, and eaten. It is the world in which new inventions are tried and new businesses are tested in the marketplace for the competitive quality and price of their products. It is the world Adam Smith described in which the consumer is, if not sovereign, at least relevant to the process as a decision maker and legislator, not just a fool with funds. It is the world in which general prosperity and the approximation of intrinsic value of labor (if not of commodities) is the desired outcome, not the windfall profits of financial manipulators. The purpose of business is to provide the "things that make ordinary life easier." Business is not an isolated game, which the public may play if it will, and the point is not just to win, for the impact on the nonplayers is typically greater than the rewards for the participants.[11]

The very structure of our society, its ample leisure and personality, are created by business, by the way business spurs and makes productivity possible and the way it distributes the goods throughout society and the world. Indeed, the values of our society—for better or worse—are essentially business values, the values of "free enterprise," the values of necessity and novelty and innovation and personal initiative. But this does not mean that our society is or should be a "free-for-all," an unhampered, unregulated scramble for wealth and profits. Neither does it mean that it is "everyone for himself or herself," a "dog-eat-dog" world, or a world in which "anything goes." To the contrary, it is a

10. Some theorists actually define "capitalism" as this very restlessness, this need to grow and expand. See, e.g., Robert Heilbroner, "The Future of Capitalism," *New York Times*, Aug. 15, 1982, and *Capitalism: For and Against* (New York: Norton, 1990).

11. Thus the importance of the current concept of "stakeholders" as opposed to the more limited notion of "stockholders," where the latter are clearly willing participants but the former need not be. Insofar as a "stake" still suggests voluntary participation, I still prefer the emphasis on corporate "impact" that employed in *It's Good Business*, which presupposes no particular willingness on the part of those affected by the company.

world defined by tacit understandings and implicit rules, a practice defined, like all practices, by mutual understandings and underlying trust,
and justified not by its profits but by the general prosperity it brings
about. Productivity and serving the public and taking care of one's own
employees are neither mere means or an afterthought of business but
rather its very essence. Then, as every smart entrepreneur knows well
enough, the profits will come as a consequence.

14

An Aristotelean Metaphor: Corporate Culture

> What seems needed as a "remedy" is some institutional analogue to
> the role that responsibility plays in the human being, guiding action
> toward certain values where the ordinary legislative prohibitors are
> unavailable or, on balance, unwise.
>
> CHRISTOPHER STONE, *Where the Law Ends*

It is a sign of considerable progress that one of the dominant models
of today's corporate thinking is the idea of a "corporate culture." As
with any analogy or metaphor, there are, of course, disanalogies, and
the concept of corporations as cultures too quickly attained the status
of a "fad"—thus marking it for easy ridicule and imminent obsoles-
cence.[1] But some fads nevertheless contain important insights, and although those who insist on keeping up with the latest fashion may soon
have moved on, the virtues of this recent change in thinking may not
yet have been fully appreciated.

1. E.g., see Mark Pastin, *The Hard Problems of Management* (San Francisco: Jossey-Bass,
1986) about "why corporations should have weak cultures and strong ethics." But one is
tempted to speculate whether Pastin, who learned ethics under the tutelage of Roderick
("ideal observer theory") Firth at Harvard, might not have too little respect for the shared
mores that come of participation in cultural life and is too impressed with the dispassionate negotiations of the social contract ("The lesson is clear. Forget culture and think
about fair agreements" [p. 144]), arguing that cultures are intrinsically "conservative" and
strong cultures "put basic beliefs, attitudes and ways of doing things beyond question."
Cultures are hard to change, but this is precisely their strength. Sometimes, ignoring the
culture works best. But only within the confines of the culture (cf. families) Pastin tends
to blend ethics into culture (or vice versa) so his opposition is not as pronounced as his
initial pronouncement would suggest. He also employs a trivial sense of culture: in Cadbury Schweppes, he suggests, there are "few corporate symbols, none of the bells and
whistles characteristic of strong-culture companies, and no need to do things 'the cadbury
way.' The corporate environment is free from ceremony" (p. 140). But on the very same
page, Pastin quotes Sir Adrian Cadbury himself: "The one thing I'm sure about . . . is
that the way it's done must be related to the culture (against the 'mandarin culture.'" So
much for "weak cultures."

The concept of a corporate culture, first and foremost, is distinctively and irreducibly *social*. It presupposes the existence of an established community and established practices, and it explicitly rejects atomistic individualism. Individuals are part of a culture only insofar as they play a part in that culture, participate in its development, and fit into its structure. Cultures are by their very nature (more or less) harmonious, that is, they are not possible unless people cooperate and share some minimal outlook on life. (There could not be a completely competitive culture, only a Hobbesian jungle of mutually disagreeable animals.[2] Cultures have rules and rituals, particular modes of dress and address; and most important of all (for our purposes) every culture has an ethics, including those basic rules that hold the society together and protect it from itself. Which of these are essential and which are "mere custom" is sometimes more easily determined by an outsider than by a member of the culture itself. The various "taboos" of every culture, including our own (and most corporate cultures), may indeed (for reasons now forgotten) protect the integrity of the community, blocking out some dreadful secret or preventing some now-unpredictable disaster. But they may be only "the way we do things around here" and of significance only because they are part of the values that are accepted by and thus help define the membership of the culture. The difference here may become extremely important in the midst of corporate upheaval and cultural change, but for day-to-day purposes it is a difference that has very little *practical* effect. The important point is that cultures presuppose shared knowledge, experience, and values and they are thus cooperative enterprises. A corporate culture is an essentially cooperative enterprise with public as well as private purposes. It cannot be reduced to a legal "fiction" or an economic mechanism or the numbers in the annual report or anything else that is not first and foremost an established group of people working together.

Needless to say, there are makeshift corporations that are neither cultures nor communities at all, just as there are nations by fiat (usually of other nations, for example, the forced amalgamation of Czechoslovakia and Yugoslavia in Europe and the carving up of Africa across and in violation of tribal lines by European colonialists). But recent history show just how badly such makeshift marriages work in both nations and corporate conglomerates. "Organizations" may be put to-

2. The most famous modern counterexample, the infamous Ik tribe of the mountain ranges of Africa, has been often abused for this purpose. Colin Turnbull's careful description of the interpersonal callousness and competitiveness of the Ik shows quite clearly that beneath their selfishness there is a cultural method, a sense of coherence even in the face of a hostile and alienating environment (Colin Turnbull, *The Mountain People* [New York: Simon and Schuster, 1974]. Within the context of a culture, the Ik do indeed strike us as shockingly indifferent to one another's well-being (even to the welfare of their own children), but nevertheless the culture itself displays the requisite structure of mutual attention, shared goals, and minimally harmonious cohesion, if not exactly cooperation.

gether just for the sake of some external benefit, such as the "travel clubs" that were organized in the 1970s in order to charter airline passage to Europe, but to think of the results as workable organic units is an often fatal mistake. The real problem arises when theorists take these examples, which are both deviant and exceptional, and elevate them to the status of paradigms, as if the existence of such merely formal organizations proves that what constitutes an organization, after all, is not its people or its shared values but the legal charter that defines and limits its purpose and activities. To the contrary, I want to insist that corporations (and most other human organizations) are defined first of all by their communal and cultural status and only secondarily (and not essentially) by any formal or legal process. All of our current cost-cutting at the expense of community, or "restructuring" for the sake of survival of the corporation but not of the people that make it up, is a preliminary to slow self-destruction.

It is important to appreciate the significance of the "culture" metaphor against the backdrop of the more vulgar, sometimes brutal and either atomistic and mechanical metaphors we have been discussing. Just as business (in general) has been saddled (and saddles itself) with unflattering and destructive images, corporations—both in general and as individual entities—have too often tended to present themselves (their public relations work and advertising to the contrary) as giant juggernauts, mechanical monsters as faceless as the glass and steel buildings that typically form their headquarters. Consumers are so many numbers and employees are only so many replaceable parts. Even top management is only part of the mechanism. It is no wonder that most Americans who do not work for corporations think of them as inhuman and as inhumane places in which to work, and those millions who do work for corporations find themselves at a serious conceptual disadvantage. What kind of a life is this, being a replaceable part in a giant machine, for whom the only virtue is mere efficiency?

The conception of a corporate culture, though relatively recent, has its origins in the more familiar model of the *bureaucracy*, developed during the French revolution and the Napoleonic era as a correction to inherited privilege and incompetence (but with its roots in Rome, in the labyrinthine organization of the medieval Catholic Church and, long before that, in the ancient civilization of the Middle East). The concept of the bureaucracy was extensively promoted and popularized (though with considerable misgivings) by the great German sociologist Max Weber at the turn of this century. The imagery of the bureaucracy provided something of a compromise between the juggernaut and machine imagery of the eighteenth-century Enlightenment on the one hand and the Renaissance and romantic demands for "humanization" on the other. (Indeed, the whole of the Western Enlightenment was something of an odd mix of machine metaphors and humanism, but that is another story.[3] But "bureaucracy" has become something of a "dirty word" for us, suggesting inefficiency instead of the model of efficiency it was once intended to be. It calls up images of Soviet ineffectiveness and Kafkaesque catacombs. And yet, modern corporations are in large part bureaucracies, and this is not necessarily to say something against them. But what is important and progressive about bureaucracies is not just their traditional and now largely discredited emphasis on efficiency, or even their still essential emphasis on meritocracy. It is rather the humanization of the bureaucracy as "culture" and the all-important shift of emphasis from machinelike efficiency to interpersonal cooperation and human productivity.[4]

Bureaucracies, like cultures and unlike machines, are made up of people, not parts. Bureaucracies have purposes. Bureaucracies involve people in making judgments, employing their skills, working together in an organized way to produce results. Those results may be the maintenance of the status quo, no easy trick in modern societies. For all of the obsessive talk about "innovation" and "competition," the essential function of most corporate bureaucracies—that is, the larger part of the corporation by far—is just this maintenance of the status quo. One can understand and sympathize with the fear and uncertainty about the future that is part of most markets without joining the myth-making chorus of "future shocks" and "megatrends." To be sure, change these days is both very real and very fast. Maintaining the status quo in a fast changing society requires being adaptive and organically tuned to the times, but it also requires a durable structure and a stable organization. Overemphasis on change and the sacrifice of stability—as evidenced in so many corporate "shake-ups" and "restructurings" today—weakens the corporation and makes it a far less efficient competitor.[5] However "leaner" (and often "meaner") it may be, this "new" corporation is likely to be far more embroiled in internal politics and the personnel problems of coping with insecurity and anxiety than facing the competition or improving its products. What maintains the stability within a corporation, however, is precisely that much-despised locus of inefficiency, the bureaucracy. Or, now in more enlightened terms, this essen-

3. See S. Toulmin, *Cosmopolis: The Hidden Agenda of Modernity* (New York: Free Press, 1989).

4. The familiar misunderstanding of the nature of bureaucracy extends even to those who are most sympathetic with the idea of corporate culture, notably, A. Kennedy and T. Deal, *Corporate Cultures* (Reading, Mass.: Addison-Wesley, 1982) (whose book began the recent "culture" fad), p. 108: "The process culture. A world of little or no feedback where employees find it hard to measure what they do; instead they concentrate on how it's done. We have another name for this culture when the processes get out of control—bureacracy."

5. Again, a word of wisdom from the Roman procousul Arbiter: "a wonderful method it [reorganizing] can be for creating the illusion of progress while producing confusion, inefficiency and demoralization."

tial continuity is provided by what we recognize as the corporate culture, an enduring security founded on interpersonal cooperation and a structure demanding mutual respect.

The idea of a corporate culture is an improvement over the more staid and impersonal image of the bureaucracy in several respects, but in one respect in particular. A "culture" is first of all a structured community of individuals and their interrelationships. Bureaucracies, on the other hand, remain subtly individualistic as well as mechanistic. People may work together in their various capacities but this "togetherness" is a function of the organization and not a relationship between them. They may not be cogs in a machine but they are functionaries who are readily replaced by anyone else with the same skills and knowledge. Our image of the bureaucracy, accordingly, is lots of people isolated in little offices (or "bureaus") doing their jobs and, if they are conscientious and efficient, not stopping to talk to one another or chitchat over the coffee machine. Our image of a culture, by way of contrast, essentially involves people emotionally involved with and attached to one another.

In the bureaucracy, the pursuit of efficiency depends on the impersonal, unemotional processing of information. Personality and character (as opposed to mere dependability) and interpersonal relationships are out of place. But however familiar this textbook "flowchart" conception of business may be, we in fact demand much more of our jobs than this, and we are certainly right to do so. The conception of a corporate culture allows us to understand such demands and justify them. It has often been pointed out but too rarely appreciated that most people spend almost half of their adult waking life in their work, and for people in corporations half of their life is that of the corporation. The very idea that we should spend so much of our lives as mere functionaries, as anything less than whole human beings, is intolerable. (This is not a new protest. Friedrich Schiller complained about the fragmentation and alienation that accompanied the division of labor two hundred years ago. Karl Marx was one of his most avid students.) The idea of a corporate culture allows us to (reintegrate our business lives and our lives, our special skills and duties, and our place in a community).

In modern corporate society, we are still struggling to integrate our work and our lives, our roles as employees and managers with our roles as citizens, neighbors, and parents. Without in the least sacrificing our bureaucratic ideal of a "meritocracy" (employment and advancement on merit rather than merely personal "connections"), we want to insist in some hard-to-define but inalienable sense that we be hired "for ourselves" and "as a whole person" and not *just* as someone who can program a computer or type ninety words per minute or develop a marketing plan or run a company. The difficulty here is that we are so

used to and steeped in the misleading metaphors we have been rejecting that we have a hard time justifying our humanistic sense of ourselves and our work. Except for a relatively small number of very specialized and autonomous managerial tasks, almost all organizational
duties—and their success or failure—depend upon our personal relations with other people. And the most important feature of almost any
job—and typically the most important reason why someone loves or
hates what they do—is the success or failure of an individual to fit in
with others, "the people I work with." Yet so many of our conceptions
of the corporation turn this basic and obvious truth into a purely secondary matter, a distraction or a sure sign of irresponsibility.

That is why I keep insisting that the basic fact about business is that
people in corporations *work together,* an utterly trivial but often forgotten principle in so much business talk and theory. People do not just
specialize in one skill or another in an impersonal "division of labor,"
efficiently (or inefficiently) distributed and arranged by some superior
management committee. Even in the most authoritarian and top-heavy
corporations, the instructions are always incomplete, specializations are
never completely distinct and independent, decisions are rarely autonomous, and personalities cannot be subdued. People can be embittered,
of course, and they can be so alienated—by physical separation into
isolated cubbyholes (or even grand corner offices)—that they become
out of sync with the others, possibly paranoid and counterproductive,
but this simply reinforces the point that personalities and personal concerns and relationships are as essential to the workplace as the stated
functions and duties of the job description. This is just that inscrutable
ingredient that American corporations, restricted and rigidified by machinelike conception of efficiency and a militaristic organizational hierarchy, find so enviable in many Japanese corporations. But there is
nothing mysterious or peculiarly "Eastern" about it. It simply has to do
with the recognition that *people* comprise corporations and live much
of their lives under corporate auspices. Impoverished and truncated
lives lead to impoverished productivity and excessive competition,
whereas rich full lives tend to be productive and cooperative.

Of course, within any organization, one expects to find office politics.
But here, too, what one recognizes on the job as an ineliminable and
sometimes full-time concern for one's people and projects as well as
one's own status becomes in most business talk and theory just another
distraction, as if organizations *should* be impersonal, frictionless machines in which each cog has its place or every bureaucrat his or her
isolated function and office. But at least some of the time in every office, office politics is the issue of the day; all other projects become
weapons or instruments and everyone else may well become either an
ally or part of the opposition. This is no distraction from business, however costly and counterproductive it may be. It is an essential part of

business as a human endeavor, even if it is typically bad business—and the result of poor organization, inattentive hiring, inadequate incentives, excessive confidence in competition, overly manipulative management, or ambiguous ethics. But there is politics, and there is a sense in which any relationship between people, even at its most harmonious and cooperative, involves the politics of recognition and self-esteem. The ideal is thus not to eliminate politics but to democratize and civilize our power relationships, to avoid jungle and battlefield metaphors and promote a culture in which politics is mutually supportive instead of antagonistic and destructively competitive.[6] There will, of course, always be those happily rare Rambo and Chuck Norris types, whom Michael Maccoby rightly called the "jungle fighter" type, but to take them as the paradigm of good business, to elevate them as cultural heroes (as in Michael Lewis's *Liar's Poker*), is to guarantee an organization mostly filled with hostile, frustrated, and embittered employees, whose devotion to the company and its interests stretches only as far as their next paycheck (or next job offer).[7] To live and to recognize oneself as a member of a corporate culture, on the other hand, is to see one's own interests and values as part of the interests and values of the corporation, and one's devotion to the company then becomes not a sacrifice or an act of faith but rather the assertion of one's own identity and self-esteem.

In a corporate culture, people, not functions or mere functionaries, work together for their shared and not merely mutual benefit. People, unlike functions and mere functionaries, have personalities, personal ambitions, and outside interests. They make friends (and enemies). They need a moment to unwind, catch their breath, relieve themselves, express themselves, renew their personal contacts around the office. (How quickly an office can be disrupted when a manager fails to say "hello" to everyone that morning.) Anal-compulsive types may see this (wrongly) as inefficient, and such interpersonal behavior as gossip and "chitchat" as a distraction, but this betrays a fatal misunderstanding of both people and organizations. That is why I have insisted that corporations are first of all communities, social groups with shared purposes. A person's position is not just a function defined by duties but a role in the community, a role that comes to have as its attributes (whether by design or evolution) such strictly interpersonal virtues as charm, attractiveness, and a good sense of humor as well as this or that job to be done.

But "community" is a very general term for interconnected and mutually interested individuals, and it contains no commitment or even a suggestion of development or internal structure. A community may be just a particular bunch of people gathered together for some period of

6. Tom Peters, in *Ethics Digest* 7, no. 2 (1990).
7. Michael Maccoby, *The Gamesman* (New York: Pocket Books, 1975); Michael Lewis, *Liar's Poker* (New York: Norton, 1989).

time to enjoy themselves and each other. Indeed, it is not altogether clear whether the same community exists over time, as individual members enter and leave the group—thus the importance of the additional concept of a culture, a corporate culture. Corporate cultures are not only distinctively and irreducibly social and opposed to atomistic individualism. Cultures have a history and a structure, and thus can remain "the same" over a substantial period of time despite the coming and going of any or even all individuals within it. And among those essential structures are the various demands of ethics. It is, above all, shared values that hold a culture together. And these values concern not only the "internal" cohesion and coherence of the culture. They also concern the sense of mission that the corporation embodies, its various stakeholder obligations and its sense of social responsibility and social (not just corporate) values.

This said, we can now come down hard on one of the most prominent confusions and controversies in business ethics. The question is whether corporations can and should be treated as moral agencies, as bearers of responsibility and obligations. It has been argued, for instance, most vigorously by John Ladd some years ago, that organizations in general (and corporations in particular) are not the right sorts of entities to be responsible. ("We cannot and must not expect formal organizations or their representatives acting in their official capacities, to be honest, courageous, considerate, sympathetic, or to have any kind of moral integrity. Such concepts are not in the vocabulary, so to speak, of the organizational language game.")[8] On the other hand, Peter French, in particular, has argued vigorously for a sense of "collective responsibility" that allows corporations straightforwardly to be blamed (and praised) for what they do.[9] Kenneth E. Goodpaster and John B. Matthews, Jr., have answered in the affirmative their own version of the question, "Can a Corporation Have a Conscience?"[10] They argue that corporations, by analogy to individuals, can be shown ("by projection") to share the three central senses of "responsibility" (causal blame, something to be done, and trustworthiness). ("If we analyse the concept of moral responsibility as it applies to persons, we find that projecting it to corporations as agents in society is possible."[11]

Goodpaster and Matthews quote a spokesman for a southern steel company, an admirable and socially concerned citizen in his own life but as a corporate spokesman the promulgator of an all-too-familiar argument: "As individuals we can exercise what influence we have as citizens, but for a corporation to attempt to exert any kind of economic

8. John Ladd quoted in Kenneth E. Goodpaster and John B. Matthews, Jr., "Can a Corporation Have a Conscience," *Harvard Business Review* (Jan.–Feb. 1982).

9. Peter French, *The Spectrum of Responsibility* (New York: St. Martin's Press, 1990).

10. Goodpaster and Matthews, "Can a Corporation Have a Conscience?" pp. 132–41.

11. Reprinted in Iannone, *Contemporary Moral Controversies in Business* (New York: Oxford University Press, 1989), p. 126.

compulsion to achieve a particular end in the social area seems to me quite beyond what a corporation should do." He goes on to call this "an abuse of corporate power." But this is, as Goodpaster and Matthews point out (in more moderate language), a two-faced argument. Corporations always do affect social relations and situations by virtue of their effectiveness in many ways that have no direct connection to their products or profits; the question is only whether they do so with their eyes open or closed, according to plan or without planning or predicting their own social impact. Why is it "irresponsible" and even "socialism" to take responsibility for one's impact on society but perfectly proper to simply let the chips fall where they may?

To be sure, corporations may overreach themselves in their social planning just as they often do in their plans for market expansion. (How many airlines, to pick but one industry have gone under in the past few years by buying too many planes, gates, and routes and burying themselves in debt?) And, to be sure, corporations "have no business" in areas where they have not the competence, but in many of the social arenas in which corporations have the most impact they clearly do have or can readily obtain the competence they need—for job training (and retraining), for industrial solutions to pollution problems, for personnel management and the control of their own products. Of course, there are disanalogies and exceptions to the "corporation as moral agent" view; not every feature of individual responsibility translates or projects onto a feature of corporate responsibility. Indeed, one problem with the Goodpaster/Matthews argument is precisely their insistence on this "analogy," rather than holding out (as French does) for a much stronger claim that corporate responsibility is not based on an argument by analogy at all but proceeds quite straightforwardly from the nature of the corporation as such.

So long as the corporation is viewed merely as a legal fiction created exclusively for the protection of its owners and their pursuit of profits, then, to be sure, the notion of "responsibility" will be limited to certain legal and contractual, merely fiduciary obligations. But once we appreciate the importance of viewing the corporation as first of all a community (within larger communities) and as a culture with shared values and larger social concerns, then the odd questions Where do corporate values come from? and How can corporations be socially responsible? simply disappear from view. It was only from a peculiarly narrow, overly legal, and inhumanly restricted understanding of organizations and institutions that such questions could make sense in the first place.

Corporations, as cultures, have built-in ethics. Not only individuals have responsibilities and values; movements and cultures, institutions and organizations do too. The Judeo-Christian tradition, for example, embodies a system of values quite independently of any particular individuals who hold those values. The Red Cross is an organization that is not reducible to any number of individual organizers or volunteers, but it clearly has values and social aims. Does it detract from the argument because this particular institution was founded as a nonprofit, charitable organization for the purpose of being responsive to social emergencies? In what sense is an institution limited to the intentions of its founders? And how explicitly need these be spelled out? The United States or France has responsibilities quite apart from the responsibilities of any particular citizens or people in power. Why? Because of its history, its prior commitments and obligations, and, especially, *what it stands for*. Why should corporate officers take such pride in insisting that they don't stand for anything, that their organizations exist for one and one purpose only, to maximize profits for a largely anonymous group of stockholders? Of course, they will gladly say (on behalf of their companies) that they stand for quality, that they are proud of their products and they are pleased that their company was not indicted by the EPA or sanctioned by Greenpeace. But this already establishes a bridge between the supposedly separate realms of business and social responsibility. Why do we insist on seeing the purpose of business in such a narrowly restricted and self-effacing way, when there is so much better that can be said for it and done with it as well?

But the "culture" metaphor has limitations too, and one of them is that it still tends to be too self-enclosed. A corporation is not like an isolated tribe in the Trobriand Islands. A corporate culture is an inseparable part of a larger culture, at most a subculture (or a sub-subculture), a specialized organelle in an organ in an organism. Indeed, it is the tendency to see business as an isolated and insulated endeavor, with values different from the values of the surrounding society, that characterizes all of these myths and metaphors, and in this sense, the "corporate culture" metaphor is not an adequate improvement on them. Another problem with such talk of corporate cultures is our tendency to confuse what we too readily take to be the supposedly standard American corporation as our paradigm and evaluate all other cultures and business arrangements accordingly. But there are other corporate cultures with other values. In New Zealand there are Maori values that coexist with colonial British values. In the southwestern United States there are strong Mexican values along with those values imported from New Jersey and Michigan. And before we indulge our clichéd superior sense that such values seem to be opposed to corporate business practices—too relaxed, not sufficiently competitive, too little personal ambition, and too much concern for family and community—let's remind ourselves that this is just the line of smugness that circulated about the Japanese thirty years ago.

We should always remember that the free market economy and the prominence of business and business thinking is an ongoing experiment, not an indelible aspect of society or a writ of God. We might not have the best way of doing it. We could even be wrong. A colleague of mine at an international conference in Bucharest recently heard a West German businessman, after listening to a number of suggestions concerning the exportation of American management skills to Eastern Europe, argue that American management was too rigid, mechanical, and hierarchical to work well even in America, much less in the more humanistic cultures of Europe. The Americans, of course, were shocked. Not only was their paradigm of a corporate culture being thrown back in their faces as inhuman; it was also declared to be dysfunctional. If no philosophical or humanitarian concerns are sufficient to prompt a new way of thinking about business, the new American situation in the world market should be ample motivation. One more management fad or marketing miracle is not going to do it, and the continuing denial of our own humanity and sociability is only going to leave us more isolated and more desperate. What we really need is a renewed sense of solidarity and shared cultural significance.

15

Business as a Profession: People in Business as Professionals

> If the profit-seeking paradox is to be avoided, the business person must see herself as a professional and the service motive must dominate. Business can only really do well if it seeks to do good.
>
> NORMAN BOWIE, "The Profit-Seeking Paradox"

People in business should think of themselves as *professionals*. To already professional managers, this may seem obvious, though many business critics will find it outrageous. My aim, once again, is to enlarge the scope of our thinking, away from a narrow and in most cases false image of grubby individual competitiveness toward a more holistic sense of social engagement, respectability, and responsibility. Corporations are not legal mechanisms for the maximization of profits and most people are not in business merely to make money. Once again (for those who refuse to give up bad arguments), this is not to say that people in business are indifferent to making money, any more than to insist that a corporation is a culture is to deny that one of the baldest necessities of corporate success is to make a profit. But making money and the need to make money are as common to the practices of medicine and law as they are to business, and business should be considered—like these time-honored (and also much-criticized) practices—a profession.[1]

1. To be sure, there is a long tradition—now instituted in the structure of our universities as well as in the popular vocabulary—that designates medicine and law, perhaps engineering and architecture, as professions, business as a trade. Indeed, there has long been a significant move to push business schools off university campuses on just this ground and assign them their rightful (and considerably more pedestrian) place as trade schools along with secretarial schools, technological trade schools, and institutes for plumbers and electricians. Business schools themselves contribute to this, of course, by pretending to teach undergraduates the language of business without requiring even a modicum of literacy and facility in their own natural language and literature (not to

Norman Bowie has argued a similar thesis in his controversial 1988 Ruffin Lecture.[2] I do not want to evade that controversy here, but I do want to begin (as he did) with a reasonable specification of what it means to be a professional—and what advantages accrue to business people who accept this designation for themselves. Bowie borrows seven criteria from Professor Abraham Flexner concerning the designation of a "professional"[3]:

1. Possess and draw upon a store of knowledge that is more than ordinarily complex.
2. Secure a theoretical grasp of the phenomenon with which it deals.
3. Apply its theoretical and complex knowledge to the practical solution of human and social problems.
4. Strive to add to and improve its stock of knowledge.
5. Pass on what it knows to novice generations not in a haphazard fashion but deliberately and formally.
6. Establish criteria of admission, legitimate practice, and proper conduct.
7. Be imbued with an altruistic spirit.

Most of these concern the specialized knowledge and skills that a professional must have ("epistemological criteria"). A physician, to say the obvious, needs extensive study in the anatomy and physiology of the body and the many malaises it suffers. A lawyer needs to learn what is virtually a new language as well as an ominous library full of prior cases and decisions. Moreover, each needs training—in diagnosis and "bedside manner," in writing and arguing and courtroom tactics. None of this is "natural," and all of it requires extensive education. But it seems to me that the complexities of modern accounting and financial analysis, to name but two of many such business specialities, are such that there can be no valid claim that business lacks similarly special knowledge and skills essential to a profession. When one adds (as one should) the considerable knowledge of production and management that is becoming necessary to feel at home in almost any industry, it should be obvious that business is and should be regarded as a profession. The fact that some very successful business people have had very little for-

---

mention the languages and literatures of the other cultures with whom they will, if successful, surely be doing business). (Both medical and law schools, by contrast, require a college education as a prerequisite for admission; engineering is sometimes denied its status as a profession because it does not do so; and medicine has been under heavy fire lately for allowing and encouraging its students to concentrate on "premed" science subjects to the exclusion of humanities.)

2. Bowie, "Business Ethics as a Disciple: The Search for Legitimacy," in *Business Ethics: The State of the Art*, ed. R. Edward Freeman (New York: Oxford University Press, 1990), pp. 17–41.

3. Abraham Flexner, "Is Social Work a Profession?" quoted in Bowie, ibid., p. 18.

mal education seems to me not to undermine this claim, and the charge that some of this knowledge is bogus or warmed over (and jargonized) common sense is not a sufficient argument against it. (Otherwise, it would bode ill for psychiatry and a good deal of the legal profession as well.) But, one might challenge, isn't it also true of electricians, plumbers, and computer repairmen that they require considerable education and training in their fields. One might in turn argue that the fund of knowledge and skills they must master is much less ominous than medicine and law, and so too the knowledge and skills of business, however full the business school curriculum. But with this question we begin to suspect that the difference between the profession and a mere "trade" may be primarily one of status rather than qualifications.

With the accumulation of knowledge and skill in any profession, there is also the need to pass this knowledge and these skills on. Education again becomes a critical ingredient in the specification of a profession, and a professional is as such concerned not just with his own competence but with the competence of succeeding generations and his or her own colleagues. Professions, accordingly, impose requirements and credentials on their practitioners, which determine who may practice and who may not. One might object that this interferes with "the free market" (an objection that many physicians and lawyers are happy to make when anyone—including their own professional associations—dictates the terms of their practice), but the obvious counterargument is that an unfettered free market is not always the best way to dispense services, particularly when the "consumers" (clients) cannot reasonably be expected to form sufficiently knowledgable judgments. (Most patients pay far more attention to their doctors' body language and looks than they do to what he is saying, which is for the most part incomprehensible.) The point, of course, is that professionals have serious impact on the lives of their clients, and a profession has a reputation to defend. Trust is essential to a successful practice, and the elimination of quacks and frauds is necessary for the success of everyone in the profession as well as for the sake of everyone else. But shouldn't business be similarly protective of its reputation, and are not people in business similarly concerned with the impact of their products and the trust they engender among their customers (and other stakeholders)? Think, in particular, of brokers and brokerage houses, how important the element of trust is and how extensively the client depends on the knowledge of the broker who wouldn't otherwise be needed. Think (just over the last few years) how many people's lives have been destroyed by disastrous investment advice and the backlash against the brokers. Think, too, about what happened during the same period as our savings and loans institutions passed out of the hands of professional bankers. Why the emphasis on the public good in law and medicine but not in the case of business? Could it be the (obviously false) assumption that the impact of business on its clientele is always more trivial than the impact of law and medicine? Could it be some residue of the old bromide— long since gone from law and medicine—that the buyer should beware? Or could it be simply one more ploy to avoid the obvious need for regulation essential to any profession in the name of "free enterprise"?

One could argue, rather cynically, that self-regulation in the established professions is nothing but a means of restricting the free market in those professions by enforcing limits and keeping down the number of licensed practitioners. (The American Medical Association has often been so accused, the American Bar Association more recently, despite the apparent glut of lawyers coming down the road.) Self-regulation through credentials also eliminates the competition (homeopaths and folk doctors in medicine, mediators and lay advisors in law). Wouldn't our health care system be much better off, one could argue, if more people with some training and skills could enter the market and do many of the tasks that most physicians avoid anyway, despite their efforts to maintain a monopoly (inoculations, treatment of routine ailments, housecalls)? And wouldn't our legal system be similarly improved if more people could carry out the more mundane functions that lawyers typically hand over to paralegals anyway? To be sure, a persuasive case can be made in both instances, but it leaves open the general point about the need for regulation and the protection of the public. One of the essential features of a profession is the enforced qualifications and competence of its practitioners where the public good is concerned, and any adequate conception of the free market must be construed *within* the frame of this demand.

It is this emphasis on the public good that lies at the heart of my campaign for the recognition of people in business as professionals. ("Altruism," I have argued, is a misleading way of stating this concern for others and too readily suggests excessive self-sacrifice.)[4] Professionalism involves a sense of social service. Professionals pledge themselves to the public, in Hippocratic oaths, in their alligiance to—and not just use of—the Constitution. (What do engineers do?) The main thrust of my insistence on the recognition of business people as professionals is precisely this emphasis on public service. Norman Bowie writes,

> Traditionally the motive for professional conduct is the service motive; the professional skills are service skills, specifically skills that benefit humankind. Doctors, lawyers, teachers, and the clergy—the standard paradigms of professionals—exercise a special skill for the benefit of human beings. The Harvard Business School has as its motto, "To Make Business a Profession." Business persons who view themselves as professionals are motivated to do good and in doing good the firm will do well. If a manager emphasizes the production and distribution of quality products that customers need and if

4. See my *Passion for Justice* (Reading, Mass.: Addison-Wesley, 1990), ch. 1.

she is honest and fair with suppliers and lenders, and most importantly if she provides meaningful work for employees, then both the manager and the firm will be profitable.[5]

This argument, that people in business should see themselves as "professionals rather than mere profit maximizers" is the heart of my argument here. We have heard quite enough about the pursuit of profits and the all-obsessive bottom line. It is time to turn our attention to what business actually accomplishes in the world and not just the rewards it accumulates in return.

But can't one accept the idea that business serves the public interest and business people have social responsibilities without insisting on calling them "professionals"? In a recent issue of *Newsweek*, Robert Samuleson argues against the identification of business as a profession. (His overall polemic is against business schools and professional M.B.A. students.) He writes,

Medicine, law and engineering are professions," says Henry Mintzberg, a management professor at McGill University. They demand mastery of a core body of knowledge. Business is different. Business schools instruct students in the mechanical skills of accounting, financing, and marketing. But the essence of business—taking sensible risks, creating valuable products, motivating people and satisfying customers—lies elsewhere and cannot be taught in a classroom. "Leadership," as Mintzberg puts it, "is not a profession."[6]

But this characterization of business as "leadership" is surely too narrow, as is the implied characterization of a profession. But is my own characterization adequate to the notion of professionalism, or is it too broad or, perhaps, too narrow? Should people in business indeed be called professionals, and, if so, doesn't this obscure the term? Indeed, what about plumbers? Are they too professionals? And is it necessarily a good thing to be a professional?

One current meaning of "professional" could indeed cause us a problem. Professionals are often lauded as "cool," controlled, capable in even the harshest conditions. But along with this, often as a matter of necessity, professionals may be cold, unemotional, uncaring. And this, in conjunction with the already dubious description of business as a ruthless, competitive world, gives rise to an unappealling portrait indeed. It is a typical if tragic scenario in many corporations: a manager is fired and breaks down in tears. "Be professional!" he is firmly instructed. "Don't get emotional" (presumably like the person who fired him). When the victim is a man, of course, the demand is doubly de-

5. Bowie, "The Profit Seeking Paradox," in *Ethics of Administration*, ed. N. Dale Wright (Provo, Utah: Brigham Young University Press, 1988).

6. Robert J. Samuelson, *Newsweek*, May 14, 1990.

meaning, a challenge to his masculinity as well as his professional status. When the victim is a woman on the other hand, such "unprofessional" behavior may be tolerated but only because it underscores the chauvinist prejudice that women just can't be professional. But why should "professional" carry with it such inhuman demands? To be sure, there is good reason why a physician who is surrounded with hysterical and possibly dying patients has to avoid becoming "emotionally involved" if it interferes with his judgment and competence as a doctor, and there is good reason why lawyers should not get too "emotionally involved" with their clients. But emotional control too readily slides into indifference, and "keeping your cool" is not to be contrasted with being inhuman to those who emotionally depend on you. Insofar as professionalism turns into callousness, I think that we can agree that professionalism taken too far is not a virtue. The business world already has enough respect for callous efficiency, and the insistence that they think of themselves as professionals is not intended to encourage this further.

"Profession," as we use the term, is another metaphor, a social metaphor with a particular cachet. According to the *Oxford English Dictionary* (seventh Edition), "to profess" literally means "to lay claim to." In other words, it refers to self-presentation rather than to an accomplishment or any credential as such. Originally, the verb referred to a profession of faith, and professors, accordingly, were religious believers. They were often, but not necessarily, educated, and they were often, but not necessarily, teachers. Are what we now call "professors" professionals? To be sure, they are not necessarily believers, but are they professional teachers (and would that mean that teachers who are not professors are thereby unprofessional?) or are they not primarily teachers at all (a view that a majority of university faculty would no doubt endorse)? Why should education and the complexity of a subject be so critical to professionalism? Indeed, education seems to be secondary in traditional usage: divinity, law, and medicine used to be called "the learned professions," suggesting that there are less learned and unlearned professions as well. ("The world's oldest profession," for one, requires little if any formal schooling.) But if education is secondary and self-presentation primary, we start to suspect that the designation of a professional is a matter of prestige and social status rather than accomplishment. In most societies, education is the privilege of the upper classes, and we should not be surprised if education were not so much the mark of the professions as a kind of added benefit; one cannot be called a professional unless he or she deserves a certain elite status, and the mark of that status is education. On this account, of course, the ideal of professionalism takes on an unhealthy dose of class-consciousness, which one could argue permeates our taxonomy of careers and professions.

For example, American high schools typically distinguish between academic and trade (or commercial) programs, and there is no question which is more prestigious. Colleges too divide themselves into academic and trade, and again the supposedly broad humanistic focus allows the former to "look down on" the latter (despite however many pleas from parents that their children be "trained for a career.") So do publishers divide themselves, and in the arts, there is a seemingly age-old (but in fact very recent) distinction between "the fine arts" and a mere "craft," a caste distinction that was invented (according to Arthur Danto) during the supposedly egalitarian French revolution by the classical painter–art world dictator Jacques-Louis David. We get the story backward if we think of these divisions first of all in terms of degrees of difficulty and only secondarily in terms of prestige. The prestige comes first, and any study of the history of the professions presents the critical reader with a keen sense of elitism and the protection of privilege as well as the quite defensible concern with competence and quality. Thus, why do we so confidently insist that physicians and lawyers are professionals but plumbers are not? Much of this is a matter of status and the familiar prejudice against those who work with their hands in blue collars as opposed to those who work exclusively with their minds (ideally they do not even have to write or type out their own ideas) in clean white collars and cuffs. People in business occupy a middle ground, spread as business is between shopkeepers and tradespeople whose business is the hands-on production and distribution of commodities or nitty-gritty services and executives whose business is strictly verbal and cerebral. But to designate those at the executive end of the spectrum as professionals and deny that designation to those at the productive end only makes the arbitrary elitism of "professionalism" all the more obvious.[7]

With elitism and privilege, however, comes a sense of noblesse oblige, the special obligations of the privileged. And the business world, more than anything else, desires and demands respectibility. Even if there are no strict criteria for the designation of a professional and professionalism is more a matter of proud self-presentation than education or credentialism, there is an obvious beneficial consequence: the exepctation of some obligation to society that is larger than grubby self-

---

7. This elitism regarding "service" (and production too) goes back to ancient times, and we would well be done with it. Aristotle both praised and belittled service, in his life with the aristocrats praising its doing but belittling those who did it. So, too, a New Zealand friend diagnosed the sometimes rude service in that otherwise friendly and delightful country by pointing to New Zealand's colonial past and the residue resentment of once being servants, which engendered a confusion between service, servility, and servitude. But there is pride in accomplishment and doing a job well, which is professionalism—very different from submission. But professionalism may be found among holders of low-prestige occupations, such as waiters and service station attendants (was it Texaco that was "your automobile professional"?), and it is not as such a class-conscious concept.

interest. In this sense, we can see that it is quite a good thing to designate plumbers and electricians as well as managers as professionals. The idea that being in business is nothing but being "out to make money" (even without the added vulgarity, "lots of it") is a terrible self-presentation, devoid of social concern or personal pride and not worthy of respect. Besides, it just isn't what business is about at all.

One of the most common current meanings of "professional" is that "one is getting paid for it." The distinction between an amateur and a professional athlete, for example, is wholly based on the question of remunerative reward, even if the remuneration (according to the strict rules of most college associations and formerly of the Olympics, for example) is not as such for playing or winning a game. (Giving a basketball player a convertible compromises his or her amateur status, whether or not it is a reward for winning a specific game.) So, too, the distinction between an amateur and a professional artist (according to the rulings of the Internal Revenue Service, for instance) turns entirely on one's intent and consequent success at making money. So construed, being professional means simply "getting paid for it," and managers and shop stewards, floorwalkers as well as plumbers are, by this easy criterion, professionals. But then, so is almost everyone who receives a salary. The honorific mantle of "professionalism" surely cannot be earned so easily.

Being in business is not opposed to professionalism, conceived of in terms of serving the public interest and not "just making money. Consider physicians as professionals. Are they also in business? We can see here how complex the question of business and professionalism becomes; on the one hand, they surely are, and on the other they emphatically are not. If a physician were to withhold treatment from a desperate patient on the grounds that he or she had not paid a previous bill, the doctor in question would be guilty of a serious breach of professional conduct. (If your physician confided to you that he really hated medicine but was staying in it for the money, you would surely look for a new doctor, possibly even before the end of the visit.) If "professional" is sometimes defined in terms of "getting paid for it," it is also defined in terms of "not doing it [just] for the money." If this strikes us as paradoxical, it is, perhaps, only because we are so addicted to those "either/or" accounts of motivation: *either* one is in it for the money *or* one is in it out of sheer devotion, *either* a corporation exists to maximize profits *or* an organization exists to promote the public good.

Professionals as well as nonprofessionals, people in business as well as many who are not "in business," are in it, in part, for the money. But what is the proper balance between financial self-interest and public service? I once overheard a conversation between two physicians who were discussing "socialized medicine" (which they seemed to conflate with life under Stalin). One said, "If the government limited our fees, why should we bother working so hard?" The same story has many variations, but are they all offensive insofar as they indicate a shift from "professionalism" to sheer commercialism—the offer of skilled labor and advice for (and *only* for) financial return. Are the doctors I overheard professionals, or are they just technically trained businessmen? ("High-class plumbers," as the popular expression goes.)[8] It is not only the mark of a professional but of everyone who does a job worth doing that the motivation is or should be something more than just "making a buck" or "earning a living."

Professionalism means service in return for compensation but not just because of the compensation. To be sure, the market for commodities is by no means so secure as the market for medicine or education, and the risks, accordingly, are much greater in that range of professions we call "business" than in that much smaller group of services that we call "professions." In return for that risk, the compensation can be greater as well. But in either case, whether one tries to sell a new breakfast cereal in an already glutted inelastic market or practices medicine in a poor, isolated rural town, one works for money but not exclusively. And on the other side of the relationship, our clients and customers pay because it's worth it, and that's what business is all about.

8. I am reminded of what Molière said about writing, a profession "like prostitution: First you do it because you enjoy it; then you do it for a few friends, then you do it for money"—an instructive sequence regarding the profit motive.

16

The Six Parameters
of Aristotelean Ethics

> To argue, in the manner of Machiavelli, that there is one rule for
> business and another for private life, is to open the door to an orgy
> of unscrupulousness before which the mind recoils. To argue that
> there is no difference at all is to lay down a principle which few
> men who have faced the difficulty in practice will be prepared to
> endorse as of invariable application, and incidentally to expose the
> ideas of morality itself to discredit by subjecting it to an almost in-
> tolerable strain.
>
> R. H. TAWNEY, *Religion and the Rise of Capitalism*

I want to organize my introduction to the Aristotelean approach to
business by summarizing the essential parameters that circumscribe and
define the virtues in business ethics, a half-dozen concerns typically ignored in the more abstract and principle-bound discussions of ethics
and policy discussions that so dominate the field. Together, they form
an integrative structure in which the individual, the corporation, and
the community, self-interest and the public good, the personal and the
professional, business and virtues all work together instead of against
one another. I will discuss each of the following six parameters in turn:

- community
- excellence
- membership
- integrity
- judgment
- holism

THE CORPORATION AS COMMUNITY

It is not at all bad being a businessman. There is a spirit of trust
and cooperation here. Everyone jokes about such things, but if

businessmen were not trusting of each other the country would col-
lapse tomorrow.

WALKER PERCY, *The Moviegoer*

The Aristotelean approach begins with the idea that we are, first of all,
members of organized groups, with shared histories and established
practices governing everything from eating and working to worshiping.
We are not, as our favorite folklore would have it, first of all *individuals*—that is, autonomous, self-sustaining, self-defining creatures who,
ideally, think entirely for ourselves and determine what we are. The
"self-made man" (or woman) is a social creature, and he or she "makes
it" by being an essential part of society, however innovative or eccentric
he or she may be. To say that we are communal creatures is to say that
we have shared interests, that even in the most competitive community
our self-interests are parasitic on and largely defined in terms of our
mutual interests. To think of the corporation as a community is to insist
that it cannot be, no matter how vicious its internal politics, a mere
collection of self-interested individuals. To see business as a social activity is to see it as a practice that both thrives on competition and presupposes a coherent community of mutually concerned as well as self-
interested citizens.

To be sure, communities in the contemporary "Western" world are
anything but homogeneous or harmonious, and the heterogeneity and
cacaphony of different voices and cultures is what gives the urgency to
our insistence on community. Corporations are not (or should not be)
"melting pots," but neither can they long contain factions of mutually
resentful minorities.[1] It seems to be one of the staples of conservative
social thinking that communities are and ought to be uniform and defined by consensus. But it seems to me that there have been few such
communities of more than tribal size and that every community from
the rural South to the Northeastern ghetto has had to accommodate
minorities and class differences, flourishing by virtue of rather than in
spite of a mixture of cultures, customs, and mores. I do not pretend
that we could or should go back to the imaginary good old days of
authoritarian homogeneity. The claim I am making here is metaphysical rather than nostalgic, and the claim is that what we call "the individual" is socially constituted and socially situated. "The individual" today

---

1. There is a substantial but often ignored problem here concerning affirmative action
and justice. We argue for a meritocracy, but the truth is that interviewers are looking for
someone they would enjoy working with, and for the most part that means someone like
them. In the typical, mostly white male corporation, there is a natural block against women
and minorities, and anyone who would raise the discomfort level. "Merit" often refers to
comfort. How to develop pluralistic communities is critical here, but neither the shrill
multiculturalism and ethnic identity debate nor the equally obstinate assimilationist success rhetoric is going to help us here.

is the product of a particularly mobile and entrepreneurial society in which natural groups (notably the extended family or tribe) have been replaced by artificial ortganizations such as schools and corporations. Movement among them is not only possible (as it is usually not among tribes and families) but encouraged, even required. But as traditional bonds are broken, the person who was once defined simply as "the daughter of Yanni" or "the son of Zeke" now becomes known as "the expert from Reno" and "the new vice president." Our credits and credentials accumulate, making us not so much unique as the product of a dozen or more competing and overlapping social groups and influences. That is "the individual," not an ontological atom but part of a complex interwoven metaphysical social fabric.

"The individual" was an invention of the eleventh and twelfth centuries in Europe, when families were separated by war and the tightly arranged structures of feudalism were breaking apart. The individual became increasingly important partly with the advent of capitalist and consumer society, but (as so often in the overly materialist history of economics) mainly because of changing religious conceptions during the Reformation, with increased emphasis on personal faith and individual salvation. But "the individual" was always a relative, context-dependent designation. An individual in one society would be a sociopath in another. ("The nail that sticks out is the one that gets hammered," says a traditional Japanese proverb.) But what we call "the individual" is, from even the slightest outside perspective, very much a social, even a conformist, conception as well. To show one's individuality in the financial world, for example, it may be imperative for men to wear ties of certain colors or patterns that they might not have chosen on their own. To further emphasize individuality (which connotes creativity, even genius), one might sport a mustache or beard (though the range of styles is very strictly circumscribed). But getting beyond trivial appearances, even our thoughts and feelings are for the most part defined and delineated by our society, in our conversations and confrontations with other people. Princeton anthropologist Clifford Geertz once wrote that a human being all alone in nature would not be a noble, autonomous being but a pathetic, quivering creature with no identity and few defenses or means of support. Our heroic conception of "the individual"—often exemplified by the lone (usually male) hero—is a bit of bad but self-serving anthropology. There are exceptional individuals, to be sure, but they are social creations and become exceptional just because they serve the needs of their society, more often than not by exemplifying precisely those forms of excellence most essential to that society.[2]

2. There is always the *Star Trek* myth, of course, the benign "outsider" who brings to a civilization some virtue that is sorely missing but wholly lacking (e.g., Kirk's courage, Spock's rationality), and the more generic Joseph Campbell myth of the hero who leaves

We find our identities and our meanings only within communities, and for most of us that means at work in a company or an institution. However we might prefer to think of ourselves, however we (rightly) insist on the importance of family and friends, however much we might complain about our particular jobs or professional paths, we define ourselves largely in terms of them, even if, in desperation, in opposition to them. Whether a person likes or hates his or her job more often than not turns on relationships with the people one works for and works with, whether there is mutual respect or animosity and callousness or indifference. Even the lone entrepreneur—the sidewalk jeweler or the financial wizard—will succeed only if he or she has social skills, enjoys (or seems to) his or her customers or clients.

The philosophical myths that have grown almost cancerous in many business circles, the neo-Hobbesian view that business is "every man for himself" and the Darwinian view that "it's a jungle out there," are direct denials of the Aristotelean view that we are first of all members of a community and our self-interest is for the most part identical to the larger interests of the group. Competition presumes, it does not replace, an underlying assumption of mutual interest and cooperation. Whether we do well, whether we like ourselves, whether we lead happy productive lives, depends to a large extent on the companies we choose. As the Greeks used to say, "to live the good life one must live in a great city." To my business students today, who are all too prone to choose a job on the basis of salary and start-up bonus alone, I always say, "to live a decent life choose the right company." In business ethics the corporation becomes one's immediate community and, for better or worse, the institution that defines the values and the conflicts of values within which one lives much of one's life. A corporation that encourages mutual cooperation and encourages individual excellence as an essential part of teamwork is a very different place to work and live than a corporation that incites "either/or" competition, antagonism, and continuous jostling for status and recognition. There is nothing more "natural" about the latter, which is at least as much the structuring of an organization (whether intended or not) as the cooperative ambience of the former.

The first principle of business ethics is that the corporation is itself a citizen, a member of the larger community, and inconceivable without it. This is the idea that has been argued over the past few decades as the principle of "social responsibility," but the often attenuated and distorted arguments surrounding that concept have been more than

---

his society and wanders off on his own, later returning with new virtues to save the society. But the fact that these are *myths* should already tell us something about their sociological status. The virtues supposedly imported are already celebrated as such.

enough to convince me that the same idea needed a different foundation.[3] The notion of "responsibility" (a version of which will, nevertheless, be central to my argument here too) is very much a part of the atomistic individualism that I am attacking as inadequate, and the classic arguments for "the social responsibilities of business" all too readily fall into the trap of *beginning* with the assumption of the corporation as an autonomous, independent entity, which *then* needs to consider its obligations to the surrounding community. But corporations, like individuals, are part and parcel of the communities that created them, and the responsibilities that they bear are not the products of argument or implicit contracts but intrinsic to their very existence as social entities. There are important and sometimes delicate questions about what the social responsibilities of business or of a particular corporation might be, but the question whether they have such responsibilities is a nonstarter, a bit of covert nonsense. Friedman's now-infamous idea that "the social responsibility of business is to increase its profits" betrays a willful misunderstanding of the very nature of both social responsibility and business. (Not surprisingly, the author of that doctrine has elsewhere protested, alienating his friends along with his critics, that he is "not pro-business but pro–free enterprise.")

These claims are closely akin to the ideas captured in the punlike notion of a *stakeholder,* that broadening conception of the corporate constituency that includes a variety of affected (and effective) groups and all sorts of different obligations and responsibilities. The term has become something of a coverall, and so what considerable advantages it has provided in terms of breadth are to some extent now compromised by the uncritical overuse of the word. For example, the notion of "stakeholder" suggests discrete groups or entities whereas the primary source of dilemmas in business ethics is the fact that virtually all of us wear (at least) two hats, for example, as employees and as members of the larger community, as consumers and as stockholders, as a manager and as a friend, and these roles can come into conflict with one another. As a program for ethical analysis in business, the standard list of stakeholders is notoriously incomplete where it concerns one's competitors rather than one's constituents. In an obvious sense, no one is more affected by one's actions (and, sometimes, no one is more effective in determining one's actions) than one's competitors. "Good sportsmanship" and fair play are essential obligations in business ethics. And yet it seems odd to say that the competition "has a stake" in the company. The idea of community thus goes beyond the idea of partic-

3. Ed Freeman and Jeanne Liedtka have made much the same argument with a more radical conclusion, that we should abandon the overworn concept of "social responsibility" altogether in their "Corporate Social Responsibility: A Critical Approach," *International Association for Business and Society Proceedings,* 1991.

ular responsibilities and obligations, although it embraces the same impetus toward larger thinking and citizenship endorsed by stakeholder analysis.

If we consider corporations first of all as communities—not legal fictions, not monolithic entities, not faceless bureaucracies, not matrices of price/earnings ratios, net assets and liabilities—then the activities and the ethics of business become much more comprehensible and much more human. Shareholders are, of course, part of the community, but most of them are only marginally rather than, as in some now-classic arguments, the sole recipients of managerial fiduciary obligations. The concept of community also shifts our conception of what makes a corporation "work" or not. What makes a corporation efficient or inefficient is not a series of well-oiled mechanical operations but the working interrelationships, the coordination and rivalries, team spirit and morale of the many people who work there and are in turn shaped and defined by the corporation. So, too, what drives a corporation is not some mysterious abstraction called "the profit motive" (which is highly implausible even as a personal motive, but utter nonsense when applied to a fictitious legal entity or a bureaucracy). It is the collective will and ambitions of its employees, few of whom (even in profit-sharing plans or in employee-owned companies) work for a profit in any obvious sense. Employees of a corporation do what they must to fit in, to perform their jobs, and to earn both the respect of others and self-respect. They want to prove their value in their jobs, they try to show their independence or their resentment, they try to please (or intentionally aggravate) their superiors, they want to impress (or intimidate) their subordinates, they want to feel good about themselves or they try to make the best of a bad situation. And, of course, they want to bring home a paycheck. To understand how corporations work (and don't work) is to understand the social psychology and sociology of communities, not the logic of a flowchart or the organizational workings of a cumbersome machine.

I have already commented on the great deal of finger pointing concerning the supposed loss of competitiveness, noting that the real problem is lack of cooperation and a coordinated business community. It is within the context of a discussion of community, accordingly, that one should raise the usually restricted set of questions about the desirability of much of the recent mergers and acquisitions activity. The primary defense of "hostile takeovers"—often articulated by such masters of the craft as T. Boone Pickens and popularized by the fictitious but infamous Gordon Gekko in *Wall Street*—is the need to spur competition, get rid of bad management, and, of course, "to be fair to the stockholders." But competition is not the "bottom line" of corporate success, and management (even bad management) is not simply extraneous or contingent to the corporation. Managers, with some reason, typically identify themselves *as* the corporation, and what has received far too little attention in the debate over the public interest of unfriendly mergers and takeovers and the distraction of "golden parachutes" for a few top executives is the utter disaster precipitated by the disruption of corporate communities. It is no surprise that a good many of the new entities created (or "liberated") by takeover activity fail, and not just because of the mountain of debt typically accumulated in the process. What work force can keep its morale in the face of the continuous threat of layoffs? What manager can function as either an authority or as a team player when his or her authority is clearly contingent and it is not even clear what "team" he or she is playing for? Such threats may encourage the *appearance* of hard work (and a great deal of derrière covering) but it cannot possibly encourage dedication or loyalty. By virtue of the excessive emphasis on competition to the exclusion of cooperation, by ignoring such "intangible" features of business life as company morale and coordination in favor of the measurable quantities listed in the financial pages, we are destroying the corporation as a community and, consequently, as a fully functional human institution. As one Japanese executive said to me recently, "We don't have to compete with American companies. They do themselves in all by themselves."

What is a corporate community? To begin with, it is heterogeneous conglomerate that is bound to be riddled with personality clashes, competing aims and methodologies, cliques and rivalries, and crisscrossed loyalties. The very fact that a corporation requires specialization and the division of labor makes inevitable such heterogenity. Two young men working in a garage, pooling their resources and their knowledge to produce a successful commodity, may, in the throes and thrills of development and struggle, experience an uninterrupted sense of oneness that would impress even a Buddhist. But once the product is launched and marketing people and managers are brought in to do the job, that primeval corporate unity is shattered and, as in the most famous recent case of this kind, one or both of the founders of the company may find themselves displaced or even fired by the assistants they brought in to help them. There is an intrinsic antagonism—to be explained in terms of social class rather than economics and in terms of our mythologies of work rather than the nature of the work itself—between the shop floor and the managerial office, just as there is an obvious opposition (not entirely financial) between those divisions of the corporation that always need to spend more money (advertising and research and development teams, for example) and those whose job it is to save it. Add to this the many different characters and personalities who populate even the most seemingly homogeneous company (although these differences too are already preestablished in the social types and classes who tend to one or the other position or profession) and one can appreciate the foolishness in our popular treatment of corporations as monolithic entities with a single mind and a single motive.

And yet there is an emergent phenomenon that does often speak with a single voice and deserves to be treated (and not just by the law) as a singular entity, "the corporation." Groups have personalities just as individuals do, the heterogeneous, even fragmented groups can nevertheless have a singular character just as conflicted people do. It is a mistake to speak of corporations as only collections of individuals, both because the "individuals" in question are themselves the creatures of the corporation and because the corporation is one of those sums that is nevertheless greater than its many constituent parts. Aristotelean ethics takes both the corporation and the individual seriously without pretending that either is an autonomous entity unto itself. Corporations are made up of people, and the people in corporations are defined by the corporation. Business ethics thus becomes a matter of corporate ethics, emphatically *not* in the sense that what counts is the ethics of the corporation, considered as an autonomous, autocratic agent, ruling over its employees (perhaps exemplified by its "corporate code"), nor in the more innocent but naive sense that the ethics of the corporation is nothing but the product of the collective morality of its employees. The morals of the executives, particularly the exemplary morals of those who are most visible in the corporation, are an important influence on corporate morality, but it is the nature and power of institutions—particularly those in which a person spends half of his or her adult waking life—to shape and sanction the morals of the individual. There may well be (and often is) a gap or dichotomy between a person's sense of ethics on the job and his or her sense of right and wrong with friends and family. There may well be real ethical differences within a company, particularly between its various departments and divisions. But even in diversity and conflict the ethics of a corporation becomes clearly and often soon visible to those most closely attached to, affiliated with, or affected by it. Corporations can (and often do) get a bad rap, an institutional black eye caused by a tiny percentage of its employees. (Hertz Rent-a-Car was caught up in a monumental car-repair scandal a year or so ago, which turned out to involve some twenty dealers out of twenty thousand. Nevertheless, it was the name "Hertz" that took the brunt of the abuse, and numbers were simply not the issue.) Such apparent injustices throw a revealing light on a company and its ethical standards, however, and give the best corporations a chance to show their moral mettle. Communities are essential units of morality, and corporations are ultimately judged not by the numbers but by the coherence and cooperation both within their walls and with the larger communities in which they play such an essential social as well as economic role.

IN SEARCH OF EXCELLENCE

> Unfortunately, you don't get what you deserve, you get what you negotiate.
>
> DR. CHESTER L. KARRASS,
advertisement for Karrass Seminars

"Excellence" has become something of a "buzz word" in business, a marketing term rather than a definition of purpose. Like "quality" (its close kin), it implies good value without any particular substance or commitment. But, both practically and philosophically, it is a word of great significance and indicates a sense of mission, a commitment beyond profit potential and the bottom line. It is a word that suggests "doing well" but also "doing good." It is a word, therefore that synthesizes the demands of the marketplace and the demands of ethics. It might be worth noting that the Aritotelean word *arete* is sometimes translated as "virtue" sometimes as "excellence," and that ambiguity is significant. And it is assumed, in Aristotle's accounts of the virtues, that success and happiness will be commensurate with excellence. In business life, this assumption—so basic that it is rarely even discussed as such—is that excellence (like quality) sells, that excellence is the key to success. In other words, our emphasis on excellence also presupposes a particular sense of justice, a *meritocracy*, in which merit—excellence—is rewarded in the marketplace.

To insist that the business world is a meritocracy seems to be saying the obvious, but the truth is that merit has a problematic and ambiguous role in the business world.[4] To be sure, an employee expects a reward in return for his or her contribution and an exceptional reward in return for an exceptional contribution, and with that in mind one would like to think that the entire system functions on the basis of merit and merit alone. But merit sometimes has to give way to the exigencies of the market, notably when severe cost-cutting requires the release of employees and managers of unquestionable skill and accomplishment. Sometimes alternative considerations of justice (such as need) take precedence, for example, if an unemployed but fully qualified applicant is hired for a job instead of a person who is slightly more accomplished but already well-positioned person.[5] In entrepreneurship and investment, as well as in job-hunting and promotion, there may be

4. See Norman Daniels, "Merit and Meritocracy," *Philosophy and Public Affairs* 7 (1978): 206–23. On special problems concerning affirmative action and justice see Lisa H. Newton, "Reverse Discrimination as Unjustified," *Ethics* 83 (1973) and the reply by Sterling Harwood, "Affirmative Action is Justified," American Philosophical Association, 1990.

5. Here is where the affirmative action controversy becomes extremely difficult, pitting need, merit, and compensatory justice against one another. See Robert K. Fullinwider, *The Reverse Discrimination Controversy* (Totowa, N.J.: Rowman and Littlefield, 1980).

a sizable element of luck involved. Indeed, in almost every aspect of business and life there will be some learned skills and inherited advantages that give some people considerable advantage over others. Rarely do we find a level playing field. Talent too often fails to find its opportunities. Hard work too often is not rewarded. Luck too often is confused with merit. Smooth talk and connections too often substitute for accomplishment. Nevertheless, the correlation between hard work, skill, and success is so much a part of our vision of the world—and consequently so convincing—that we cannot tolerate the idea of an economic system that would depend upon luck alone ("manna from the sky," according to philosopher Robert Nozick).[6] The prosperity of the corporation as well as of the larger community requires knowledge, skills, and hard work, which must come from its members. (The intolerable exception here is the slave state, defended by Aristotle, in which much of the talent and effort expended toward the prosperity of the community is not that of the members of the community at all. But the hatefulness of this counterexample underscores just how important the notion of a meritocracy is for us.[7]) Though it may be true, therefore, that some great fortunes have been made through dumb luck and mere bumbling has lead to some great discoveries and breakthroughs, the heart of the free enterprise system remains not luck but pluck, knowledge, skill, and hard work. We put too much emphasis on profits and the results of successful business activity and pay too little attention, except by way of rhetorical flourishes, to the process and procedures of the practice itself. Fairness in rewarding good work is the single most important part of the practice of business.

One of the critical problems in corporate life, and in the free market system in general, is the apparent failure of meritocracy, along with the increasing suspicion that hard work is not rewarded and good ideas are more likely to be ignored or stolen than rewarded.[8] Position becomes more important than ability or skill. "Schmoozing" and "going along to get along" replace efficiency as the way to success. Personal public relations and publicity become more prudential than the project that actually gets developed. Indeed, the "fast-tracking" ideal often involves the mere plan of a project, developed just enough to demonstrate one's abilities and allow one to move along. The project is not yet implemented, but it is just far enough along to cause considerable disruption and confusion in one's abandoned company. And in the wake of massive "downsizing" and the uncertainty of mergers (both "friendly" and "unfriendly"), executives and employees alike lose faith in their own

6. Robert Nozick, *Anarchy, State and Utopia* (New York: Basic Books, 1974), p. 198.

7. Aristotle's meritocracy, by contrast, concerned the aristocratic merits of those who ruled. Productivity was not at issue, but rather statesmenship and the virtues associated with high social status, including wit, charm, and generosity.

8. See Robert Jackall, *Moral Mazes* (New York: Oxford University Press, 1988), ch. 2.

abilities to get ahead on their merits. The obvious result: strategies for "survival" start to replace devotion to tasks. Research and development are replaced by the search for short term results, and managers worry less about their effectiveness and much more about their appearance and placement. Virtue may be its own reward, but if it is not also rewarded by its beneficiaries, it may well turn a resentful cheek. There is nothing more destructive to productivity than the failure of meritocracy and nothing more productive of inner office resentment, envy, and spite.

Of particular concern here is the peculiar nature of managerial talent and skills. The skills involved in good management are not always so evident as the tangible results of a trade or profession, carpentry, computer programming,, or accounting. Management skills are "people skills," matters of facilitation and, at their best, inspirational rather than productive as such. Thus an excellent manager knows that excellence in management is often evident in what does not happen or what seemingly happens with little effort rather than in any dramatic or breathtaking performance. The best manager, accordingly, may be marked by an absence of troublesome situations rather than by any dramatic skill in fire fighting. And he or she may well seem to sit by the sidelines while the employees he or she has nurtured present their rather spectacular products to the world. The insecurity that inevitably results from this should not be taken to mean that "excellence" has no place in managerial life, however, or that management circles are by their very nature doomed (as some seem to be) to an insistent mediocrity, a "don't rock the boat" mentality. Managerial genius may also be manifested in productive anarchy, and we all know that the absence of troublesome situations may be a sign of totalitarian mismanagement rather than anticipatory insight. What is necessary is top management that knows how to see and evaluate managerial performance without simply assuming that flash is substance, that silence is efficiency, or that chaos is unproductive. In other words, it is managerial virtue that needs to be examined, and not the mere consequences or short-term products of management.

One of the key injunctions of the Aristotelean approach to business is to encourage and insist on excellence and to defend the ideal of a meritocracy, a system in which excellence is rewarded and mediocrity ("not rocking the boat") is not. In managerial circles, "excellence in management" is too often such a mask for mediocrity. Robert Jackall writes:

> What if men and women in the corporation no longer see success as necessarily connected to hard work? What becomes of the social morality of the corporation—the everyday rules-in-use that people play by—when there is thought to be no fixed or, one might say, objective standard of excellence to

explain how and why winners are separated from also-rans, how and why some people succeed and others fail? What rules do people fashion to interact with one another when they feel that, instead of ability, talent, and dedicated service to an organization, politics, adroit talk, luck, connections, and self-promotion are the real sorters of people into sheep and goats?[9]

It is this question that defines the issue for a great many corporations today, not necessarily because corporations or their executives have failed to care about quality and excellence but because these are issues that remain mere abstractions, attributes (at best) of the end product, and not working principles that define the very nature of the corporation itself and everyone who works within it. Ironically, it is the undisputed virtue of *teamwork* that gives rise to the managerial measurement problem. Even in successful companies, measurement of merit in management is often exceedingly difficult, and success in many managerial positions is only tested by the absence of any trouble evident to those above. Moreover, a manager works in a nexus of interlocking personnel responsibilities and the contribution of any one person, even the person in charge, may be diffuse and impossible to ascertain. The mandate or *telos* of a given department might be nothing more definite than "keeping costs down," "keeping the shop floor safe," or "keeping top management happy," and it may be not at all evident what counts as success (although failure is usually pretty obvious). That, perhaps, is the paradox of managerial excellence: outright failure is obvious but excellence may be invisible.

The idea that individuality has to be submerged into larger collective projects and purposes too readily gives way to some terrible confusions, not only in terms of the supposed loss of self and individuality and the dreaded specter of "collectivism" (why not just call it "teamwork"?), but in terms of the self-defeating conflation of individual submersion and individual irresponsibility. To be part of a group in which one's own contributions cannot be measured except by reference to the overall effort and success of the group is not to say that the individual is not thereby responsible for his or her own efforts and the overall success of the group. Talking about collective responsibility does not undermine or oppose the importance of individual responsibility. So, too, talking about teamwork does not entail conformity or mediocrity. The members of a team do not usually have similar but rather complementary roles, and even where the roles are similar the particular contribution of each member is aimed at the success of the project, not just at "fitting in" with the rest of the group, Indeed, this distinction is absolutely essential, for the difference between mediocrity and excellence is often just this difference in emphasis between working together with the ultimate purpose of the enterprise in mind and just trying to fit in,

9. Robert Jackall, *Moral Mazes* (New York: Oxford University Press, 1988), p. 3.

to not rock the boat, to protect oneself from being singled out for blame or being caught up in one or another internal competition for power and status. Excellence is mutual inspiration and support, including contradiction and controversy, in pursuit of a shared purpose. Mediocrity is enforced conformity, timid nonaggressiveness based on mutual insecurity, losing sight of one's purpose, and retreating to suspicious collective self-protection.

The idea of merit and meritocracy is often misunderstood in the familiar language of incentives. Excellence deserves reward but, paradoxically, excellence is not performance *for* reward. An incentive is a carrot held in front of a pony, the dog biscuit held out in front of a puppy: a means, perhaps a trick, to get it to behave. But a good puppy (and, I presume, a good pony) will do the right thing independent of the incentive, and the carrot or the dog buscuit becomes a pleasant (even if expected) aftermath rather than the reason for doing right in the first place.[10] This may seem like a subtle point, but anyone who has tried to call a frisky dog without a pocket full of dog biscuits recognizes the importance of the difference. Of course, if good behavior is continuously greeted with indifference or worse, those good traits soon become extinguished. So, too, excellence in business is belied, if not undermined, by those who work "just to make a living" and by businesses that (as so many annual reports tiresomely insist) aim solely at improving stockholder value and the bottom line. True, good products and innovative marketing do (or should) result in improving stockholder value and the bottom line, but good products and innovative marketing require their own attention, and not merely as means. To see profits as incentives—except perhaps for (not all) investors for whom "merit" is not usually in question—is to get the logic of business backward. Meritocracy demands that merit be rewarded; it does not thereby suggest that the motivation of merit is the reward or that the market will always reward merit. Indeed, there may even be, as some authors have argued, a fundamental contradiction between the two.[11]

We like to think that merit and the market go hand in hand, that the market rewards excellence as readily and as efficiently as a first grade teacher rewards this morning's spelling bee champion. But the two are quite different, and a bit of a jog to our market mentality on the subject of merit could be one of the most important contributions of an Aristotelean approach to ethics. I believe the Aristotelean approach to this

10. This analogy has its obvious limitations, of course. See, e.g., the "good puppy" analysis of corporate ethics, often reprinted, in Laura Nash, "Business Ethics without the Sermon," *Harvard Business Review*. For a more informed account of "good puppies," however, see Vicki Hearne, "How to Say 'Fetch,'" in *Adam's Task* (New York: Random House, 1982).

11. Friedrich von Hayek, *The Mirage of Social Justice* (London: Routledge and Kegan Paul, 1976).

subject is far superior to our own ever-worsening reward system—that as much as we talk about excellence and its rewards we in fact defer excellence, leaving both its inspiration and its rewards to the magic of the market, magic not just because it occasionally produces miracles but because justice in a market system is quite unplanned and even unexpected, including those much touted rewards for merit. But the free enterprise insistence on an "unplanned" economy is very different from one that systematically rewards the wrong kind of behavior and encourages only one of several essential business skills and talents. There will always abe a gamble in any enterprise that depends, as the market does, on timing and popular preferences, but behind the gamble must be a wealth of knowledge, skills, and effort and the confidence that, most of the time, the best idea, product, or service will in fact win. To reward only results, to ignore the virtues that go into every effort, is to further the game and gambling aspect of business and discourage the pride and prosperity that in fact constitute its justification.

On Adam Smith's classical model of localized supply and demand, perhaps the marketplace rewards merit and quality and efficiency are appropriately rewarded. But in these days of mass advertising, financial wheeling and dealing, and corporate anonymity, this classic connection has been twisted and broken in a dozen different ways. Celebrities earn far more than they deserve and hyped-up products (whatever their quality) create their own demand (children's "action" toys advertised on Saturday morning television); brokers don't "earn" a commision but simply take it; stockmarket players are in a lottery, not a job, no matter how good they are; and injustice seems to be endemic to the corporation, credit going not to the deserving but to the undeserving, the self-serving. it is true that a great many jobs, salaries, and bonuses in America are determined by competitive market value and not by merit. But even here, Michael Lewis rightly wonders how it can be that Wall Street salaries are so high when there are thousands of applicants for every job, while there are too few good teachers (a profession where effectiveness is readily measurable) and yet their salaries remain pitifully low. It would seem to be obvious, but it must be said again and again: the market as such is *not* a meritocracy. But business must be. Which is just to say, in a different way, that the business world is not the free market alone. It consists of communities within communities and constitutes a way of life in which merit as well as the freedom of the market is essential.

This is not to say—as we too readily conclude—that excellence is always or necessarily measured by means of competition. Of course, one can prove one's excellence in competition, and competition sometimes (but not always) inspires a person to perform better or more efficiently. But excellence is measured by its *telos* or purpose, and except where the explicit purpose is to beat the competition or to "be the best" that *telos* or purpose need not involve any competition whatever. Indeed, our cultural obsession with competition and "being the best" (as opposed, for example, to the Boy Scout "do your best") may be a recipe for *lack* of competitiveness and oblivion to higher purposes. Rival companies have too often competed with one another into oblivion. Rival managers bucking for promotion, executives competing for "the top spot," and "raiders" (whether or not in the name of the stockholders) have too often dragged a whole company down with them. Competition, at least the American sense of competition, too readily encourages only short-term thinking, and it is this false sense of competition— sometimes used by otherwise incompetent managers to "rally the troops— that fuels so much of business enterprise these days. Competition too often leads to teleological blindness and replaces the search for excellence with mere desperation. One thinks of cats being drowned in a bag who in effect drown one another instead of collectively clawing open the bag. Excellence is first of all cooperation and competition. It essentially represents a contribution to the larger whole. It is not skill for its own sake, not merely "winning," and not simply a source of personal pride.

There is in every activity, practice, or profession, of course, the excitement of internal competition, arts and games the sole purpose of which is to test the ability of its practitioners and, at its best, its masters. Indeed, there is little that is more inspiring (if sometimes only for a few minutes) than seeing a master at work, in virtually any harmless human endeavor. (Indeed, there is something fascinating watching even a skilled con man at work—preferably in a work of fiction.) But internal competition is secondary to certain external requirements and standards that explain the origins and place of the practice in the first place. Surgeons, no matter how skillful, would not be allowed to practice if they did not in fact save people's lives. (Thus the morbid absurdity in the familiar crack, "the operation was a success, but the patient died.") Athletic games promote good health, sportsmanship, and coordination as well as entertainment for the players, and athletes if they are worth watching must display not only skill but provide inspiration or entertainment. Again, excellence must be attached to an activity. True, some activities seem comparatively passive. For instance, one might be an excellent listener, but to think that listening is a purely passive activity is to show that one does not understand what it is to listen. Being an excellent manager typically entails being a good listener, but only a fool (or a managerial failure) would confuse such seeming passivity with an absence of effort and activity. The purposes of management are best so served, however more impressive (but less effective) the flurries of activity that often masquerade as "work" may be.

It is the centrality of excellence that defines the virtues in business and in business ethics. Excellence implies effective action, and excellence in business is bound up with productivity. It is not enough to do no wrong. "Knowingly do no harm" *(Primum non nocere)* is *not* the end of business ethics (as Peter Drucker suggests).[12] This is a purely negative, "side constraint" view of ethics, which is the very contrary of the Aristotelean view. One can usually do no harm by doing nothing, but virtue in business means, precisely, doing good, as measured, presumably, by the market. "Ethics and excellence," the hardly original slogan I have used as my title, is not just a tag-along with Peters and Waterman, a pop managerial catchphrase. Excellence means doing one's best and motivating others to do their best too. In the odd but essential role of "mediator" that is the manager's job, excellence is necessarily a group accomplishment, and managerial virtue, accordingly, is or should be mainly measured as "facilitation" rather than accomplishment as such. Many business virtues, accordingly, are social virtues—congeniality, reasonableness, and a sense of propriety and politeness. Some business virtues, such as skill in hard-headed negotiation, are more specific to business and somewhat ludicrous if taken beyond their proper domain. (Being a "tough negotiator" is a virtue in business but not in babysitting.) The businessman (now businesswoman too) who carries his (or her) tough negotiating skills beyond their proper context has become something of a stock comic figure in our society. It does not follow, however, that the virtues of business are therefore opposed to the ordinary virtues of civilized life—as Alfred Carr infamously argued in his *Harvard Business Review* polemic of several years ago. The virtues of business ethics are business virtues but they are nonetheless virtues, and the exercise of these virtues is aimed at both the bottom line and ethics. Indeed, our Aristotelean insistence on the place of the virtues in business is aimed in part at bringing these sometimes antagonistic concepts of "the bottom line" and ethics together. Except when under severe threat, we think too lazily of our large corporations and of the business world itself as permanent installations that require only minimal effort and attention to keep them going. We have to learn again to think of business as a grand experiment, which has been carried out in earnest for only a few hundred years, and whether or not the experiment works will depend on whether it does indeed encourage excellence and inspire virtue in its practitioners or only fosters a mad scramble for survival and quick profits.

THE INDIVIDUAL IN THE ORGANIZATION

> The idea that the moral life is largely a matter of carrying out the duties which attach to one's "station" in society presupposes an unacceptably conformist attitude towards established social arrange-

---

12. Peter Drucker, *Management* (New York: Harper and Row, 1974), pp. 366–67.

ments. F. H. Bradley's "My Station and its Duties" strikes the modern reader as a curiously dated piece of moral philosophy.

ALISTAIR M. MACLEOD

Community and teleology capture the essence of the Aristotelean framework, in which a sense of collective purpose and social well-being defines the aspirations and virtues of the individual. But the happy image of harmony does not adequately capture the reality of most socioeconomic institutions, and even the best corporations are riddled with tensions and conflicts. There are personality differences and disagreements about the priorities and purpose of the organization. There are power struggles and clashes of ambitions. There are miscommunications and inconsistencies, and there are difficult situations in which two equally demanding but seemingly incompatible courses of action seem required. And, most serious of all, there are all sorts of conflicts of loyalties and obligations that are so serious that they become ethical dilemmas, contradictions within the community, and contrary conceptions of responsibility. The last four parameters, therefore, are not so much concerned with the basic framework of the Aristotelean perspective as they are with the navigation of virtue throughout the sometimes convoluted passages of community, corporate purpose, and personal virtue. (Much of this discussion will be continued in Part III.)

One of the most abused parameters of the Aristotelean view is the concept of *membership*, the idea that an employee or executive develops his or her personal identity largely through the organizations in which he or she spends most of adult waking life. It is not hard to find the origins of this prejudice: it is our insistence on individualism and the idea that each of us has his or her own complete identity, quite apart from any external affiliations we may choose or roles we may play. But the obvious fact is that what we think of ourselves and how we behave is molded through and through by the various groups and institutions of which we have been members, beginning with our family and our schools and culminating, for millions of people, in the corporation. To think of ethics simply in terms of one's "personal values"—and to juxtapose these against something ominously referred to as "corporate values"—is to miss the obvious, that our most personal values are also social and that we join, stay, and succeed with one organization rather than another because our values fit. This is not to deny the tensions and conflicts that inevitably occur within any organization (including the family), but only to point out the bad faith involved in the usual distinction between "who I really am" and the person I am on the job. *Corporate role identity* is genuine identity, and to deny this is to alienate oneself from the corporation (and probably from any possibility of success or happiness within it) from the start.

Much has been written, for example, by Norman Bowie in his good little book on *Business Ethics,* on the importance of "role morality" and "my Position and its duties."[13] It is the situatedness of corporate roles that lends them their particular ethical poignancy, the fact that an employee or an executive is not just a person who happens to be in a place and is constrained by no more than the usual ethical prohibitions. To work for a company is to accept a set of particular obligations, to assume a prima facie loyalty to one's employer, to adopt a certain standard of excellence and conscientiousness that is largely defined by the job itself. There may be general ethical rules and guidelines that cut across most positions but, as these get more general and more broadly applicable, they also become all but useless in concrete ethical dilemmas. Robert Townsend's cute comment that "if a company needs an ethical code, use the Ten Commandments" is thus not only irreverent but irrelevant too.[14] The Aristotelean approach to business ethics presumes concrete situations and particular people and their places in organizations. There is little point to an ethics that tries to transcend all such particularities and embrace the chairman of the board as well as a middle manager, a secretary, and a factory worker.

Insofar as we define ourselves (as well as finding ourselves already defined by others), we do so in terms of group affinities and identities, our roles in communities and organizations. These may be as formal as a designated position (for example, the president) or as informal as the "jokester in the class." Our individual identities are composed of a converging network of such identities, comparisons, and contrasts—the funniest one, the tallest one, the handsomest one, and so on. There is virtually no context, except perhaps that noncontext in which we talk about the ultimate reductionist concept of "the soul," in which an individual is such, much less uniquely such—without (at least implicit) comparison and contrast with others with whom he or she is affiliated and identified. In the context of the corporation, we are our roles, our positions, that convergence of identities imposed by the company and the people we work with, from the contractual obligations of the job itself and the various perks and responsibilities of its position in the hierarchy to the informal interpersonal roles and contrasts that are an essential part of any group that spends much time together—the department slowpoke, the division wiz-kid, the company flirt, the bossy one (as opposed to "the boss"), or the butt of the jokes. The Aristotelean approach to business, as opposed to the more atomistic classical approach, begins with the corporate conception of people working together and gaining their identity in groups rather than the image of isolated rational negotiators bargaining, buying, and selling from one another in discrete transactions. For it is the presupposition of business

---

13. Norman Bowie, *Business Ethics* (Englewood Cliffs, N.J.: Prentice-Hall, 1982), pp. 1–16.

14. Robert Townsend, *Up the Organization* (New York: Knopf, 1970).

that business in even its simplest transactions is a complex practice in which our relationship to one another (and not just as business partners) is essential. Business itself is an organized system in which "buyer" and "seller" as well as "entrepreneur" and "employee" are established roles.

Our roles define our duties. A financial officer has a set of duties that constitutes the control and management of the finances of the firm while the director of human resources has a set of duties that directs all personnel decisions. The director of human resources has a responsibility not to waste money, but it is not exactly one of her duties, and the financial officer has an obligation to the employees of the firm, even though he does not, as such, have a duty to them. Duties are quite specific, defined by (and definitive of) one's job or position. They need not be (and usually are not) spelled out in a contract as such, but they are (or should be) clearly understood as a prerequisite for the job. (It is only as a joke that one can imagine a financial officer complaining, "Oh, I didn't know that I was supposed to *save* money.") But the concept of "duty" has been greatly distorted in modern ethics and with it such kindred concepts as "obligation" and "responsibility." In the philosophy of Immanuel Kant, most famously, duty (in German *Pflicht*) is turned into a matter of abstract, universal principles, and the idea of role-specific, job-defined duties gets either discarded or relegated to derivative status. So, too, the favored moral concept of "obligation"—which makes perfectly good sense, for example, as specified in a contract but progressively loses its significance when there are no explicit or implicit agreements and the circumstances become increasingly impersonal and nonspecific. "Responsibility" is no doubt the broadest of these three notions, covering a great deal of territory, but it too is essentially based in specific relationships and agreements. The tendency in philosophy has been to turn these essential moral concepts into top-heavy, rule-based abstractions; the important thing in business ethics is to see them instead as ground-level, role-specific aspects of one's position in the company and, at the same time, one's place in the overall community.

The range of duties may be as large as the variety of jobs and positions. They will be different in different size firms, more or less demanding, more or less flexible. There are certain "metaduties," such as loyalty to the company, that may more or less transcend any number of jobs, but these are still context-bound (for example, loyalty to the company that is paying your salary) and it would be a mistake to restrict business ethics to just these very generally defined duties. When a concrete activity such as physically producing a product is concerned, one's duties are largely defined by the notion of "quality." When the activities are more abstract, for example, accounting or financial analysis, accuracy and honesty tend to define one's primary duties. When one's job is mainly concerned with interpersonal relationships (the jobs of most managers), one's duties tend to be facilitative and straightforwardly ethical—concerned with fair dealing, respect and proper consideration, a decent modicum of compassion. Considerable confusion and the likelihood of unethical behavior emerge when these different sorts of jobs are mixed up or mixed together, when accountants start dealing with people as numbers or when managerial skills are conflated with productive skills. To appreciate the role of duties in business ethics is to appreciate the range and variety of jobs and their responsibilities. It requires an understanding of what people actually do and not an abstract a priori calculation of what is right.

The definition of duties in terms of roles has at least two disturbing consequences for traditional rule-bound ethics. The first is the familiar sense of distrust of any context-bound ethics, the suspicion that this might too easily turn out to make morals "relative" to different contexts and make absolute judgments of right and wrong impossible.[15] I have tried to suggest that this does not follow as a consequence, that all jobs share some more general context (for example, working for someone to produce or do something) and all human activities share some even more general context (living together, depending on one another, being vulnerable creatures who can be injured, need food, shelter, and affection) that dictates moral principles and virtues that are as general and as universal as a reasonable person would like.

The second disturbing consequence has had much less play in the literature and in the media but it is in fact a much more pressing and practical problem. To what extent do we really want to let ourselves be defined (on the job) by an impersonal (even if very particular) set of duties and demands? To what extent do we want our personalities to become not only secondary to but submerged in our positions? (Thus the distasteful images of "the faceless bureaucrat" and the "gray men" in the executive suites.) And to what extent do we want our relationships in business to be restricted to those that are defined only by the contracts and the numbers? Here is a very familiar and practical example, which touches almost every corporate person with any responsibility for buying supplies or negotiating contracts. A number of bidders have made offers to supply the company with wazzits. One of these suppliers has in fact been supplying the company for many years. Your people know his people, and the representative has gotten to be one of your favorite acquaintances. Their bid (which is as low as they can go

---

15. This point has often been made in philosophy, and public pundits still love to use the bogeyman of "relativism" to terrify voters and school boards. But the contextual nature of virtue ethics, in particular, does not entail that all virtues are merely local and not universal as well. See, e.g., Martha Nussbaum, "Non-Relative Virtues," in *Ethical Theory: Virtues and Character*, ed. Peter French, Midwest Studies in Philosophy, vol. 13 (Notre Dame, Ind.: University of Notre Dame Press, 1988).

and about what it's been for years) is marginally higher than several others. Should you—can you ethically—make your decision on the basis of your good feelings about the company and its representatives? Granted, if there were an enormous difference in the bids and your own company was vigorously cost-cutting, you would have no choice. Granted too, if there were any suggestion of sleaze—for example, that you would personally benefit from the deal with the past and ongoing supplier—you would judge the decision to be unethical. But surely part of business and its routine decisions must be personal comfort, a sense of ongoing loyalty, and other "personal" factors that cannot easily be computed into the bottom line. On the other hand, the duties of the job, narrowly construed, specify "the lowest bidder." I find this kind of case troublesome, not because I encourage a more flexible approach to ethics, but, to the contrary, because I believe that ethics in business is always broader than the narrow economic definition of "fiduciary responsibilities." But, as always, we try to take such cases and make them easier by imposing some rigid impersonal criterion.

Such examples abound in any aspect of business—which is to say, most of business—where personal relations are not only inevitable but essential, between a bank loan officer and her long-standing clients, between any retailer and his customers, between every manager and his or her reportees. For example, Arthur Andersen uses a training tape in which a young manager's boss instructs him, first subtly, then with increasing bluntness, that he should give an account to one of his old friends, despite the fact that his is not the low bid. The way the video is directed, the boss is sufficiently crude about this that we are, in effect, prompted to conclude that he is guilty of wrongdoing and the young man is caught between doing wrong and staying employed. But the question is whether we want to turn all business transactions into purely impersonal bureaucratic decisions. Is "favoritism" always a bad thing? (So, too, we need to ask, again and again, about the much-touted fiduciary duties that managers [and all employees] have to the stockholders. How narrowly are these to be construed? How "trump" are they with regard to internal corporate comforts and values? If stock shares could be improved by a point or two by selling all of the [usually quite fancy] furniture and having all executives sit and work on cardboard boxes and wooden crates, should they be obliged to do so? Is the need for a friendly work atmosphere and a pleasant ongoing relationship with suppliers like this? Where does "favoritism" end and "corruption" begin?)

These two complications are not objections to the Aristotelean view of business but rather reasons to underscore the importance of the virtues and the need for maintaining the larger picture of the place of one's job and the corporation in society as a whole. "Relativism" is not a threat to ethics unless the various roles and positions in which we find ourselves are taken as absolutes, without further reason—I'm just doin' my job". The Aristotelean point is that particular differences in roles, goals, and values only make sense because all are subordinated to some larger social purpose that gives them their meaning. (The division of labor and duties was not invented in the time of Adam Smith. Aristotle was well acquainted with the need for distinctive social and economic roles.) And, regarding the second complication, the rigidification of rules emphasizing uniform standards and encouraging impersonality is not a consequence of the concept of role identity but rather a breakdown of the sense of virtue (and "judgment," which we will discuss shortly). In their place, we get rules, impersonal standards, roles defined by formal structures instead of by the people who fill them in light of the larger organization. There need be nothing "impersonal" about role identity; indeed, one's personality defines (as well as gets defined by) a role well filled. To say that someone "was made for the job" is high praise, not a personal offense.

There is a further complication with the Aristotelean approach to business ethics and its emphasis on roles and specific contexts, and that is the possibility of a clash of contexts, a conflict of duties. The problem, of course, is that people in business inevitably play several roles or wear several hats at once, and these roles may clash with one another as they may clash with more personal roles based on family, friendship, and personal obligations. This is a pervasive problem in business ethics. Some of the pressure for very general principles that apply to all situations both in and out of business comes from the desire to deny the possibility of such conflicts (which in some extreme cases are called "tragedy"). But if ethics is contextual and we find ourselves in several contexts (several overlapping jobs with different duties, on the job but still the head of a family), there is always the possibility that our duties will conflict and our virtues will undermine one another. A kind heart in the midst of a vicious battle may be a liability, just as "the competitive edge" in a friendly situation may turn out to be brutal.

Discussions of the virtues have been hamstrung since Aristotle by a kind of wishful thinking—not itself a virtue, especially in supposedly hard-headed philosophers. The presumption has been, only sometimes accompanied by argument, that there is, at least ideally, a *unity of the virtues*, a happy harmony that the virtuous man or woman will enjoy. Put crudely, the view is that, if one (truly) has one virtue, he or she will have all of them. In part, this is the result of a long-standing need for optimism in moral matters, the ideal (summarized by Kant as the *summum bonum*) that the good is good "in itself" and (under some pain of contradiction) that virtue will be rewarded, that the pursuit and triumph of virtue will not be frustrated by ill fortune or, much worse, by other virtues. I think that this is, however, just a special case of our general tendency in both business and in ethics to leap to the singular solution

that it's just a business (or legal) problem, or purely moral consideration. In all such reductions, the aim is to eliminate conflicts and contradictions and reduce the debate to a single dimension and a single criterion, "the bottom line," "whatever the lawyers tell us" or "the right
thing whatever the cost." But in the context of any organization of any
complexity (even the family) there will be very real conflicts and no
single criterion. Loyalties often conflict on the job, particularly in any
politicized company or institution. (Does that leave anyone out?) One's
duty to superiors may well conflict with one's obligations to subordinates, and in any but the best-organized company there is always the
possibility of conflicting, even contradictory but equally obliging orders
from two different superiors. One's sense of loyalty to an aging and no
longer effective manager who provided one's job opportunity in the
first place may well clash with a more general sense of obligation to the
company. The seriousness of these conflicts and clashes, this "disunity
of the virtues," is documented in detail by Jackall in his *Moral Mazes,*
although I think he ultimately makes this out to be too much of a clash
between morality and corporate politics. But an essential part of "corporate morality" is loyalty to the organization and to one's superiors,
and not all of corporate politics is vicious or counterproductive. Indeed, we too easily tend to forget that loyalty demands politics, including the strife caused by honest disagreement, and loyalty to one's superiors may, contrary to prudence, require contrariness. But the point
is that in any less than perfect organization or society, there is no guaranteed unity of the virtues and no easy distinction between virtue or
morals as such and the duties of one's job or position.

Virtues tend to be context-bound, but contexts overlap and clash with
one another. In any organization, there are overlapping and concentric
circles of identity and responsibility, and a virtue in one arena may
conflict with a virtue in another—indeed, it may even be a vice. This is
a painful realization, and it may even tempt some to declare an Aristotelean ethics to be impossible. Indeed, it is all too easy to retreat in
desperation in either direction, to promote a false sense of virtue that
is too detached or divorced from the realities of one's role identity in
the company (as philosophers, standing on the outside—in their own
safe identities—are too prone to do), or to encourage total absorption
in one's company role so as to be incapable of seeing beyond it (a favorite strategy of militaristic managers). But there is no such easy answer. We always wear multiple hats and have potentially competing responsibilities. There is no denying the disunity of the virtues. But neither
is there any denying the fundamental importance of role identity in
establishing the contextual basis for virtue in business.

THE MEANING OF INTEGRITY

> An honest man . . . the noblest work of God.
>
> ALEXANDER POPE, *Essay on Man*

It is because of such internal conflicts and the clash of loyalties that the word "integrity" is so important to business ethics. Integrity is not so much a virtue itself as it is a complex of virtues, the virtues working together to form a coherent character, an identifiable and trustworthy personality. Unfortunately, "integrity" is a word, like "honor"—its close kin—that sometimes seems all but archaic in the modern business world. To some business executives, it suggests stubbornness and inflexibility, a refusal to be a "team player." But to reject integrity and the importance of unity of character, to find fault with employees who insist on drawing the line because they may well refuse to carry out commands they believe to be unethical, is short-sighted and self-destructive, at best. For every employee who is a "troublemaker" there will be ten who are congenial and loyal but insist on "drawing the line somewhere," and it is such employees and their judgments that prevent many a company from taking a dangerous or disastrous step over the bounds of good taste or good citizenship. Good management is not preventing ethical employees from causing trouble (nor is it avoiding hiring such people in the first place), but rather it is respecting the integrity of others as a partial guide to one's own actions.

Integrity is often understood as honesty. But honesty is too limited for integrity, and there may be times when integrity requires being less than candid, even lying. (A standard example depicts someone being questioned by the bad guys and tempted to betray his comrades.) Integrity is sometimes understood as resisting temptation. But integrity often requires action and "pro-active" behavior; it is not just "not giving in." Integrity is often understood as resisting or refusing the orders of others, but, more often, integrity requires obedience and loyalty. Either way integrity is essentially *moral courage*, the will and willingness to do what one knows one ought to do. The key, of course, is that the orders one obeys and the person or organization that commands our loyalty must be compatible with one's own values and virtues. When one willingly joins an organization (a corporation), agrees to act on its behalf and in its interests, and agrees with its aims and values, obedience and loyalty are part and parcel of integrity. But when one comes to disagree with those aims and values, integrity instead requires disobedience and disloyalty, at least in the form of a resignation. Thus is seems that "integrity" has two very different meanings, one of them encouraging conformity and obedience, the other urging a belligerent independence. But this is a misleading contrast. Integrity includes both one's sense of membership and loyalty and one's sense of moral autonomy.

The very word suggests "wholeness," but insofar as one's identity is not that of an isolated atom but rather the product of a larger social molecule, that wholeness includes—rather than excludes—other people and one's social roles. One's integrity on the job typically requires the following of the rules and practices that define that job, rather than allowing oneself to be swayed by distractions and contrary temptations. And yet, critical encounters sometimes require a show of integrity that is indeed antithetical to one's assigned role and duties. This is not the place to work out this complex and central ethical issue, but the point that must be made is that such considerations are a far cry from the sorts of quandary debates that define much of traditional ethics. The question of integrity is not a question of obligation and it is certainly not a matter of utility. It is rather a matter of who one is, coupled with the fact that, on the job, each of us is (at least) two persons at once.

It is the divided self that makes integrity so important to us, a kind of coordination problem as well as an ideal in ethics. On the one hand, there is a kind of public integrity of the sort we expect of our colleagues in business and hope for in politicians—telling the truth, avoiding shady and illicit dealings, remaining loyal even under pressure, refusing to take bribes, and so on. So considered, having integrity means more or less the same thing as being ethical, so long as we leave some room for differences in opinion about what is ethically proper and what is not (for example, in controversial matters concerning sexual behavior). But what makes the issue of integrity so important and so difficult is the interpretation of "wholeness" as "being true to yourself." In *Portrait of the Artist as a Young Man,* James Joyce has his hero Stephen Dedalus declare his independence and his integrity: "I will not serve that in which I no longer believe whether it call itself my home, my fatherland or my church: and I will try to express myself in some mode of life or art as freely as I can and as wholly as I can."[16] Here the notion of integrity puts itself at arm's length (without actually rejecting) the standards of ethics as such. Integrity becomes much more a question of one's own standards, one's own authority, and it may be the case, at least on occasion (or in certain corrupt or oppressive situations) that one's sense of being true to self will permit or even require some breach of the moral rules. Even if one sticks to the path of the straight and narrow, however, the significance of this sort of integrity is that one doesn't just *follow* the rules but one makes them his or her own.[17]

16. James Joyce, *Portrait of the Artist as a Young Man* (New York: Viking, 1968), quoted by Lynn McFall in her "Integrity," *Ethics* 98 (Oct. 1987): 5.

17. This distinction between following and "making one's own" is the central tenet of many existentialist philosophies. The nineteenth century Danish philosopher Søren Kierkegaard thus distinguished between "Christendom," which involved unthinking obedience to Christian beliefs and values, and truly becoming a Christian, which involved a passionate personal commitment. So, too, more recently Martin Heidegger in Germany

This gives the specific meaning of integrity a great deal of breadth, indeed as broad as the range of individuals, institutions, and practices in which the quest for "wholeness" can be found.

The contrary of integrity—lack of integrity—can take on many forms. We should note, first of all, that integrity is something a person "has" or "lacks," it is not a particular act or activity that one does or does not do. So, too, although a single action may utterly betray the lack of integrity, there is no single action (or, indeed, any number of actions) that will definitively establish a person's integrity. This is, perhaps, why integrity is so heavily guarded, and why people will go to such lengths to deny their own misdeeds and corruption. A single slip can be fatal, while a lifetime of good deeds still leaves open the question of one's ultimate righteousness. (Thus the peculiar self-suffering of saints, not out of guilt but from doubt, the question of whether that single fatal temptation may yet lie ahead of them, or whether they *might* have yielded under different circumstances before.) The tenuousness of integrity explains why it is too that a single flaw or failing typically leads to others, indeed, to a system of rationalizations and cover-ups that betray a lack of integrity more demonstrably than the original misdeed. For example, *hypocrisy* stands at direct odds with integrity, not because it necessarily involves dishonesty or any other overt breach of ethics but rather because it stands to misbehavior as perjury stands to an indictment; even if a person is not guilty of the alleged crime, he or she becomes guilty of a violation of justice on the behalf of that (real or only suspected) crime. A hypocrite fails to "practice what he preaches," but the lack of integrity is most obvious in the fragmentation of the self, the break in wholeness, that is required by saying one thing and doing another. But it is not simply a reach between action and language, as we so often make it seem. Language is already action and our actions are already language-pervaded, so that hypocritical behavior involves an enormously complex deception of not only other people but of the hypocrite himself or herself. When the hypocrite does what he or she has prohibited, we expect a number of sophisticated strategies, only the simplest of which is straight-out denial. More often, the action in question will be redescribed in language that slips around the stated prohibition. ("I wasn't really stealing it; I was just borrowing it for a while." "That was no bribe; that was a token of my appreciation for services already rendered.") Hypocrisy often hides behind self-deception, and the hypocrite may not recognize what seems to be obvious. ("Oh, well, surely that doesn't count as breaking a contract. After all, he . . .") Pushed to the wall, the hypocrite may cover up inconsistency

---

and Jean-Paul Sartre in France insisted on "resolution" and "authenticity" rather than mere rule following. And although none of them use the word as we do, one might well summarize this aspect of their philosophies by calling it "integrity."

with self-effacing humor, of the "do what I say, not what I do" variety. But this isn't to undo the hypocrisy, it is only to distract from it.

Two familiar examples of the lack of integrity in the corporate setting are the opportunist and the "chameleon."[18] What is striking about these two modes of corruption is the fact that neither of them needs to involve any dishonesty or hypocrisy whatever (although, like many vices, they often welcome such company). Neither do they involve any obvious inconsistency, at least from the person's own point of view. The opportunist does not usually have any principles that we would readily recognize as ethical, and therefore there may be no standard to which he or she can be faithful. Of course, there is something of a selfish *telos* or generic goal that the opportunist tends to follow and make his or her own: "Do whatever it takes." There is also a modus operandi: "Always keep your eyes open and your feet ready." None of this indicates principled behavior. But why should such behavior indicate a lack of integrity. Isn't such a person being particularly true to self? Indeed, isn't all of this flexibility designed just for that purpose? But here we see how the public and the personal senses of integrity tend to come together, for consistency requires something more than fidelity to a single, selfish goal. It also involves coherence and respect for other people, and even Stephen Dedalus's declaration of independence does not and cannot be interpreted as an "other people be damned" philosophy. It rather requires fidelity to self in the midst of others and together with them. Integrity is not heightened by hermitage, and the opportunist is in fact an ethical hermit who merely uses others as his or her instruments. But if integrity is in part independence ("true to self") it is also the very contrary of using other people to one's own ends.

The "chameleon" displays a similar lack of integrity in his or her total absence of not only principles but goals as well, unless we want to accept "fit in and do whatever seems to please other people" as some sort of purpose in life. A chameleon is a lizard, of course, who has the remarkable ability to change its colors depending on the context, and the typical corporate "yes-man" is like a lizard, crawling from executive to executive and changing colors accordingly. (Luckily for the lizard, the colors within a corporation often tend to be more or less uniform.) But when questions of method and purpose are opened up and equally powerful voices disagree, the chameleon is in trouble—as if the reptilian version were to find itself on a background of plaid. Thus the fragile consistency of the chameleon, whose tenuous appearance of integrity depends on the uniformity of other people, fractures into incoherence. This is how one distinguishes the vices of the chameleon from the virtue of loyalty, of course; loyalty is stalwart and (within reason)

18. For these prototypes, see Martin Berman's excellent book on compromise, *Splitting the Difference* (Lawrence: University Press of Kansas, 1990), esp. ch. 3.

unshifting. The chameleon has no integrity because he or she has no self, only a reflection of the social situation.

The lack of integrity, however, may involve neither hypocrisy nor the looseness of principle so evident in the opportunist. It is perhaps most painfully problematic and evident where we expect to find it the least. And that is in the "person of integrity," for whom integrity is a self-conscious badge to be worn in public, and for whom any and every challenge to his or her opinions (on whatever subject) is considered a moral challenge (reflecting a lack of integrity in the challenger, of course.) Perhaps the worst boss to work for is the person of integrity, not the Simon Legree or the bully who prides himself or herself on toughness. The person of integrity insists not only that he or she is right but *morally* right, and you, by contrast are morally wrong or, at best, morally confused. Of course, the person of integrity has principles to which he or she is ruthlessly obedient, but the odd thing about principles is that the more general they are the more they admit of interpretations and exceptions. And so long as the person of integrity has principles to defend his or her interpretations and exceptions, he or she remains, as always, the person of integrity, impossible to argue with, dangerous to disagree with, and as unpredictable as the opportunist or the chameleon. For whereas the latter shifts with the winds and the situation, the person of integrity pretends not to shift at all; it is rather the world that moves around, leaving the principles in place and requiring only a new application or interpretation. Personally, I recommend working for someone who realizes that integrity does not mean being the moral rock around which the rest of the earth revolves.

The suggestion that integrity is not hermitage and involves other people deserves to be put in stronger form, for the unity that integrity demands is not just a self-contained unity, a unity in spite of other people or aimed against them. One way to see this is to question the sorts of unifying principles that can constitute integrity. One cannot, for instance, imagine calling someone a person of integrity because he or she lives for the pursuit of pleasure or the amassment of wealth.[19] The chameleon might be characterized as someone who lives for approval (or, at least, to avoid disapproval) but that hardly counts as a unifying principle for the sake of integrity; so, too, the opportunist has his "principles" and modus operandi but these do not constitute integrity. Lynn McFall suggests that these sorts of principles are simply not *important* enough to be candidates for integrity—but, she asks, "important to whom?"[20] The answer cannot simply be personal. That is, one does not have integrity just because he or she sticks by a principle or passion that is of great personal importance. (One can think of all sorts

19. McFall, "Integrity," p. 9.
20. Ibid., p. 10.

of ludicrous examples, such as the classic of Captain Queeg in *The Caine Mutiny*.) We eliminate candidates that are "expedient, artificial or shallow."[21] We readily recognize principles or personal policies that concern the virtues, for example, honesty, generosity, trustworthiness, courage, and kindness. But this recognition of the relevance of the social virtues indicates that the social is already interwoven into the seemingly individual notion of integrity. Stephen Dedalus makes sense to us, in fact, only because we too belong to a society in which autonomy is recognized as essential to integrity, and the search for "one's own way" and the insistence that one be "true to self" are as much a part of our social ethics as of his. (It is quite different, I suggest, from the seemingly similar concept of "honor," which depends upon group membership rather than individuality.) Integrity for most of us is the search for our own way within the context of a group or a choice of groups and within the roles and positions defined by our jobs, careers, and professions. It is only at the extreme—probably on the day we quit—that we adopt Joyce's hero's defiant stance and declare our independence from the mores of the corporation. But it is only at the other extreme that one confuses integrity with unquestioning obedience, for then one faces the danger of becoming a mere chameleon, camouflaged from itself by the fact that there never seems to be a need to change.

The problem of integrity in corporate life is the fact that, because we inevitably wear at least two hats and answer to a number of very different and sometimes contradictory demands and principles, that wholesome image of a unified life is often an impossible illusion, not even an ideal.[22] In any organization or institution, but especially in the context of today's corporation, the notion of integrity as wholeness must not be confused with that one-dimensional version of uncompromising self-righteousness that I sarcastically referred to as "the person of integrity." Integrity requires the will to negotiate and compromise as well as conviction and commitment, and the idea that integrity means being *closed* to outside influences and temptations as opposed to *open* to others is a grotesque and dangerous misunderstanding. Whatever else integrity means to us today, it involves getting along with other people and defending the institutions one represents. This is subject to some rather extreme moral constraints (the usual "living in Nazi Germany" ex-

21. Webster's Third International Dictionary, s.v. "integrity," quoted in ibid., p. 11.

22. British philosopher Bernard Williams has argued that this image of integrity (a concept that he defends first and foremost in his philosophy) is nevertheless "simpleminded" (*Problems of the Self* [Cambridge: Cambridge University Press, 1973], p. 149). So, too, even so enthusiastic an advocate as Alasdair MacIntyre, who insists that we see our lives in narrative terms "as a whole," expresses grave doubts about whether such a notion is any longer possible to us (*After Virtue* [Notre Dame, Ind.: University of Notre Dame Press, 1981], p. 191). But see also Berman, *Splitting the Difference*, on the role of compromise and its relation to integrity.

amples), but for most of us integrity means cooperation, not resistance. Integrity involves openness and affection and flexibility, and (not surprising) an organization or corporation that has integrity will be one that is composed of open-minded, caring individuals. Integrity involves principles and policies, to be sure, but it also involves a pervasive sense of social context and a sense of moral courage that means standing up for others as well as oneself. Otherwise, it becomes mere self-righteousness, not a corporate virtue at all.

We will have more to say about the supervirtue of integrity in Part III. But the central point is that integrity, far from being a special virtue, peculiar to saints, is the essential virtue to a decent life. It is, in the recent vernacular, "getting it all together," not being torn by conflicts and doubts such that one cannot enjoy the fruits of what for most of us is an enviable life. It is an illusion to think that a busy life in business could be entirely trouble free, of course, and so is the idea that integrity is a magical preventative, an innoculation against ethical dilemmas. But a sense of one's own integrity is what allows us to navigate the treacherous waters of those dilemmas, and though integrity does not guarantee success, there can be no success without it.

DECISION MAKING AND GOOD JUDGMENT

> What makes good judgment
> Experience.
> What makes experience?
> Bad judgment.
> GUILIELMO FERRARO

The fact that our roles conflict and there are often no singular principles to help us decide on an ethical course of action shifts the emphasis away from our calculative and ratiocinative faculties and back toward an older, often ignored faculty called "judgment." Against the view that ethics consists primarily of general principles that are applied to particular situations, Aristotle thought that it was "good judgment" or *phronesis* that was of the greatest importance in ethics. Good judgment (which centered on "perception" rather than the abstract formulation and interpretation of general principles) was the product of a good upbringing, a proper education. It is always situated, perhaps something like Joseph Fletcher's still much referred-to notion of a "situation ethics," and it takes into careful account the particularity of the persons and circumstances involved. But I think the real importance of *phronesis* is not just its priority to ethical deliberation and ratiocination; it also has to do with the inevitable conflicts of both concerns and principles that define almost every ethical dilemma. Justice, for example, may sound (especially in some philosophers) as if it were a monolithic or hierarchically layered and almost mechanical process. But, as I have argued elsewhere, there are a dozen or more different considerations that enter into most deliberations about justice, including not only rights and prior obligations and the public good but questions of merit (which themselves break down into a variety of sometimes conflicting categories) and responsibility and risk.[23] There is *no* (nonarbitrary) mechanical decision procedure for resolving most disputes about justice, and what is required, in each and every particular case, is the ability to balance and weigh competing concerns and come to a "fair" conclusion. But what's fair is not the outcome of one or several preordained principles of justice; it is a judgment call, always disputable but nevertheless well or badly made. Cutting corners may be wrong but rounding them off may be an inevitable aspect of any practice with its rules-in-use. I have often thought that encouraging abstract ethical theory actually discourages and distracts us from the need to make judgments. (I actually heard one of my academic colleagues say—without qualms—that, since he's been studying ethical theory, he no longer has any sense of ethics.) And if this sounds implausible, I urge you to remember your last department or board meeting, and the inverse relationship between the high moral tone of the conversation and the ridiculousness of the proposals and decisions that followed.

Decision-making is one of the great arts of management, and it is both strange and unfortunate, therefore, that so many executives and managers have so much trouble with it, are so troubled by it, or try to avoid it altogether. Part of the problem is that for so much of our lives, we are treated as children or as students who are incapable or "not yet ready" to make decisions, and then, not surprisingly, we find ourselves not quite sure how important decisions are to be made. And so we make rash decisions, taking the first option to come to mind, or we follow the (not always good) example of our predecessors, or we rely on tradition, or we pick something just because it is new. In business life, those who began and continued their careers in the corporation found themselves evaluated not on the basis of bold or original thinking or decision making but by virtue of their obedience, and, again, when they finally arrived in a position of great responsibility the art of decision making was largely unknown to them. Decision making, like responsibility in general, takes practice. There is no age too young to begin, and there is no position in the corporation too lowly or too insignificant to be left out of the decision-making process. Making decisions is not a "natural" talent, and indeed recent research has shown that our natural temptations are rather irrational—quite the contrary of the teachings of overrationalized game theory. For example, a per-

---

23. Robert C. Solomon, *Passion for Justice*, (Reading, Mass.: Addison-Wesley, 1990), ch. 2.

son confronted with a great many options—for example, too many new models of new cars—will tend not to choose the best but, if the field is not somehow narrowed down, refuse to choose at all.[24] Or, people under pressure, especially hard-pressed executives, will often tend to make decisions precipitously, even priding themselves on their ability to make off-the-cuff or seat-of-the-pants decisions. In doing so, however, they often follow principles or policies that may well go unexamined, ignore the data or the evidence, and neglect important constituencies and miss attractive options and alternatives. Procrastination, dwelling too long on and "overstudying" a decision is, without a doubt, a serious and sometimes fatal corporate flaw, but haste and lack of deliberation can be equally serious. Good judgment cannot, perhaps, be taught, except by experience. But it can and should be encouraged, emphasized, and practiced, not just in academic case studies but in real-life situations, with personal consequences, people complaining, and all of the other confusions and distractions that make many people prefer not to have to make decisions at all.

An essential part of every business ethics seminar is some version or other of an ethical decision-making model. No reader of this book will be surprised to learn that the very idea of a decision-making model, the analysis of proper deliberation and choice into distinct steps and inferences, was invented by Aristotle, who developed a "practical syllogism" with precisely this in mind.[25] Since then, of course, the development of decision-making models has become a minor industry. The exact form varies considerably, as do the number of steps and the claims made on its behalf, but this much is central to them all. A decision-making model is a reminder to slow down and deliberate, consider the consequences, the constituencies, the options. It would be foolish to insist that someone actually sit down and fill out the blanks for each step for every decision. Many decisions, especially those that are more or less repetitive, can indeed be made "off the cuff," and one need not list all of the consequences or constituencies when these are obvious and familiar. But it is very easy to miss some evidence and attractive options because one has already "decided" before making the decision, and part of the process of following a model is to stoke the moral imagination and encourage us to think beyond the familiar and the obvious. With that in mind, I offer one such model here, not with any bold claims about its uniqueness or superiority and not to claim that following these steps will make you wealthy and wise. What is important is the overall emphasis on the importance of careful and considerate de-

24. Louis Harris, *Risk in a Complex Society* (New York: Marsh, 1980); Jon Elster, *Ulysses and the Sirens* (Cambridge: Cambridge University Press, 1990).
25. Aristotle, *Nicomachean Ethics*, Book VII, in *The Works of Aristotle*, trans. T. Irwin (Indianapolis: Hacket, 1985).

cision making in a complex world of tangled and often conflicting interests and considerations.

An Ethical Decision-Making Model

1. Identify the problem.

> What makes it an *ethical* problem? (Questions of rights, obligations, fairness, relationships, integrity)

2. Identify the constituents.

> Who has been hurt?
> Who could be hurt?
> Who could be helped?
> Are they willing players or are they victims?
> Can you negotiate with them?

3. Diagnose the situation.

> Is it going to get worse (or better)?
> Who is to blame? (Possibly no one)
> Who can do something now?
> What could have prevented it?
> Can the damage now be undone?

4. Analyze your options.

> Imagine the range of possibilities.
> Limit yourself to the two or three most manageable. (Too many are discouraging)
> What are the likely outcomes of each?
> What are the likely costs of each?
> How can you achieve them?
> Which is most desirable, given the circumstances?

5. Act.

> Do what you have to do.
> Don't be afraid to admit errors.
> Be as bold in confronting a problem as you were in causing it.

The importance of decision making and good judgment in business ethics cannot be overestimated. Following the rules is always a handy guide to right action but it is never enough and in some exceptional cases it may be disastrous. Rules conflict with each other and with our aims and goals. It is not always the case that a rule trumps self-interest. Where enormous stakes are at issue—for instance, the survival of the company or the life of a fellow employee or executive—some routine ethical considerations may have to be cast aside. When the company faces an emergency, for example, the usual recognition of and respect for an employee's or an executive's right to spare time and time away from the office may well be sacrificed. (How often such emergencies justify such a sacrifice, however, is another question that calls for good judgment on the part of managers.) When an employee faces a crisis or an important situation—a serious illness, a death in the family, or the birth of a baby, for instance—special considerations may well be due even though they conflict with the usual company policies. This is not to say that emergencies and desperation justify ignoring ethics (indeed, it is in emergencies that one's ethical mettle often is tested.[26] It is only to say that there are a great many ethical demands and principles, some of them much more important than others and it is only good judgment, not some all-purpose hierarchy of rules, that instructs us what is the right thing to do.

Not only can loyalties and obligations conflict, but ethics itself has its internal conflicts. The most dramatic manifestation of this, perhaps, is the past several hundred (or several thousand) years of ethical theory. To put it crudely, if ordinary people and managers waited for the philosophers to settle the issues of ethics before they acted, the human species would have vanished long ago. The fact is that neither philosophers nor everyone else agree about ethics.[27] If ethics were so singular, how is it then that the brightest minds of the Western tradition (there is no greater consensus in the East) have not agreed on a single ethical system. Instead, we find deontologists defending their absolute ("a priori") rational principles against utilitarians defending the greatest good for the greatest number and virtue advocates attacking both of them. Each group thinks that its formulation of the "highest principle" or "most basic concept" of ethics is the correct one. In daily practice, we see the same disputes at work, causing disagreements, wreaking havoc, even without the theoretical sophistication and arguments. One executive insists that the company play by the book and follow the rules to the letter, even if the rule in question is of dubious merit. Another accuses him of pigheadedness and insists that the company ought to do what is practical, whatever the rules or policies dictate. Still a third insists that the company has no obligation except to do what is best for the company itself and its stockholders, and a fourth accuses all of the others of being "heartless" and not making decisions "based on people." Theoreticians will recognize the nature of such disagreements in terms of differences in criteria rather than merely a dispute over what to do, but most practitioners (including most ethical theorists, in their daily discussions) will not recognize the nature of their disagreement as such. What we find here is a difference in *ethical styles*, the very different ways in which different people approach ethics and ethical situations. Each of us (quite naturally) thinks of the way we approach ethics as the *right* way. If we are compassionate and make ethical decisions by

26. See David Norton, "Moral Minimalism," in French, *Ethical Theory*.

27. See, for instance, Alasdair MacIntyre's opening arguments in *After Virtue*, and his discussion of disagreements about justice in Chap. 18.

putting ourselves in the other person's shoes, we expect that everyone ought to do likewise. If we feel compelled to follow the rules to the letter, we will probably not understand those who do not respect the rules as such but see them merely as rules of thumb or as prohibitions whose only sanction is the fear of getting caught when breaking them.

The idea that there is no "right" way of thinking about ethics but rather a variety of forms of judgments, each of them "ethical," makes the notion of ethical judgment all the more important (along with the related virtue of integrity). The idea of ethical styles does not mean, emphatically, that there are no clearly wrong ways of thinking about ethics. The pursuit of pure selfishness may entail "take 'em if you can" and "kick 'em when they're down" philosophies, which are not *ethical* styles, whatever else they may be. But there are different ethical styles just as there are different managerial and personal styles, and to understand the role of judgment in business ethics is to appreciate this diversity and to understand that our differences do not necessarily signal unethical thinking (we will discuss ethical styles at greater length in Part III).

Judgment is essential to both business and business ethics because business is so bound to context and so subject to so many confluent and competing interests and demands. There is no simple calculus or decision procedure for choosing the best business deal, and those who try to follow such a calculus or procedure will almost inevitably get caught up in its simple-mindedness—no matter how sophisticated or complicated it may be. So, too, those who try to reduce ethics to a simple principle or rule of thumb will find themselves thumb-tied and accused of pigheadedness and inflexibility—which they may too readily misunderstand as "integrity." In those many cases in which obligations or loyalties conflict there may be no right answer, and when one checks on the rules he or she will probably find that the rules conflict as well. In a pessimistic tone, one might say that sometimes there is no way to make the right decision. (Indeed, moral pessimists have defined an "ethical dilemma" in just that way.) But good judgment only means making the best decision available, which means making the decision in the right way.

HOLISM: BEYOND STAKEHOLDER ANALYSIS

> The man of wisdom delights in water; the man of humanity delights in mountains. The man of wisdom is active; the man of humanity is tranquil. The man of wisdom enjoys happiness; the man of humanity enjoys long life.
>
> LAO-TZU, *Tao-te-ching*

It more or less follows from what I've said that the ultimate aim of the Aristotelean approach to business is to cultivate whole human beings, not jungle fighters, efficiency automatons, or "good soldiers." But one of the problems of traditional business thinking is our tendency to isolate our business or professional roles from the rest of our lives, a process that Marx, following Schiller, described as "alienation." The good life may have many facets, but they are facets and not mere components, much less isolated aspects of a fragmented existence. We hear more and more in managerial circles, despite the tiresome emphasis on task techniques and "objectives," that a manager's primary and ultimate concern is *people*. It's gotten trite, but as I watch our more ambitious students and talk with more and more semisuccessful but "trapped" middle managers and executives, I become more and more convinced that the tunnel vision of business life encouraged by the too-narrow business curriculum and the daily rhetoric of the corporate community is damaging and counterproductive.[28] Good employees are good people, and to pretend that the virtues of business stand isolated from the virtues of the rest of our lives—and this is not for a moment to deny the particularity of either our business roles or our lives—is to set up that familiar tragedy in which a pressured employee violates his or her personal values because, from a purely business point of view, he or she "didn't really have any choice."

This search for wholeness in the individual employee or manager extends to the corporation itself, and here we come back to the now-familiar notion of a *stakeholder*, which embraces the idea that corporate responsibilities and obligations involve not only stockholders but embrace a wide variety of affected (and effective) groups. The great virtue of the notion of the stakeholder, however, is its sense of *holism*. Holism (not "wholism") is concern for the whole rather than some of its parts, an emphasis on the big picture rather than the analysis of narrowly circumscribed details such as profits. We have to reject all of those false dichotomies and antagonisms between business and ethics, between profit and doing good, between personal and corporate values and virtues. If I may once again reintroduce the tiredest term in business ethics, the "social responsibility" of business, properly understood, is not an odd number of extraneous obligations of the businesses and corporations. It is the very point of their existence. Social responsibility does not mean sacrificing profits to "do-gooding" or fleecing the stockholders. (Milton Friedman, in one of his more apoplectic moments, called even the most innocent corporate efforts to improve public life "pure theft" and "unadulterated socialism.")[29] Social responsibility only means that the pur-

28. Again, see Earl Shorris, *The Oppressed Middle* (New York: Doubleday, 1976).

29. Milton Friedman, "The Social Responsibility of Business Is to Increase Its Profits," *New York Times*, Sept. 13, 1970.

pose of business is to do what business has always been meant to do, enrich society as well as the pockets of those who are responsible for the enriching.

"Holism" is a term that has been coopted by New Age thinkers and mystics, but it deserves to become an important term in ethics and in managerial thinking as well. Holism encourages and ultimately requires reference to "the big picture," to the overall context in which a business decision and in fact business itself is engaged, to the "whole" rather than just a part (which leads, predictably, to many misspellings). Much of my argument here has been an argument against atomistic and analytic individualism, the temptation to understand ourselves each as an isolated whole and to understand the world around us by breaking it up into discrete little parts or pieces. We are, of course, "individuals" in some sense, but it is important to recognize that even our individuality is the holistic product of our culture and its concepts. And, of course, understanding does proceed through analysis, whether scientific analysis in which complex wholes are broken or dissected into parts to see how they work and fit together, or strategic analysis in which the complex possible consequences of a decision are broken into discrete chains of causation and evaluated one by one. But such understanding has its limits, and understanding how the parts fit together is not quite the same as understanding the operation as a whole. Scientists understand more and more about the parts (organs) of an organism and how they fit together, but they are nevertheless a long way from understanding the nature of life itself, and it has been often argued that no amount of analysis will ever provide the answer to such a question. And in business, attempted theories of business in terms of isolated and in fact organic components such as "profit" and trying to understand human behavior in terms of economics (profit maximization and consumer desires and their fulfillment) lead to a rather total misunderstanding of business.

It is only by embracing holism that we will get an adequate grasp of such perennial business ethics concepts as "social responsibility," which cannot be analyzed (as is so often attempted) in terms of individual obligations. Moreover, the character of the corporation itself—even the business world—cannot be understood if, as we do, we insist on thinking of "the corporation" either as a fictitious legal entity (leaving in question the conceptual identity of all of those buildings and people) or as a collection of a people (leaving the ways in which they interact and the structures of the corporation something of a derivation). Corporations are neither abstract entities nor mere collections of individuals. Holism, accordingly, means seeing beyond all of those contextually useful but ultimately self-defeating or otherwise inadequate dichotomies that have ruled modern philosophy since the scientific revolutions of the seventeenth century.[30] In straight philosophical terms, this means questioning and overcoming such familiar dichotomies as "reason versus passion," "culture versus nature," "self versus others," and "duty versus self-interest." Thinking about work and management as purely "rational" activities all too readily blinds us to what Friedrich Nietzsche called the "human-all-too-human"—that is, emotional and often "irrational" ways in which people actually behave, particularly where status, power, and money are at stake. To think of emotional behavior as "weakness," however (for example, the embarrassed reaction provoked by an executive who breaks down in tears when he is fired from a job he has held for fifteen years), indicates how far overboard the corporate world has gone in the direction of Weberian "rationality" and away from our ordinary sense of propriety and responsibility where such traumatic situations are concerned.[31] In part, I admit, this can also be attributed to a misunderstood insistence on "professionalization," in which "professional" is mistaken for "cold and calculated" rather than "dedicated and competent." So, too, the standard contrasts between "self and others" and "duty versus self-interest," which have defined modern philosophy and political thought for centuries, introduce vicious dichotomies that lock us into destructive "either/or" modes of thought. At the heart of much business thinking is the "Hobbesian" assumption that people are essentially selfish and, as such, in brutal competition with one another.[32] It was Hobbes who saw "the state of nature" as "a war of all against all," and his efforts to soften that conclusion by appealing to some mythical contractual agreement ("the social contract") in which we all adopt mutual obligations and respect one another's rights, however revolutionary and politically beneficial it may have been in the seventeenth and eighteenth centuries, was not only a dubious retreat to the "nature versus culture" dichotomy but an even more dubious presumption about human nature—that we are all, by nature, isolated individuals out for ourselves rather than essentially social creatures who have group affinities and affections as well as the need to cooperate built into our very genes.[33] The twin concepts of obligation and rights are intended as compensation for this tragic opposition between self and others, as if once we are hopelessly alienated from one another we can nevertheless adopt a "rational" arrangement in which we promise not to hurt or interfere with one another. But this is not the sort of creatures we are, and the opposition between duty and self-interest is just as metaphysically phony as the dichotomy between self and others.

30. See, e.g., Stephen Toulmin, *Cosmopolis: The Hidden Agenda of Modernity* (New York: Free Press, 1989).
31. On changes in the Puritan ethic to Weberian rationality, see Jackall, *Moral Mazes*, ch. 1.
32. After Thomas Hobbes, who popularized it in his *Leviathan*.
33. See my *Passion for Justice*, ch. 3.

The very existence of the business enterprise and the prosperity and power of corporations suggest not the power of Hobbesian selfishness but rather the human capacity—both natural and cultural—to cooperate and organize, to serve one's own interests by serving the interests of others. Indeed, except in the exceptional competitive circumstance, it is impossible to distinguish these.

Such dualistic thinking permeates corporate life and business thinking in a number of more specific ways as well. The "us versus them" mentality that defines so much of intraindustry competition and the "every man for himself" philosophy that spouts in so many corporate hallways clearly harks back to the larger philosophical issues that we were just discussing, but the philosophical issues are often subtler than that. For instance, the emphasis on intraindustry competition typically ignores (particularly in the "heat of battle") the extent to which companies in the same industry are mutually dependent, and what is fatal or successful for one might well be fatal or successful for them all. Airlines scrupulously follow the rule that no company will ever mention the accident record of another, not because airline executives are necessarily wedded to the rules of fair competition but rather because they recognize a basic rule of prudence—that if people are afraid to fly they do not feel any more secure by paying attention to one airline rather than another. The veritable explosion of the desktop computer industry provided a boom for hundreds, perhaps thousands of new (and old) companies, even if, eventually, intraindustry competition and mergers forced many of them out of business. So, too, because of our intense (and largely mythological) individualism we tend too readily to maintain not only a distinction but an antagonism between our concept of the individual and our notion of the corporation, as if corporate life essentially robs people of their individuality and turns them into anonymities, with the only proper reaction being rebellion (even that means only wearing obscene or otherwise outrageous underwear as an unseen gesture of defiance). But we all know the disaster that ensues when employees really do start thinking of themselves as exploited victims and of the corporation in terms of "this damn company." That is probably the common "excuse" for employee theft (10 to 15 percent in many businesses) and no doubt costs the corporate world much more in terms of time wasted and tasks pursued with a fraction of the energy that would be be devoted to tasks that one considers "one's own." But this disastrous way of thinking is not the invention of disgruntled employees alone. The antagonistic concept of the individual versus the corporation is often promulgated by managers and corporate leaders themselves, when they emphasize "sacrifice" and even "dedication" rather than shared identity and projects. The "family" metaphor is often thought to be corny and clichéd (and, no doubt, it is often employed hypocritically) but it underscores perhaps the single most important point in both good business and business ethics—that a sense of cooperation that does not presuppose an antagonistic sense of "individual versus the corporation" is essential. Of course, there may always be an occasion when integrity means standing up and saying No to the corporation that has nourished and supported you, but this (often tragic) circumstance only shows us how corporations can go wrong. It does not demonstrate any deep underlying distinction between individual and corporation.

The antagonistic dichotomy of "labor versus management," has been criticized and commented upon for many years and by many business writers, so I do not want to belabor the obvious here. To be sure, trade unions played and continue to play an essential role in the fight for justice and fairness in the business world, and the fact that union demands may on occasion be "bad for business" is a short-sighted vision of what counts as "good business." It may not have been obvious in earlier decades, but international competition has made us keenly aware of the need to see labor and management not as adversaries but as essential partners in a productive enterprise. So, too, the antagonistic dichotomy of "business versus government" has all but withered in the competition with Japan, Inc., which has made it all too clear that the eighteenth-century "laissez faire" model of economics is all but dead. To be sure, the nature and extent of government regulation of business are still and will continue to be a legitimate source of concern and debate, but we are now becoming much more keenly aware of the extent to which government must set the competitive ground rules for some industries—and not only those that are politically sensitive or intimately connected with national security. Pollution and other environmental problems can only be solved if government is willing to provide guidelines that competitive industries cannot possibly provide for themselves (which does not mean, of course, that government should propose impossible regulations). But government is not just a brake on business, a setter of standards and limitations. It also provides support and protection, subsidies and loans (such as the mammoth Lockheed and Chrysler loans of a few years ago). And, ideally, it can and should provide organizational impetus and foster cooperation as well as competition. But, once again, it may be that the dichotomy of "business versus government" is itself outmoded and obsolete. As corporations grow into small countries in their own right and spread multinationally across the globe, dictating government policies not only here but elsewhere as well, it is clear that the traditional distinction between business and government is harder and harder to discern and may soon become impractical as well as indefensible. What that will do to the old rhetoric of "free enterprise" and the "laissez faire" distrust of government regulation remains to be seen, but in the more holistic sense of the business world that is emerging, we can already see a larger sense of business and a more inclusive, intrinsic sense of social responsibility.

To say that the distinction between business and government is breaking down is not to deny that each has its legitimate and exclusive domain. It is only to reject the adversarial antagonism that is expressed by so much archaic business rhetoric and insist that a more synthetic and cooperative way of thinking would at this point in history be far more productive. So, too, with the other distinctions I have suggested submerging into a more holistic scenario. All of them—emotion and reason, self and others, nature and culture, employee and firm, labor and management, business and government—are useful in context, but they are distinct only by way of "dialectic," by virtue of their play against one another. Distinctions are useful and necessary, but every distinction should also be viewed with caution. There is a point at which the convenience of a distinction turns into an obstacle and is no longer an aid to understanding and progress. The concept of the individual is, without doubt, one of the most important and beneficial conceptual advances in human history, but we have reached a point where it blocks rather than aids our insight and closes off the vision of a more harmonious society. The dominant metaphor of "competition" also presupposes too many Hobbesian antagonisms as basic truths and thus misses that larger, underlying cooperative structure that makes competition possible. To be sure, an overly "moralistic" attitude toward the rough-and-tumble of business is often counterproductive, but this only means that morality too must be integrated into business. Indeed, the very notion of business ethics as a special subject in business is bound to be a disaster for both business and ethics. Business is, at its very core, ethical, and our ethics, in this society, is very much bound up with our sense of fair business practices. A young business student today needs specialized classes in finance and marketing, but it is a gigantic mistake to move from the need for specialization to the current narrowness of business studies and the consequent shrinking of the business personality. Holism is not itself another philosophy so much as it is simply the insistence that wherever we find antagonism and competing concepts we should expand our vision until we see the whole context. In the case of business and economics, this means that our vision should take in the whole of human nature and society, not just profits, costs, and benefits and the law of supply and demand. Business is not an isolated enterprise, and to insist that it is so is only to support and strengthen the attack on business as an antisocial activity. The Aristotelean approach to business, by contrast, is ultimately nothing other than the recognition of business as an integral part of the larger society.

The portrait that is framed by these six parameters (along with such subsidiary concepts as "merit," "teleology," "duty") suggests an ethics

that is defined by people working and living together, not an abstract
set of principles or legal claims, not a bureaucracy where impersonality
and efficiency are especially important, not a world of competitive individuals working against one another for a limited supply of goods,
not a mediocracy in which "teamwork" is reduced to mere mutual protection based on mutual suspicion. It is a conception of ethics that is
not imposed on business "from the top" (with too little respect for the
real-life struggles of business people and corporations) but extracted
from business as a successful ongoing practice. And this, of course, is
the basic point. Business is a practice. It presupposed a (more or less)
organized society (or societies) that shares all sorts of agreements about
the good life and how to get there, about what is a fair exchange and
what is not, about how to interact and what must be, what must not be,
and what need not be said. People in business are ethical, therefore,
not on the basis of some "external" standard but by virtue of the very
activity in which they are engaging.

III

THE HEART OF THE CORPORATION: BUSINESS VIRTUES AND VICES

> To argue, in the manner of Machiavelli, that there is one rule for business and another for private life, is to open the door to an orgy of unscrupulousness before which the mind recoils. To argue that there is no difference at all is to lay down a principle which few men who have faced the difficulty in practice will be prepared to endorse as of invariable application, and incidentally to expose the ideas of morality itself to discredit by subjecting it to an almost intolerable strain.
>
> R. H. TAWNEY, *Religion and the Rise of Capitalism*

Business is a human enterprise. to be good in business is to be a good human being. One can make money without virtue, of course, but success requires much more—a good and decent life, friends and respect, love and a little admiration. Too many of our strategies are mock Machiavellian ("better to be feared than loved") while our fantasies insist on exactly the opposite. The key to the good life is not power (which by its very nature is always there to be challenged and therefore tenuous) but mutual respect and a sense of solidarity. In business, it is by virtue of the satisfaction of needs and desires and his or her importance in the community, not by virtue of wealth alone, that the business person has become the "pillar of the community." (A few centuries ago, it was still easier for a camel to go through the eye of a needle than it was for a newly rich businessman to get into high society, much less heaven.) In the corporation, we all know that life can be hell because of only one or two people with vices—a dishonest colleague, an unfair supervisor, an untrustworthy assistant, not to mention a mean or unappreciative boss. And where life is hell, productivity levels will not be divine, although adrenalin levels will undoubtedly run sky-high. In the complex interpersonality of the corporation, there are limits to the good that formal codes or principles can do. Corporate life and consequently corporate success will be determined by the character and personality of the individuals who are its constituents, and though the nature of the corporation will have much to do with the formation of that character, it will also be the product of the totality of personalities that guide and run it. That is what the Aristotelean approach is all about: a renewed emphasis on the character of the people who make up the world of business and the structures and influences that mold them.

The renewed emphasis on the virtues in ethics is a recent phenomenon, dating back only a decade or so. Curiously enough, that is just about the time that business ethics has been developing its new status both as an aspect of "applied" ethics and as a required subject for business students and corporate executives. But the ethics of virtue (or "virtue ethics," clumsily named) has not until now been applied to business ethics, which has remained largely in the grip of just those ethical paradigms that the renewed emphasis on the virtues is aimed to dispel—an obsession with ethical dilemmas or "quandaries" instead of day-to-day ethical behavior, an emphasis on actions and policies rather than the people who are their agents and authors, an insistence on universal rules that make no reference to particular people, roles, or relationships, and a reliance on rational principles instead of emotions and character.[1] Of course, one can view this vision of ethics as itself a modern flash-in-the-pan, a passing phase of philosophy that dates back only to the late eighteenth century, and virtue ethics has a lineage that dates back to Plato and Aristotle. But longevity is hardly the conclusive test of validity in such matters, and what counts are the benefits that an ethics of virtue can bring to our understanding of business and the particular concerns of business ethics.

"The virtues" is a short-hand way of summarizing the ideals that define good character. There are a great many virtues—in fact, it would be a daunting task to try to list them all. Just for a

---

1. See, for a good argument against "quandary ethics," Edmund Pincoffs, *Quandaries and Virtues* (Lawrence: University Press of Kansas, 1986).

start, we have honesty, loyalty, sincerity, courage, reliability, trustworthiness, benevolence, sensitivity, helpfulness, cooperativeness, civility, decency, modesty, openness, cheerfulness, amiability, tolerance, reasonableness, tactfulness, wittiness, gracefulness, liveliness, magnanimity, persistence, prudence, resourcefulness, cool-headedness, warmth, and hospitality.[2] Each of these has subtle subtraits and related virtues, for example, honesty and truthfulness, dependability and trustworthiness, and there are a great many virtues of strength, energy, and skill as well as attractiveness, charm, and aesthetic appeal that we have not included. There are "negative" virtues, that is, virtues that specify the absence of some annoying or antisocial trait, such as nonnegligence, nonvengefulness, nonvindictiveness and unpretentiousness, and there are virtues of excess and superiority, such as superconscientiousness and superreliability. From such a variety of virtues, one of the most important impressions for anyone interested in ethics and business ethics is the impoverished nature of any moral language that limits itself to such terms as "good" and "bad," "right" and "wrong." To be sure, most of the virtues are "good" and lead to "right" action, and most of the contrary vices are "bad" and lead to "wrong"-doing. But not only does such ethical language lead us to ignore most of what is significant and subtle in our ordinary ethical judgments, it tends to lead us away from just that focus on personal character that is most essential to most of our interpersonal decisions, whether it is to trust a colleague, make a new friend, hire or fire a new assistant, speak out against a problematic policy, respect a superior, or invite the boss over to the house for dinner. Ethics is not the study of right and wrong, anymore than art and aesthetics are the study of beauty and ugliness.[3] Ethics, like art and aesthetics is a colorful, multifaceted appreciation and engagement with other people in the world. In business ethics, it is only the extreme and sinister misdeed that we label simply "wrong"; more often, we invoke a palette of imaginative descriptions such as "sleazy" and "slimy." Even the phrase "good character" (or "good

2. A complex taxonomy of many virtues is in Pincoffs, ibid., p. 84. My own discussion of the virtues, summarized in the following chapters, is taken from *Ethics: A Short Introduction* (Madison: Brown and Benchmark, 1992).

3. See Frithjof Bergmann, "The Experience of Values," in *Revisions*, ed. Hauerwas and S. Macintyre (Notre Dame, Ind.: University of Notre Dame Press, 1983), pp. 127–59.

person") strikes us as uninteresting and vacuous; it is the details that count, not the gloss. And there are many details, any of which might become more or less significant in some particular situation.

One of the most important features of the virtues is the fact that they are context-bound, "relative" to various practices and activities, and that means that not only will new practices produce new virtues (as the new practice of business investment encouraged by John Calvin encouraged the virtue called "thrift") but that a virtue that is of little importance in one situation may be a cardinal virtue in another or vice versa (as anyone who has been transferred from a sensitive position in human resources to one in an efficiency-driven manufacturing division can testify). A virtue, to repeat our earlier simpleminded summary, is a good trait to have, in a given context and given a certain sort of situation. Of course there are general virtues—such as honesty and courage—that will no doubt be virtues in virtually any situation or context, but even these take on special meaning depending on circumstances. Despite the military rhetoric, courage in the corporation is very different from the courage required on the battlefield, and honesty in strategic planning is quite different from honesty in personnel. But that does not mean that virtues are "relative" in the more insidious sense—that there are ultimately no virtues and no virtue and in certain circumstances, such as the hard-headed world of business: "anything goes." On the contrary, it is when times get tough and when heads get hard that the virtues become most essential.

17

The Nature of the Virtues

> If you want to understand the ethical ideals of the Greeks, do not
> think of a virtue as having to do with what a person does. Think of
> it, instead, as having to do with what one is.
>
> RICHARD TAYLOR, *Virtue Ethics*

Business ethics is too often conceived as a set of impositions and constraints, obstacles to business behavior rather than the motivating force
of that behavior. So conceived, it is no surprise that many people in
business look upon ethics and ethicists with suspicion, as antagonistic if
not antithetical to their enterprise. But properly understood, ethics does
not and should not consist of a set of prohibitive principles or rules,
and it is the virtue of an ethics of virtue to be rather an intrinsic part
and the driving force of a successful life well lived. Its motivation need
not depend on elaborate soul-searching and deliberation but on the
easy flow of interpersonal relations in a company that respects and honors
the virtues and condemns (and discharges) vice. On the Aristotelean
view, living well, becoming successful, and being happy already incorporate ethics not as a set of constraints contrary to our inclinations but
rather as a set of virtues that, as part of our character, is very much in
tune with our inclinations. Business is ruled by the virtues as well as by
the need to make a profit, and these virtues are not obstacles but the
ultimate standard in business. Anyone can make money in a society in
which most people still presume that others are honest and allow wishful thinking ("an unbelievable price") to get the best of them. But it is
how one makes money that matters, and one does not aim first of all to
be rich but rather to be good and respected. The rewards will follow,
but this does not mean that the point and purpose of the enterprise
are the rewards. It would be a cliché to say that virtue is its own reward,
but what this suggests is not the pleasures of self-righteousness but an
optimum strategy for happiness that understands its priorities and ends
and means.

Virtues are essentially social traits, even though our vision of a paragon of virtue is often a man or woman standing alone. A virtue fits in

with people in a particular kind of community. It may provoke temporary animosity and opposition (for example, when someone uses his
or her freedom of speech to attack courageously and honestly a popular but flawed or unjust public policy) but the virtue itself, nevertheless,
is essential to the life of the community and socially sanctioned. David
Hume and later Adam Smith defined a virtue as a special trait of character that is pleasing both to other people and to ourselves. This is,
perhaps, a bit too genteel—the product of an overly "gentlemanly" vision of the virtues and the modest hedonism that ruled ethics in Edinburgh, but it does capture the essential sociability of the virtues that is
not only good for business (congeniality, honesty) but essential to the
very life of business (trust, dependability). What quality is to products,
the virtues are to those who produce and distribute them. And within
the corporation, we need not and should not think of the virtues as
particularly noble, outstanding traits. They are the ordinary shapes of
daily intercourse, the courtesy of a casual conversation, the trust that
lies behind every casual promise and assurance. To emphasize the virtues is not, therefore, to put a special premium on heroism or sainthood. It is to emphasize the familiar—the complex harmony and mutual respect that makes a company efficient and successful. The test of
virtue, so conceived, is "getting along," not in the often timid, conformist, or merely strategic sense of "going along" but in the much more
important sense of always keeping in mind the larger community and
its well-being. This is not opposed to integrity but part and parcel of it.
Too often we think of integrity as the virtue that separates us from
others. In what follows I want to interpret that "wholeness" precisely
in terms of group sensibility and social harmony, or what in a more
sportsmanlike and less musical metaphor we often refer to as "team
spirit." Once again, this is no argument against individuality or excellence but rather the basis of both.

A virtue, according to Aristotle, is itself an excellence; not, perhaps,
a very specialized skill or talent (like being a good carpenter or basketball player) but an exemplary way of getting along with other people,
a way of manifesting in one's own thoughts, feelings, and actions the
ideals and aims of the entire community. Thus honesty is a virtue not
because it is a skill necessary for any particular endeavor or because it
is "the best policy" in most social situations but because it represents
the ideal of straight dealing, fair play, common knowledge, and open
inquiry. What is public is probably approved of and what is hidden is
probably dangerous. So, too, courage is a virtue not just because it requires a special talent or just because "somebody's got to do it" but
because we all believe (with varying degrees of commitment) that individuals should stand up for what they care about and in. But not all
virtues need be so serious or so central to our idea of integrity. Aristotle listed charm, wit, and a good sense of humor as virtues, and I

think that we would probably agree. To be sure, the circumstances in which congeniality is a central virtue and in which courage becomes cardinal will be very different, but it is a troubled organization that requires the more heroic virtues all the time and does not have the relative security and leisure to enjoy those virtues that make life worthwhile rather than those that are necessary for mere survival. Indeed, part of the folly of the familiar military, machine, and jungle metaphors in business is that they all make business life out to be something threatening and relentless. But the truth (even in the military and in the jungle) is that there are long and sometimes relaxed respites and a need for play and playfulness as well as diligence. Camaraderie and the virtues of "getting along" are just as important to group survival as the coordination needed for fighting together. There are reasons why we want to survive, apart from sheer Darwinian obstinacy, and the fact that we relish and enjoy the social harmony of our life and our jobs is one of them. One of the most powerful but most ignored arguments against hostile takeovers and unfriendly mergers is the desire on the part of the members of a corporate community to maintain that community, and this is not the same as executives "fighting to keep their jobs."

The fact that many of the virtues are social virtues of congeniality suggests that we should not insist on virtue as a particularly "moral" category, nor is it obvious that we should draw a sharp distinction between moral virtues (such as honesty) and nonmoral virtues (such as wit). Many virtues (such as loyalty and generosity) seem to be ambiguous in terms of morality, and the very notion of "morality" has been so distorted by a century or two of conflation with a very specialized and overly principled conception of morals and confusion with very narrow questions of behavior (particularly sexual behavior) that it is, perhaps, no longer a useful term for understanding the subtleties of social harmony. What is important is rather the place of a virtue (along with other virtues) in the living of a meaningful, fulfilling life, and what is important for a business virtue is its place in a productive, meaningful life in business. And this does not simply mean, How does it contribute to the bottom line? but rather, Does it contribute to the social harmony of the organization? Does it manifest the best ideals of the organization? Does it render an employee or manager "whole" or does it tear a person to pieces, walling off one aspect of a personality from another and leaving one part to apologize to or feel ashamed before the other? One might speculate that the more "moral" virtues are those that, when violated, put one in a position of "disgrace" in the eyes of one's peers. (Having a lousy sense of humor, on the other hand, is certainly undesirable but hardly a disgrace.) But this is a largely negative characterization of character, and note that the very word "dis-*grace*" suggests the religious origins of much of our conception of morality. Nevertheless, disgrace is not an adequate test even for the moral virtues however essential it may be to the moral life.[1] It would be probably better to emphasize the importance of the virtues rather than their violation. Despite the insistence of many moralists to the contrary, it would seem that the congenial virtues are just as essential to corporate well-being as the more moral virtues. We typically forgive a certain amount of exaggeration and fictionalization for the sake of humor, and we recognize in Shakespeare's Falstaff, for instance, the convincing principle that a display of humor can sometimes take priority over valor. We tend to be overly absolutist about certain moral principles, and the cost of that absolutism is the neglect of the congenial virtues and a consequent dreariness in both social life and ethical discourse.

Unfortunately, the convoluted history of morals has resulted in a confusing ambiguity for the term "virtue." On the one hand, a virtue is a particular feature of a person's character, such as honesty, wittiness, generosity, or social charm. On the other hand, there is a general all-encompassing designation of a person's "virtue" and talk of "virtue" in general, where the word is used as a synonym for "morality." (Kant, for example, uses the word "virtue" in this way.) Of course, a person who has virtues will very likely be virtuous, and a virtuous person will no doubt have at least some virtues. Nevertheless, the two conceptions are distinct. A person may have many virtues but, nevertheless, lead a sufficiently wild and unconventional life (even assuming no *im*morality as such) to prohibit that person's being called "virtuous." On the other hand, a person, perhaps out of fear of punishment and general inhibition, may well live a life that is wholly virtuous in the moral sense, and yet be an utter bore.[2] Some terrific people may live in a morally gray world, and some indisputably good people may nonetheless be intolerably dull. That should give us pause, for it provides an appealing reason for preferring a broadened Aristotelean ethic that recognizes the entire range of virtues and does not become obsessed with singular virtue.

It is important not to see the virtues as merely instances of more general ethical principles. To be sure, any virtue will usually admit of generalization ("it would be good if everyone were so generous, honest, brave") and by its very nature a virtue will contribute to the general good. But though the virtues may be generalized and may even instan-

---

1. Later in this discussion, I will similarly emphasize the importance of the odd Aristotelean virtue of *shame*. The point is not that it is desirable to be ashamed, of course, but rather that the capacity to be shamed is essential to having a virtuous character in the first place. As the Ethiopian proverb says, "Where there is no shame, there is no honor." The difference between shame and disgrace, however, is significant here. Disgrace suggests dishonor before God. Shame is secular and suggests rather a "letting down" of your colleagues and others who trusted or depended on you.

2. Several of Jane Austin's characters come to mind here, notably the insufferable but very proper Mr. Collins in *Pride and Prejudice*.

tiate some general principle, it would be a mistake to think of exemplifying a virtue as acting on principle. "Be honest" looks very much like
"do not lie," except that a truly honest person probably never even
thinks of lying. Whereas the concept of morality (whether Kantian or
utilitarian) seems to entail the use of general principles (whether "treat
people as ends, not means" or "serve the greatest good for the greatest
number"), one might have a virtue and never think about it as such,
acting "spontaneously" whenever the appropriate occasion arises. So,
too, it is a mistake to think of the virtues as self-sacrificing or selfless,
although certainly some may be. In most of the virtues, the opposition
of "self" to "others" does not arise. A trait that counts as a virtue will
be desirable and pleasing to others, presumably because that virtue
benefits (and does not harm) them, but it would be wrong to think of
virtues as essentially "altruistic." A generous person may take delight
in the well-being of others, but he or she need not do so, and, if he or
she also takes tremendous pleasure in the act of giving (for any number
of reasons), that does not undermine or subtract from the generosity.
He or she may simply *be* generous—one might say "overflowing"—or
take great pride in being a generous person. To be generous is to act
and to be motivated by generosity, to be sure, but no further claim
need be made distinguishing self-interest, altruism, and concern for
others.

If the practice of the virtues is often spontaneous and requires little
thought, it certainly does not as such require deliberation. Indeed, too
much deliberation ("Should I be generous? Am I supposed to leave a
20 percent tip or can I get away with less?") is evidence that one does
not have the virtue in question. In general, the virtues (as opposed to
"morality") are not concerned with abstract rules or principles. Many
of the virtues would seem to be rather silly if they were preceded by
the sorts of deliberation insisted upon by many moral theorists. ("The
rule is that one ought to be generous; therefore, I ought to give more";
or "One ought to have a good sense of humor; therefore, *laugh!*") Of
course, there are some virtues that quite clearly involve principles (triv-
ially, "being a principled person"), and a thoughtful person might well
generalize about his or her virtues or formulate various "rules of thumb."
But the focus on the virtues is not primarily concerned with such
thoughts and guidelines. Rather, it is the hallmark of a virtue that it be
engrained in one's character and—perhaps after years of cultivation
and practice—seem perfectly "natural."

Even the most common virtues, such as courage and temperance,
turn out to have very different meanings in different societies. Courage
in Homer's Greece could be measured by one's stalwart behavior in
hand-to-hand combat. We most often mention courage in the context
of "courage of one's convictions," which is quite something else. President John F. Kennedy once wrote a book entitled *Profiles in Courage*,

but the courage of many politicians today will not even stand up to the
risk of losing reelection. That is not the same virtue as the courage of
Achilles facing a hundred Trojans in battle. Indeed, one might even be
led to wonder whether the two uses of the word "courage" have much
in common. And yet, we expect a certain agreement on the virtues
even in societies that are very different, in part, of course, because the
broadest parameters of human life (physical vulnerability, the need to
eat and drink and sleep, our need for others, the awareness of death)
are common to all of us. Nevertheless, we can and should expect to
find many significant and sometimes fascinating differences, and this
will be particularly important to us as we try to summarize some set of
virtues that is definitive of business life. In a moment, we will consider
one well-developed list of virtues that is quite different from our own,
a list that as you may have anticipated, comes from Aristotle. He canonized for all time the virtues of a very particular Athenian society at
a very particular moment in its history. It is important to keep in mind
that Aristotle's Athens was no longer the Greece of Homer's *Illiad,* no
longer a crude tribe in conflict with other crude tribes, but a *polis,* a
free and sophisticated city-state (compared with any other society in
ancient history) with a relatively representative government and a rich
heritage of art, philosophy, and statesmanship. Courage in battle was
still an important virtue—in fact, the first virtue that Aristotle mentions—but it was by no means the only or the most important one.
Achilles and Agamemnon, two heroes of the Trojan War, would have
been considered barbarians in Aristotle's Athens.

The fact that a virtue must be considered good within the context of
one's particular society means that the virtues will vary from context to
context, whether because they serve some specific practical function
(having a good business sense in the corporate world or knowing how
to handle snakes on a snake farm) or because they appeal to the particular ideal or *telos* of the culture (being faithful in a religious society or
being effective and efficient in the office). Being able to fight well with
a sword and being the fastest gun in the West are no longer virtues in
late twentieth-century America. At most, they might be salable skills in
Hollywood. Having the talent to be a crack computer programmer would
not have been a virtue during the Trojan War and having a superb
sense of humor would not have been a virtue in a medieval Carmelite
monastery. Philosophers have often argued that morality is defined in
part by its universality, but few ethicists have been tempted to say that
about the virtues. Indeed, the most striking thing about the virtues is
how they vary from culture to culture and through history. We take a
sense of humor to be of paramount importance; it is hard for us to
accept the fact that there are societies in which our sometimes-raucous
laughter is considered both foolish and obnoxious. We, on the other
hand, take a dim view of tragedy and overconcern with death, but there

are many cultures in which proper attitudes and behavior toward death are core virtues, permeating all of life.[3] Attitudes toward food and sex vary enormously from culture to culture, and what counts as gluttony and perversity in one culture is normal and desirable behavior in another. Even friendliness, which we consider a virtue, varies considerably from culture to culture for not every society prides itself on being as "open" as we are. What Americans call "friendliness" is greeted in many parts of the world as foolishness, and it is all too common for Americans to declare another people "unfriendly" because immediate intimacy with free-spending Yankee tourists is not forthcoming. But even here, despite the often mawkish paeans to friendship that proliferate in the press and on weekend camping trips, it is often said in business as in international politics that one has no friends, only interests. This is, I believe, a serious error (in politics as in business), but it gives us fair warning that the nature of the virtues in business cannot just be taken for granted. Could it be, as some people are always saying, that the virtues of business are not like those in the rest of life, that they require deviousness and brutality that otherwise (for example, with friends or in family life) would be deemed intolerable?[4]

To understand the complexity of business virtues, we must from the outset remind ourselves that the virtues, as context-bound, are determined not only by the very general and heterogeneous practice of "business" but by particular roles and circumstances. A small shopkeeper finds himself in a very different situation than an executive vice-president in charge of operations in a large commercial bank, and it is tempting to say that there may be virtually nothing they share in common and no virtue appropriate for both of them. But certain blanket or "mandatory" all-purpose virtues, notably honesty and trustworthiness, will nevertheless be essential for both, with considerable latitude in meaning.[5] One might suggest (with caution) that courage no longer has this "mandatory" status, but instead has become a virtue valued only in somewhat extraordinary situations. Even then, however, although we praise courage in the face of dire threats, we do not usually chastize the lack of courage (which is more often than not reclassified as "prudence" or "playing it smart"—Falstaff's "discretion"—rather than cowardice). Courage is still a virtue, to be sure, but it has become an extraordinary virtue, depending upon especially threatening contexts. Courage has also become something of a specialty virtue, almost a skill,

3. The ancient Egyptians are a notable if distant example.

4. Notably, Alfred Carr, in his infamous "Is Business Bluffing Ethical?" *Harvard Business Review* (Jan.–Feb. 1968). But even those critics who saw through Carr's clumsy sophistry nevertheless left open the question whether business virtues might indeed be more like those of the poker player than the family minister.

5. The classification of "mandatory" moral virtues comes from Edmond Pincoffs, *Quandaries and Virtues* (Lawrence: University Press of Kansas, 1986).

to be "hired out" in times of crisis. But virtues, though context-bound, are not just specialized skills or talents, and in addition to the technical and particular virtues specific to certain roles and professions (quick calculative ability in accounting, friendly persuasiveness in sales), there are generic virtues that deserve to be called "business virtues." Dependability and integrity would be two good examples, and though the applications may be very different for our shopkeeper and our senior vice-president, there seems to be no doubt that the virtues themselves are appropriate and important for both of them. What makes business virtues problematic is not the enormous variety and complexity of business life but rather the dramatic confluence and conflict between very different kinds of virtues.

18

Aristotelean Virtues: Warrior, Moral, Business

> [George] Washington, almost from the moment of his death, became a legend symbolizing (among other things) the "superiority" of American military leaders over foreign officers because of their great strength of character.
>
> ERNEST GREENWOOD, "Attributes of a Profession"

Military metaphors suggest military virtues, and if business life were indeed the brutal and heroic world of Homer's *Iliad* and corporations were tribes in moral conflict with one another, we would expect the business virtues to be those most closely associated with combat, not only strength and prowess but courage, imperviousness to pain or pity, frightfulness (that is, causing fright in others, not being frightened oneself). We would expect the warrior to have an appropriately insensitive personality, rather clumsy social habits, and an enormous ego. Not surprising, these are precisely the virtues often praised by and attributed to top business executives, summarized (badly) in the single word, "toughness." But, of course, warrior metaphors depend on a warlike situation, and we have taken considerable pains to dismiss that picture of corporate business life as pathological and misleading.[1] And most CEOs, however "tough," do not fit this picture at all. Consider, instead, a very different picture of the corporation, as a wealthy and prosperous *polis*, with considerable pride in its products, philosophy, and corporate culture. There would still be external threats and an occasional battle, but this would no longer be the day-to-day concern of the community. Courage might still be an important virtue, but most of the other warrior virtues and the typical characteristics of the war-

1. For good discussions of the problematic virtue of toughness in positions of leadership, I recommend William Galston "Toughness as a Political Virtue," *Journal of Social Philosophy: Virtues in Social Theory* (Summer 1991); and Thomas Nagel, "Ruthlessness in Public Life." in *Public and Private Morality*, ed. Stuart Hampshire (Cambridge University Press, 1978).

199

rior personality would seem boorish and bullish, inappropriate in most social settings and downright embarrassing in some. The virtues, in such a society, would tend to be the genteel, congenial virtues, those that lubricate a rich, pleasant social life. And these will be just as applicable to the CEO as to the boy at the loading dock or the teller at the checkout window. Consider, with this in mind, Aristotle's classic list of virtues[2]:

Courage	Friendliness
Temperance	Truthfulness
Liberality	Wittiness
Magnificence	Shame
Pride	Justice (a very general virtue)
Good Temper	Honor (a public virtue)

Aristotle's list does not include the military virtues, except courage, which he describes as an occasionally necessary virtue but hardly the central one. Far more important is justice—which in the warrior mentality means simply "to the victor go the spoils" but in genteel society involves complicated deliberations about merit, need, status, equality, and fairness. Of paramount importance is honor, which is not so much a virtue in its own right as it is the sum of the virtues, one's character as a virtuous person. To be sure, a warrior might fight for his honor, but we usually take this to mean some challenge to his fighting ability or his willingness or readiness to fight. Honor for Aristotle has much more to do with one's status in society, being recognized as a just and generous and not a miserly man, for example, and not humiliating oneself with lewd displays or excess of food, song, drink. Taken as a description not of the Greek city-state but of the corporation, we can recognize here too many of the virtues ascribed to the best executives, who are moderate and often surprisingly modest, generous with their time and money, concerned first and foremost with their and the company's reputation (honor), and loathe to risk any action that might be humiliating. So, too, such virtues as charm, wit, and friendliness are recognized as extremely important. Probably no one has reached the executive floor by wit alone, but few have succeded without it. It is necessary to lead and to lead effectively, of course, but it is more important to lead not as an Achilles or an Agamemnon charging ahead

2. The following discussion of Aristotle's list of the virtues is adapted from my *Ethics: A Short Introduction* (Madison: Brown and Benchmark, 1992) pt. III, with the permission of the editor.

on his own through the scattering Trojans but as an admirable, inspiring human being. Best-selling books to the contrary, Genghis Khan and Attila the Hun would not be successful corporate leaders today, nor would the successful executive find that much to learn from Machiavelli.

But we are not an Aristotelean society, and the corporation is not simply a *polis*. The Homeric world of the warrior is three thousand years old, and the world of Aristotle well over two thousand. Since then, a great deal has happened in the world, and as social circumstances have changed, so has our conception of the virtues. And what has happened, to condense millions of events and pages into a phrase or two, is the domination of Christianity and the rise of the individual. Put these two together (in fact our concept of the individual largely originated in the Christian conception of the individual soul) and one gets, among many other aspects of the modern world, John Calvin's unique conception of individual salvation and its manifestations in wordly success, and Adam Smith's revolutionary notion of individual enterprise serving the social good. Calvin incorporated in his philosophy a good many of the traditional Christian virtues, even as he altered the worldview of that religion to make ample room for business. Adam Smith, of course, was a good Christian too. At the foundation of his free enterprise model lay a conception of human nature that was deeply social and sympathetic, and he too was much concerned with the Christian virtues and how they might be made to fit into the rapidly expanding economy of the eighteenth century. But these virtues, although appropriately genteel for a gentlemanly Scottish bourgeoisie, were no longer Aristotelean virtues. The warrior virtues had all but disappeared (courage was now strictly a domestic virtue, and one given more lip service than attention), the congenial virtues were demoted to a kind of second place, and what we now call the *moral* virtues and had become primary. Even toughness, we will see, is best understood as a moral virtue—akin to moral courage—rather than a warrior virtue.

Aristotle used the word "moral" simply to mean "practical." But with the Judeo-Christian tradition the words "moral," and "morality" came to take on weighty, even cosmic meanings. Morality was that code given to us (or imposed on us) by God. Morality referred not to the things that make life pleasant or congenial but to a small set of essentials, rules that are not to be broken under any circumstances. Morality was cut off from its social base, the *polis* presumed by Aristotle, and became more and more a concern of God and the individual, only secondarily of society. Thus the virtues came to be identified with individual morality and, by the end of the eighteenth century, increasingly with the abstract rules of reason that dictated universal morality, a natural development of the ethics of the Ten Commandments. And like the Ten Commandments, the virtues came to be more concerned with abstinence than excellence and more concerned with "being a good person" than congeniality. A good person, depending on the severity of one's moral and religious upbringing, doesn't lie, doesn't cheat, doesn't do anything dishonest, doesn't drink or eat to excess—not only to avoid social humiliation but to avoid displaying that lack of control or self-indulgence that is the sure sign of a weak or corrupted personality. And here too, we see the virtues upon which a great many of the chief executives of our largest corporations pride themselves.

One might insist, just to waylay the argument I seem to be developing here, that warrior virtues, congeniality (Aristotelean) virtues, and moral virtues are in fact quite compatible, and there is no reason why a Lee Iococca, for example, can't display warrior toughness, Aristotelean gentility, and Christian righteousness. And indeed, this is the case. But my argument is not that these three sets of virtues are incompatible as such, but rather that they present us with three quite distinct contexts and three different ethical frameworks, and to understand business ethics is to understand the confluence, the priorities, and the potential conflicts between these. When excessive attention is paid to corporate battles and the warrior virtues, social harmony within the corporation may become a screaming alliance of desperation, and one's personal sense of integrity can be threatened or fatally damaged. Excessive attention to the congenial virtues may in fact "soften" a company so that it becomes less competitive, and an exaggerated sense of righteousness to the detriment of congeniality and competitiveness may well cause a company to shatter into a thousand rigid little moralists, incapable of working together. But what makes the framework of this book Aristotelean is precisely the emphasis on Aristotle's own perspective on the virtues, in which it is cooperation and not an isolated individual sense of self-worth that defines the most important virtues, in which the warrior virtues play an essential but diminished role, in which the well-being of the community goes hand in hand with individual excellence, not by virtue of any "invisible hand" but precisely because of the social consciousness and public spirit of each and every individual.

One of the things to notice about Aristotle's list of virtues is that it includes both moral and congenial virtues, underscoring the importance of thinking about ethics as essentially a community-bound, interpersonal concern. So, too, in business ethics, the Aristotelean view takes ethics to be not an imposition from above (reason or the divine law) nor a matter of internal, individual conscience and consciousness, but a set of virtues and values that are formed by the practice of business and cultivated (whether or not formulated) by the business community. Aristotle's list also includes virtues we would not usually consider as such: pride, for instance. We tend rather to think of pride as a vice, or at best as a kind of defensiveness. The closest we come to understanding Aristotle's virtue is in our accusation, "Have you no pride?!" But Aristotle obviously means more than the unwillingness to humiliate oneself. To be proud is to see oneself in terms of one's accomplishments and value them. It does not mean being a snob or smug and condescending. Coupled with a appropriate gratitude (too often confused with humility) pride is ultimately a communal virtue, not just an individual attitude. In the corporation, pride plays a peculiar but central role in the virtues. Pride in the product, pride in the company, pride in the people one works with—these are all not only acceptable but the ideal of every corporate employee, manager, or executive.

The pursuit of excellence is expected, of course, except in those troubled companies or departments that, despite their free enterprise status, insist on following the old Eastern European model of mutually encouraged (and enforced) mediocrity. The pursuit of excellence, in turn, requires the recognition of excellence and, in the case of one's own work, self-acknowledgment of a job well done. But there the virtue of pride comes to a screeching halt. To talk about one's own excellence, much less to *brag* about it, is considered a serious vice, indeed, in some circumstances sufficient to undermine whatever credit one deserved for the original accomplishment. And yet we notice that humility does not appear in Aristotle's list, and we can be certain that it would not have appeared in Agamemnon's list of virtues. Our sense of virtue presumes a modest sense of self, which may be why we have so much trouble dealing with excellence even while we make such a big deal about it.

Almost all of Aristotle's virtues are recognizable as business virtues, and this is, of course, not surprising. Business is, above all, a social activity, involving dealing with other people in both stressful and friendly situations (and trying to make the former into the latter). Despite our emphasis on hardheadedness and the bottom line, we do not praise and often despise tight-fistedness, and we do praise great-souled generosity ("magnificence"). But such virtues may be misleading for us. We would not praise an executive who "gave away the store"; we would instead think that executive mentally unhinged. But the virtues for Aristotle do not involve radical demands on our behavior, and the sort of fanaticism praised if not often practiced in many religions (giving away *all* one's worldly goods) is completely foreign to Aristotle's insistence on "moderation." Thus the generous or "magnificent" person gives away only as much of wealth as will increase his or her status in the community. Here we would encounter the familiar charge that such giving is not true generosity, for it involves no personal sacrifice and includes a "selfish" motive, the quest for self-aggrandizement. But Aristotle would refuse to recognize this opposition between enlightened self-interest and virtue, and we continue to enforce it at our peril. The argument here, of course, is exactly the skeptical argument leveled against generous corporations when they give to the arts, education and social welfare programs: "They're only doing it for the P.R." But here executives (and everyone else) would be wise to follow Aristotle and reject the notion that "true" generosity is self-sacrifice and that self-benefiting generosity is "only P.R." There are occasions that call for self-sacrifice, but to insist that such extreme action is essential to the virtues is to deny the virtues their relevance to life in business and most other areas.

So, too, what Aristotle calls "temperance" is not at all the abstinence that we refer to by that name; indeed, Aristotle and his friends would have looked down upon someone who refused on principle to indulge in wine and song as an insufferable bore. Such virtues for Aristotle are social virtues of congeniality, not moral virtues (in our weighty sense), and joining in and bolstering the sense of camaraderie is far more desirable than making a moralistic stance. The man who drinks too much and shouts in the streets may be an embarrassment to himself and to his friends, but he does not give any particular offense to the gods (who were more than likely amused). Temperance is tempered by camaraderie and community; it is not a commandment from God or an absolute dictate of conscience. Of course, there was that special Greek vice, *hubris,* which should not be read as mere boastfulness or lack of modesty but as an actual challenge to the gods. But this was a distinctively god-oriented vice and therefore very different from the others. Aristotle's ethics is concerned with community. Where we would identify vices first of all in terms of their violation of explicit principles of morality, Aristotle would point out their social offensiveness and their violation of ordinary reason. In business ethics, this sense is essential. The only stipulation must always be that it is not just the business community *alone* that is the arbiter of appropriate business virtues and values.

Before we go on to explore the idea of "business virtues" as such, we should take a moment to counter what may well be a growing objection in the reader's mind: couldn't all of this emphasis on community and the rejection of "externally imposed" values lead to the unwitting but nevertheless unavoidable acceptance of a pathological community that internally condoned even the most vile practices. Indeed, Aristotle's own *polis* would seem to provide just such an example. Virtually half of the inhabitants of Athens were slaves, and the prosperous economy of Athens—and the leisurely life of its statesmen and philosophers—was made possible only by the institution of slavery. Don't we need externally imposed standards to forbid such abominations? Suppose that the entire business community agreed that the use of cheap, Third World child labor was an acceptable way to lower the prices of manufactured goods. Shouldn't such a practice be universally condemned? And if not by the business community itself, then from the outside?

This is, of course, a crucial argument for any defense of the Aristotelean approach, and one of the reproaches of business ethics itself (from the Left) has been its lack of distance from the business community and its consequent failure to criticize the whole world of business and its practices "from the outside." But from where should moral criticism of the business community come? And to take the most extreme example, how would one argue against the reinstitution of slavery, if the entire business community (or at least a large majority) approved of it?

Our first response, as expected, is to repeat our insistence that the community in question is never a single company or industry or even the business community. Business is part of and beholden to the larger society, and the business community is part of a greater community. There are severe limits, therefore, to what extent business practices can deviate from more general social practices and basic social guidelines. Of course, business, like some sports, may condone a kind of brutality that would be utterly unacceptable out of the ring or off the playing field, but the essential ingredient in every such practice is that all participants have agreed to and are prepared for the brutality involved. But that eliminates the threat of slavery and exploitative child labor, in the first case because we cannot imagine that slaves, given a real choice, would themselves agree to slavery, and in the second case because children (and not only children) are not suitable or "prepared" for the harsh conditions of manufacturing—if only because they deserve a childhood.[3] Furthermore, because the values of the business community are for the most part the values of the larger society, there are "internal" values that determine the injustice of such practices. This may not have been true in Athens, but in the United States the principle that everyone is created equal was already in place and much debated by the Founding Fathers, however long it took them or their successors to apply the principle to slaves. And that means that slavery was wrong, even if it was not acknowledged to be wrong, by the same people who engaged in the practice.[4] So, too, business sometimes engages in exploitative practices that are wrong, not just from the point of view of the "outside" but by virtue of the egalitarian sensibility and the sense of fairness shared by the business community itself.

To criticize and attack such practices, therefore, does not require an

3. There are enormous disputes, of course, about attitudes toward slavery among the slaves in the American South before 1863. But it seems obvious that acceptance of an institution because one has been refused an education about one's options and alternatives in life does not count as "agreeing" to the terms of slavery, and although it might be similarly argued (with the convenience of two thousand years intervening) that the slaves of Athens themselves accepted the institution of slavery in their own provinces and only regretted their own status as slaves, it does not follow that their accepting slavery means that they implicitly agreed to their own servitude. In Athens, and elsewhere, slavery always presupposes force and suppression, not community.

4. Just to avoid regional righteousness, let's remind ourselves that slavery was still practiced in New York City until the 1820s.

external imposition of values or principles. Of course, there is the lingering possibility of an entire society, not just a community within society or a set of practices, becoming cancerous, and though this is not a problem for the specific concerns of business ethics, it is by no means a possibility to be taken lightly. My answer is that, without being romantic or utopian, there is such a thing as the human community, and there are certain foundations to our behavior in what is called "human nature." It is with reference to these large parameters that one can without intellectual humility criticize fascism and human rights abuses as well as those abuses of the multinational business community that do not seem to be easily contained within the bounds of a single society.[5] But my concern in this book is not with such global issues but distinctively local matters. The Aristotelean view presupposes a larger framework that meets with our general approval. (There is little to be said in defense of business to one who rejects the very idea of a business society). And that larger framework has everything to do with the actual function and aims of business in society.

5. For a good discussion of this thorny topic, see Tom Donaldson's *Business Ethics in the International Marketplace* (New York: Oxford University Press, 1990).

19

The Basic Business Virtues: Honesty, Fairness, Trust, and Toughness

A reasonable estimate of economic organizations must allow for the fact that, unless industry is to be paralyzed by recurrent revolts on the part of outraged human nature, it must satisfy criteria that are not purely economic.

R. H. TAWNEY, *Religion and the Rise of Capitalism*

Business is a social activity, specifically, the activity of exchanging money, goods, and services. It may be, at its most primitive, mere barter, or it may involve the extremely sophisticated sale and purchase of stock or futures options on the commodities exchange. But the very idea of exchange in business has built into it the requirement of mutual agreement, the expectation of an honest accounting, and a fair exchange. Of course, an exchange can be mutually agreed upon without being honest, but then one rightly questions (possibly in court) whether the exchange has then actually even taken place. So, too, one can have a mutually agreed upon exchange that is not fair, but this is reason for just complaint and, again, a plausible cause for litigation. In one sense, the whole point of mutual agreement is fairness, and it is often assumed by legal and political thinkers that an agreement between knowledgeable, intelligent, informed, and consenting adults is thereby fair, even if (from outside eyes) the balance of exchange is by no means equal and one person is getting a much better deal than the other. Of course, such an agreement may be compromised by duress or what Hobbes called "force," but so long as the agreement itself is not extorted or compelled, the deal is generally considered valid. (There are extreme exceptions, such as the high price of life-prolonging medicine for the desperately ill.) The importance of mutual agreement in business is absolutely essential. It is the first premise in the logic of personal freedom upon which the entire edifice of free enterprise thinking is built.

My surreptiously replacement of your worn-out radio with a brand new digital clock-radio that I know you want is not a business transaction, no matter how delighted you may be at the outcome. There has been no mutual agreement. A transaction with a child or someone mentally deficient, a "deal" with your dog or a friendly cow is not a business transaction, no matter how well intended. There has been no mutual agreement because there can be no assumption of mutual knowledge or understanding. An exchange with a stranger holds all sorts of pit-falls: assumptions of mutual knowledge and understanding that may well not be the case. (Consider a cab driver counting out change for a first-time foreign tourist.) The virtues of business are just those traits of character that make mutual knowledge or understanding possible.

In other words, the very nature of business is to be open and honest, to make one's goods or service available to others and to make them known for what they are, with a positive "spin," no doubt, but with considerable accuracy nonetheless. The precondition of business is the virtue of the participants. This is not to make an extraordinarily naive suggestion that we should trust everyone. It is only to say that without a modicum of trust and a general practice of candor and honesty there could be no exchange and no business. There are also any number of instrumental virtues involved here, which only come to our attention when suddenly we notice their absence. There is the mutual recognition of equal worth, the value of a commodity or service, the ability to recognize, count, and value money (a skill often amusingly lacking in children). There are communications skills assumed, to be able to talk, negotiate, phone, write, or fax, and with all such exchanges of information the virtue of honesty (and secondarily truthfulness) is essential. Immanuel Kant gives the example of a false promise to pay back borrowed money, and reflectively considers the consequences if everyone did that. He quickly concludes that such promises would be greeted with ridicule as vain pretenses.[1] Indeed, we don't have to ponder the overwhelming (and ultimately nonsensical) thought that "everyone did that." It would be quite enough if it happened more than once in a while. Witness the normal reaction to being taken advantage of in a shop or a mail-order catalog: "I'll never shop with them again!" Being stranded once without help by an airline or burned once with excessive rent-a-car charges may be enough to switch brand loyalties for life, and a single bank failure even on the other end of the country is enough to shake the trust of depositors. In other words, trustworthiness is not a sign of naiveté but one of the presuppositions of the business world, and dependability is not an extraordinary gesture on the part of a business but the basic criterion for its continued existence. Of course, here we always find the exceptions, the "fly-by-night" companies and the

---

1. Immanuel Kant, *Grounding of the Metaphysics of Morals*, sec. II.

one-shot deals, but, as we argued in our discussion of "game theory" in business, such exceptions are not to be taken as the general rule.

As I have stated, such notions as "honest advertising" and "truth in lending" are not simply legal impositions upon business life nor are they saintly ideals that are unrealistic for people in business. They are rather the preconditions of business and, as such, the essential virtues for any business dealing. Along with these cardinal business virtues goes a network of communicative and logical virtues as well, notably demands of relevance, coherence and consistency, the demands of clear unambiguous expression, the ability to speak and to listen—not just as a sales tool but as an essential. The loud and just complaints against so much of advertising these days (especially political advertising) is not that they spout falsehoods but rather that they spew irrelevancies, including a great many in poor taste. The standard repulsed reaction against the aggressive salesman is not so much because of what he says (as if one really listens), but because of the manner of presentation, the repetitiveness, and, most of all, the clearly intentional aim of preventing the buyer from having a moment to think things through and make an intelligent decision. Not that purchases (especially large, personal purchases) are normally made with very much rationality or intelligence, but the aggressive salesman interferes with one of our basic rights as consumers—and, again, one of the presuppositions of business as such—namely, the right to make our own stupid decisions without interference or the use of force by anyone.

So, too, one of the basic virtues of business is that broad notion that we call *fairness*. We will have more to say about fairness later on, under the more philosophically proper title of "justice." But for now, it is enough to say that fairness isn't so much an ideal in business as a basic expectation. It has to do with honesty, dependability, and trust, insofar as mutual agreement is, in business, the hallmark of fairness. It also has to do with the notion of equivalence or "equity," the equal value of what is exchanged, whether it be goods, work, or wages. But it is not as if "fair price" and "fair wages" and "reasonable returns" are marked in heaven, which once again brings us back to the importance of mutual agreement, which, writ large, is what we call "market value." What counts as "fair," accordingly, is always in some sense a subjective judgment, based not just on the individual feelings and needs of the immediate participants but on the larger collective consciousness as well. It is remarkable, however, how vigorously this sense of market has been and still is resisted. Aristotle and Aquinas really did write as if prices and the wages of labor were somehow written into the nature of things, and even Adam Smith (and after him Karl Marx) tried to tack down "intrinsic values" above and beyond market values in order to insist that some things (such as human labor) had their true worth even if certain commodities were left to the vicissitudes of supply and demand.

True, there is such a thing as an "inflated market," but typically this refers not to some transcendental value behind the market but the recognition that prices and real demand (as opposed to artificial stimulation) are out of sync.

Fairness in business, in other words, is a certain kind of "attunement," a sense of value and a willingness to exchange value for value in a market that provides no ultimately objective guideposts. It also means that negotiation skills are not nearly so incidental or special as we are often lead to believe. We are mislead, I think, by the "microeconomic" fact that most of the goods and services we buy are offered to us beforehand with a price tag, as if the value were already set (which we notice especially, of course, when it is set too high). But the nature of the free market is that even the most "set" prices are the outcome of a grand negotiation, often of thousands of consumers acting as a block even as they think of themselves acting only as individuals. The point is more obvious in many foreign bazaars, where the very idea of a fixed price (as opposed to a fair price) is nonsensical. But again, the point of all of this is that the notion of fairness in the market is ultimately a function of mutual agreement. The virtues of facilitation, or what we have called the congenial virtues (the basic Aristotelean virtues), are the essential virtues of business activity.

Honesty is the first virtue of business life. Honesty, to put it sweet and simple, means telling the truth, being told what you are getting or, at least, what you are letting yourself in for. Honesty does not, however, mean "full disclosure," and there are certain aspects of every transaction that are expected to be unknown and undisclosed. Every transaction involves a certain amount of risk and uncertainty, and that risk and uncertainty may even be the focus of the deal itself (as in certain forms of gambling and, of course, in may "securities" and commodities exchanges). If someone buys a used car or an old house, he or she cannot possibly be expected to be told everything about the liabilities about to be obtained. Indeed, the practice of buying used cars (and to a lesser extend old houses) is already riddled with high expectations about risk and low expectations about disclosure. But there are limits, of course, and a great many expectations nevertheless. A seller may not tell about a shaky transmission or a potentially leaky roof, but he or she is bound to tell the truth if asked. (The Roman philosopher Cicero worried about leaky roofs two thousand years ago, and where roofs are involved, business ethics seems not to have changed much since then.) Not knowing the answer to a direct question may sometimes be an excuse for not answering, but not always. There are some things that the buyer can be expected to ask and has the right to know, which means the seller has an obligation to find out in turn. (A record of automobile mileage, for example, is tightly regulated by law, and house-termite inspection is now built into madated purchase agreements in most states in the United States.) "Good faith" provisions often dictate what is relevant to a business transaction, but it would be a mistake to think of these as spelled out explicitly, much less formulated into law. "Buyer beware" may be a now-archaic piece of micro-economic advice, but the importance of general awareness of the specifics of the particular practice in which one is participating is an essential virtue on the purchasing side of the deal. There are others, of course—paying on time, but bouncing checks—but asking the right questions and having the knowledge to come to an informed mutual agreement is the complement of the basic virtues expected of the seller. Indeed, one of the most frustrating issues in business ethics is convincing the consumer, and not just the person in business, that he or she too has obligations and responsibilities, and knowledge—and acting on that knowledge—is first and foremost among them.

Not disclosing is different from a refusal to disclose, and this is different again from dishonesty. As so often in matters of ethics, distinctions are made in black and white, and so any adequate understanding is closed to us.[2] The contrast between honesty and dishonesty is not a simple black-and-white contrast between right and wrong but (to extend the metaphor) they are two extremes in a rich colorful spectrum, in which the presence of risk and uncertainty as well as the frequent need to not tell all render both black and white a painterly and often illusory surface of many mixed colors. Insofar as every transaction involves some risk, it also precludes total honesty, even the seemingly straightforward "I don't know." The tolerance for risk varies, of course. What the pharmacist or the surgeon says to a patient has protections and constraints that are not present for the television consumer who calls a toll-free number to buy the "surprise value of the week." Often, not disclosing means simply not having been asked the right question ("you never asked me"), but sometimes the question can be taken for granted, even if never thought of ("well, you never asked me if the automobile had an engine"). Refusal to disclose when asked is not necessarily unethical, of course, but it certainly changes the nature of the transaction. Risk then moves from being an ordinary but marginal liability to the center stage of the bargain. Thus Carr on business bluffing is at best talking about the kind of transaction that has already gone partially sour or is from the first a special case.[3] Business (like much else in life) may involve bluffing but ordinary business presumes the very opposite, candor and straightforward information. The presence or possibility of bluffing changes the focus of the transaction (as in

2. See, for example, Ezra Bowen's essay on "business and literacy" in *Business Ethics: The State of the Art*, ed. R. Edward Freeman (New York: Oxford University Press, 1991), p. 186, "the fact is that ethics, or accountability, comes in two decorator colors: black and white." I recommend Joanne Ciulla's reply in the same book.

3. Alfred Carr, "Is Business Bluffing Ethical?" *Harvard Business Review* (Jan.–Feb. 1968).

poker) to deviation and cover-up, to the psychology of the players rather than the mere commodity or service in question.

Dishonesty, finally, is not refusal to inform but the giving of false information. This is, perhaps, straightforwardly a vice—even in poker—but it does not follow that it is always a vice. Like all vices, it may become a virtue in extreme circumstances, the standard example is lying about the presence of your friend who is hiding from the Gestapo, or, in business, lying to a customer to *discourage* a purchase that might be ill-afforded or dangerous. What's more, the lie may be virtuous even if (and not because) it should turn out to be true.[4] But in any ordinary business circumstances, dishonesty undermines and invalidates the agreement. The very nature of an agreement after all, presupposes that all parties know *to what* they are agreeing. Dishonesty, accordingly, undoes the very idea of a business exchange, and despite the routine charges of rampant and widespread dishonesty in the business world there can in fact be relatively little dishonesty if that world is to continue to function at all.

Honesty isn't everything, however. One of the odder complications of honesty and truth telling is the fact that people often have vices that work against (or for, depending on your point of view) the effort to be honest. First and foremost among these is *self-deception,* that uncanny ability that we have to fool ourselves as well as (often better than) other people. When one is self-deceived, one honestly tells what he or she thinks to be the truth. Is the resulting falsehood a lie? So, too, people who are honest are sometimes weak-willed[5] and, accordingly, do not deliver on what they quite sincerely promised. And then again, some people change their minds. They meant it when they said it, but now they wouldn't say it at all. Thus dependability ranks along with honesty as one of the cardinal business virtues, particularly given the time-lag nature of most business deals. In a barter system or in small market transactions, exchanges may be simultaneous ("give it to me, and I'll give this to you"). But we often order products in advance, even have them made up especially for us, and with the time lapse between the order and the delivery, and the delivery and the payment, dependability makes all of the difference. It is not enough for the deal to be good. It has to actually come about as well. Many a sucker has been taken in by the offer of a bargain "too good to be believed" just because it was. The deal was terrific but the product advertised never arrived. Again,

---

4. Jean-Paul Sartre wrote an early short story called "The Wall," in which a captured resistance fighter lies about the whereabouts of his good friend, who will no doubt be tortured and killed if caught. It turns out, however, that the friend has moved to the place mentioned in the lie, and so he is caught after all. The virtue of the lie, however, remains, though Sartre's character is, needless to say, less than self-righteous about the outcome. See *The Well and Other Stories* (New York: New Directions, 1948).

5. What Aristotle called *akrasia,* or "incontinence."

it is not hard to see just how fragile this system can be and how few frauds it takes to wreck the system. One of my students had a part-time job selling surgical equipment over the phone, and most of her time was spent calling the supply company to find out when (if ever) the goods would be available and soothing irate purchasers when their bargain-priced goods were six to eight months late. One might debate whether such a business is dishonest as well as undependable, but the net result is the same—a paradigm of that kind of fraud which gives business a bad name and, in volume, puts one out of business.

Finally, trust is not the same as naiveté, a point that often has to be made again and again for both distrustful consumers and self-styled hardheaded business types. Trust is an attitude, a working presupposition. It is not a principle, much less the principle that one ought to trust everyone. But, mixed with experience and judgment and open to the possibility that sometimes we all get "burned," one needs trust in order to enter into even the simplest transactions and activities, indeed, even to walk down the street. It is trust that makes the system work, the fundamental supposition that most of the people are honest and dependable most of the time. That is not to say that you cannot fool or be fooled, but that network of community and shared expectations that we have taken to be the heart of the Aristotelean view of business might just as well be called "trust." Indeed, if Aristotle did not mention it as one of his virtues (and he was by no means naive about the treachery that pervaded the Athenian *polis*), it was rather because he took it for granted. No practice and no community could even begin to survive without it.

This brings us to the perhaps most misunderstood virtue in business life, the virtue of *toughness*. The word "tough" is typically used by way of admiration, though often coupled with a shake of the head and an expression of frustration. Sometimes, it is used as a euphemism, in place of or in conjunction with various synonyms for a nasty or odious human being. Not infrequently, it simply means stubborn, impossible, or meanspirited. But toughness is generally and genuinely perceived as a virtue, albeit a virtue that is often misplaced and misconceived. Insofar as business consists of bargaining and dealing with other people, toughness is essential, and its opposite is not so much weakness as incompetence. But much of what is called toughness is neither a virtue nor a vice. It is not a character trait so much as it is a skill, whether cultivated or "natural." In certain central business practices, notably negotiating, toughness is not so much a personal virtue as it is a technique or set of techniques, an acquired manner and an accomplished strategy, "knowing when to hold 'em, knowing when to fold 'em." Toughness includes knowing how to bluff and when to keep silent, when to be cooperative and when not to be. But such a skill is not, contra Carr, unethical or divorced from ordinary morals; it is a legitimate part of a certain kind of obviously legitimate activity. Yet, as a specific skill or set of skills, being a tough negotiator is not sufficiently personal or general to count as a virtue, which is not to say, of course, that it is not therefore admirable or necessary.

Very often, what "toughness" means is simply "smart," that is, knowing the business, knowing one's competitors and dealings, knowing how to get things done. Again, this is an admirable and necessary set of business qualifications but not, as such, a virtue. But toughness also means perseverance, which is a personal as well as a business virtue. As always, Aristotle's standard of moderation comes into play here, for there is such a thing as too much perseverance, which then becomes mere obstinacy or stubbornness. Of course, what seemed like obstinacy to those of little faith may well turn out to be richly rewarded by the results, and what was indeed healthy perseverance may nevertheless turn to failure in the vicissitudes of the market. But too little "stick-to-it-iveness" makes success virtually impossible and makes life intolerable for those investors, employees, and other stakeholders who naturally depend on a full-blooded effort rather than a halfhearted try. Toughness as perseverance means nothing other than having a goal and a purpose, seeing its worthiness and pursuing it to the end. What makes it "tough" is facing up to setbacks and obstacles that would discourage lesser beings; indeed, it is only in the face of failure that such toughness is truly tested, for it is no virtue to "persevere" when the market is handing you nothing but success.

Toughness in an executive also has an ethically painful element. Sometimes it is necessary to do something wrong in order to do what is right. Powerful politicians, of course, face such dilemmas all of the time, giving rise to a substantial literature on the controversial virtues of toughness and ruthlessness and the allegedly opposed domains of public and private morality.[6] Sometimes, to reach a higher goal, one must do what one otherwise would not and should not even consider. For example, in the face of debts or deficiencies that will very likely capsize the company, a chairman may need to let go perfectly qualified, hard-working, loyal employees. Viewed as an action isolated from the circumstances, letting people go for no reason whatever—that is, for no fault of their own—would be the height of injustice. But if it is a matter of saving the company, then this otherwise-unjust act may nevertheless be necessary. Toughness is being able and willing to undertake such measures. This is not to say, however—and this cannot be emphasized enough—that such decisions can or should be made with-

6. See, for example, Stuart Hampshire, ed., *Public and Private Morality* (Cambridge: Cambridge University Press, 1978), and his own *Innocence and Experience* (Cambridge: Harvard University Press, 1989). See also Bernard Williams, "Politics and Moral Character," in his *Moral Luck* (Cambridge: Cambridge University Press, 1981), and Thomas Nagel, "Ruthlessness in Public Life" in the Hampshire collection.

out guilt or pain or bad feelings. It does not mean that what one has done is not, despite its necessity, wrong. The chief executive of a large corporation once told me that "downsizing" his company was the most painful thing he had ever had to do. His toughness lay not in callousness or indifference but in his willingness to do what was necessary and in his insistence on doing it as humanely as possible. Indeed, callousness and indifference are not themselves signs of toughness but the very opposite, indications of that form of weakness that can face moral issues only by denying them. Toughness is a virtue, but callousness and indifference are not, and the two should never be confused.

In politics, toughness is the phenomenon that is sometimes called "dirty hands."[7] It is the need to do what is painful or awful, even (in a small frame of reference) immoral in order to do what is right or necessary. One chief executive was asked point-blank by an elderly stockholder if his holdings in the company were safe and secure. The CEO, knowing full well that a slash in the dividend would be announced later that week, could not help but tell a lie or, at least, seriously circumnavigate the truth. Again, his personal pain and guilt were considerable, but prevarication was unavoidable. Of course, profits alone are not sufficient as an excuse, and one might thus understand the popularity and indignation surrounding Michael Moore's movie *Roger and Me*, about the closing of GM plants in Flint, Michigan. If the reason was company survival, combined with some well-publicized cutbacks in executive positions, perks, and salaries, such closings would have hardly made a movie. But when profits and perks are the motivation, toughness is not a virtue—or, in this case, toughness is callousness.

Like almost all of the virtues, toughness is not simply self-interested, but neither can it be considered an altruistic or self-sacrificing trait of character. Toughness is ultimately having a vision and persevering in the long-term plans and strategies necessary to achieve that vision. It means not being dissuaded by threats and temptations. But it does not mean an easy willingness to step on other people or violate the basic rules of morality or sacrifice the other basic virtues of business. Toughness has its place in the constellation of virtues, and sometimes it needs to yield to compassion or generosity, to trust or fairness. Again, this is no defense of naiveté, but what toughness certainly does not mean— and is far too often taken to mean—is meanspiritedness and indifference, lack of care and concern for others. Toughness is a true business

---

7. The need to do wrong in order to do good was one of the enduring obsessions of the great German sociologist, Max Weber. See his "Politics as a Vocation," in *From Max Weber: Essays in Sociology*, ed. H. Gerth and C. Mills (New York: Oxford University Press, 1946). The term "dirty hands" was popularized by Jean-Paul Sartre in his play of that name. It can be found in the volume *No Exit and Three Other Plays* (New York: Vintage, 1946). See also Michael Stocker on "The Problem of Dirty Hands," in his *Plural and Conflicting Values* (Oxford: Oxford University Press, 1990).

virtue, and in tough businesses it may even emerge as the primary business virtue, but it is not opposed to integrity. Indeed, one might well argue that it is ultimately equivalent to integrity. Toughness is a proper sense of purpose, insulated against greed as well as weakness. As such, much of what is called toughness might better be called moral courage.

20

The Virtues of the Corporate Self: Friendliness, Honor, Loyalty, Shame

> The concept of loyalty has changed from one of "blind and obligated" to one of "insightful and earned." . . . Loyalty tends to be more easily earned in those organizations that have clearly-defined values and challenging standards. People are likely to be loyal to values that lead to outstanding achievements in products, services and relationships.
>
> ALEXANDER B. HORNIMAN,
> "Whatever Happened to Loyalty"

> Where there is no shame, there is no honor.
>
> Ethiopian proverb

Aristotle tells us that the virtues are to be defined according to the purpose (the *telos*) of a practice, of a people, of what it is to be a human being as such. Business virtues, accordingly, are a subset of the virtues, those particular to furthering the purpose and practice of business. Accordingly, its virtues are those that are essential to interpersonal relationships, to the recognition of mutual needs and desires, and to the satisfaction of those needs and desires. On this account, certain sorts of virtues, such as congeniality, will obviously be high on the list of business virtues. Friendliness is basic to business, no matter how often the grump in the boss's office may be the subject of lament and literature. Like many virtues, friendliness is important most obviously in the breach, and if it sometimes seems like a vice in business, it is only because it is so routine that it often works as a "cover" for more devious motives and, on occasion, for viciousness. The very particular business virtue of "salesmanship" contains a large measure of friendliness, not only as a successful technique but as essential to the activity itself. (Without friendliness, hostile salesmanship is called "extortion.") More generally, the atmosphere of friendliness that pervades even the most tension-

217

filled company is essential to the kind of cooperation that any organization requires. The power structure of most corporations may suggest otherwise, that militaristic hierarchy and discipline is the way to insure cooperation. But the casualties and the amount of anxiety in corporations that actually practice such managerial techniques are rarely justified by the margin of success they achieve, and the much-celebrated virtue of "toughness" makes sense and is successful only within a context more broadly defined by its friendliness. Even the most military-minded companies tend to emphasize the exhilaration of competition rather than the oppressive threats of hierarchy. According to a Pepsico personnel spokesman, quoted in 1983, "Most of our guys are having fun. They are the kind of people who would rather be in the Marines than in the Army."[1]

Friendliness is one of Aristotle's most celebrated virtues, but we should be cautious about equating Aristotle's virtue with the trait that is prized in the corporate business community. Aristotle's virtue is not at all our slap-a-stranger-on-the-back-and-give-a-big-smile sense of friendliness. Friendliness for Aristotle refers more to *being* a friend than to any superficial feeling or expression of friendship. It certainly does not mean being friendly to everybody. It is selective, even snobbish, and not that general congeniality that every employee of a company is expected to display from nine to five. As such, friendship (rather than "friendliness") remains a personal value for us, but it is very different from and extraneous to the friendliness expected in the corporation. Working as hard as we do and for so many hours, it is not surprising that many people form their closest relationships with colleagues at the office. But such friendships are emphatically not essential to or part of one's corporate responsibilities—even in a designated mentor or "buddy" relationship—and, however desirable, they are not part of the corporate practice. Indeed, an extremely close friendship on the job may even be a disruption or an invitation to injustice, somewhat akin to an office romance.

The interpersonal aspect of business dictates a number of other obvious virtues, among them fairness (or "justice") in one's dealings with people, especially one's own subordinates, compassion and sympathy in dealing with their problems, gratitude and recognition of worth in responding to their accomplishments. It is quite curious how neglected such essential virtues have become in the corporate environment, provoking an avalanche of books, such as *The One Minute Manager*, that praise the art of the casual compliment as if it were a dramatic managerial breakthrough. The virtues of interpersonal relationships also include the upward-looking virtues of respect and obedience toward one's

---

1. Quoted in Solomon and Hanson, *Above the Bottom Line* (New York: Harcourt Brace Jovanovich, 1983), p. 119.

superiors, the all-important corporate virtue of loyalty, and the enormous variety of virtues (including all of these just noted) in dealing with customers, vendors, regulators, and the surrounding community. The virtues of interpersonal relationships even include such much-attended to but unrecognized virtues as attention to dress and grooming, not just for the sake of fashion (although being up-to-date is surely an important part of a business image) but because it in turn exemplifies other virtues, including neatness (although the correlation of neatness of mind and sartorial neatness is far from established), conformity to company standards, and self-respect. A key corporate virtue, of course, is one's ability and willingness to be a "team player," which even without the sports-inclined metaphor suggests cooperation and a number of other group-minded virtues. The point of all of this, of course, is to underscore our vision of business as first of all a very human practice, involved primarily with interpersonal relationships and not only with "making money." Business includes simple exchange and barter systems as well as profit-seeking corporations, and it engages the urge for shared excitement and creative self-expression through entrepreneurship as well as the desire for the rewards that follow entrepreneurial success.

The virtue of the Aristotelean approach to business ethics, I have argued, is its focus on the virtues and the character of the individual. But there is very little that is so central or essential to the character of the individual as his or her emotions, a feature of personality that is all too often treated, especially in management circles, as a taboo topic, a source of embarrassment and unbusinesslike behavior rather than the very essence of being human. But the emotions are not, as we are often lead to believe, self-contained, merely "internal" disturbances that distance us from the world and pull us into ourselves. Quite the contrary, our emotions form our attachments to the world, notably in love and kindred affections but also in a number of emotions that lead us toward an enlargement of the self. I have defended the idea that we are—even as individuals—thoroughly social, not isolated, autonomous, or selfish beings whose places in society are up for negotiation according to mutual self-interest. The Aristotelean approach must be understood, accordingly, in terms of a certain concept of self, an "expanded" self that is constituted by and identifies itself with the larger community or society. This self is defined, first of all, by its attachments and affections, the people and things that one cares about, the people and institutions whose ideals, judgments, and opinions determine not only one's success but one's very conception of self. These form the larger personal context in which business activity is motivated and success in business is determined. The "profit motive" is in fact derivative of a number of interpersonal and institutional demands, only partly determined by the market, much more powerfully determined by the people who make up the market and a network of social, cultural, political, and religious doctrines about the nature of the individual and his or her place in the good society. But an alternative, more personal way to think about this is to think of the self as itself primarily a matter of emotions, defined, as I suggested, by its attachments and affections. But here we confront the darkest dogma of traditional business thinking, the impoverished idea of *Homo economicus* who has no attachments or affections other than crude self-interest and the ability to calculate how to satisfy that interest vis-à-vis other people. It is this sense of self that the Aristotelean view is wholly devoted to devastate, and in its place suggests a larger sense of self, which is to be characterized by a special set of emotions that are not entirely absorbed in self-interest. These emotions include, from the outset, such feelings and sentiments as caring, compassion, sympathy, and devotion. And in the corporation they come to include such organizational virtues as loyalty. Too often it is assumed without argument or discussion that emotions are merely personal, whether this means that they are merely subjective, exclusively of concern to the one who experiences them, or merely physical and of no real importance. But emotions can be "about" all sorts of things, and some emotions are not only about society but involve society in the very identity of their subject. They are emotions that would be unintelligible without this larger sense of self.

Of particular interest here is a mixed set of emotions that—with the rise of radical individualism and the loss of a sense of Aristotelean virtue, the emphasis on policies and principles, and the neglect of the person—has all but dropped out of business ethics. It includes *loyalty, honor,* and a sense of *shame.* (Guilt is the contrast here, and is not part of the set.) Loyalty is a kind of integrity, not within oneself (conceived of as a self-sufficient, integral whole) but rather with oneself conceived as a part of a larger self, a group, a community, an organization, or institution. Business ethics too often ignores loyalty in favor of the more abstract and universal concepts of rights. So long as we respect contracts, one can imagine the discussion ending, what is the point of a superfluous and perhaps childish emotion like loyalty? Of course, loyalty (like patriotism, one special variant of it) can be a refuge from responsibility or a forum for venal self-righteousness, but it does not follow—as many people seem to think it does—that it is an emotion that has lost its place in the corporate world, and that our loyalties should always be first and foremost to ourselves, or to one's conscience, or to some set of "higher" standards. Every employer wants the loyalty of the employees, but the objection of such loyalty is that the employees will thereby lose sight of their own best interests and, perhaps, find themselves bound to plans or policies that they themselves find unethical or even illegal. But the argument here is not against loyalty but rather for the need for critical self-awareness in one's loyalties. It is not an argument against loyalty any more than the dangers of love are an argument against love. (Loyalty would not be wrongly conceived as a variety of love, appropriate to groups and institutions as well as to individuals.) Against the recent "work-for-hire" approach to employer-employee relations, I argue that Aristotelean emphasis on loyalty—and that means loyalty in *both* directions—has a lot to offer to business ethics that too often gets dismissed with the usual stories of uncritical loyalty and gross corporate malfeasance.[2]

Honor is a second grand emotion of the Aristotelean self, and another emotion that is an endangered species in radical individualist thinking. Honor, when we use the term at all, usually means "pride"—a very different emotion—or even "vanity"—a very different and hardly flattering emotion indeed. (President Nixon's "peace with honor" in Vietnam meant "avoid political humiliation," not "doing what is honorable.") But pride is a highly individual emotion; it has to do (as Hume argued in his *Treatise*) with a sense of personal accomplishment, and its main focus is the individual self. Of course, it is possible to be proud of someone else by way of a slightly enlarged notion of self—when we are proud of our children or our parents or our team—but pride is too personal and too concerned with accomplishment. Honor, by contrast, need not involve accomplishment at all (though it certainly may and often does) and it makes very little sense as a purely personal notion. (That is why, when people say that they are defending their honor but are obviously nursing their pride, we find such behavior not only foolish but pretentious as well.) Honor first of all requires a sense of belonging, a sense of membership, a sense of self that is inseparable from one's group identity. Honor involves living up to the expectations of the group, whether these are spelled out as a code of honor or a set of moral rules or are simply implicit in the practices and goals of the group. (It is not obeying moral rules that makes one honorable, however; it is obeying the rules because they are the rules of one's group—very un-Kantian.) One's honor, in other words, is never one's honor alone. It is the honor of the community that one represents; to stand up for one's own honor necessarily entails defending it as a representative of that community. In business ethics, this sense of honor helps clarify both the role of the individual employee or executive in the corporation and, even more important, the role of both the individual and the corporation in society. (Tragedy in business ethics, we might add, does not usually consist of a conflict of interests but a rather a conflicting sense of honor, torn between one membership and another—as an employee

2. For a good philosophical discussion of loyalty, see Andrew Oldenquist, "Loyalties," *Journal of Philosophy* 79, no. 4 (1982): 173 n. 74. See also Josiah Royce, *The Philosophy of Loyalty* (New York: Macmillan, 1908). I have discussed the nature of the emotions of honor, loyalty, and shame at greater length in my *Passion for Justice* (Reading, Mass.: Addison-Wesley, 1990), ch. 6.

of the company, as the friend of one's immediate supervisor, or as the member of the greater community.)

Honor should not be thought of as a set of personal constraints defined by one's membership in a group. The notion of "constraints" is appropriate rather to a group of which one is not a member or, perhaps, is a member only by chance or reluctantly. One's sense of honor is, if not voluntary, at least personally acceptable, part and parcel of one's sense of self. It is one's pride in the reflective identification with that group, and pride in the accomplishments of that group (whether or not one has actually contributed to them oneself). It is, in this sense, a species of merit, but here this is very different from any sense of desert or what one has achieved. Merit in the context of honor has to do with who one *is*—namely a member of the group in good standing— and not particularly with anything that one has done (or not done), except insofar as such acts are part of one's membership in the group. So, too, there is a natural affinity between honor and self-esteem; one's self-esteem depends on one's sense of honor (though not vice versa) and one's standing in the group becomes the criterion of self-esteem. One cannot be much of a "member" if one can be humiliated in the group and nevertheless have a solid sense of self-worth. So, too, the contemporary idea that one's main objective after public humiliation is to "get over it" makes impossible any sense of honor, which presupposes that one doesn't just "get over it." One might note that one symptom of our collective loss of honor is the fact that no one seems to believe in the concept of a "ruined life" anymore. One just moves to another town or gets another job or sets up another company and "starts over." In practical terms, what this means is that the business community is notoriously poor in sanctioning its own rules and punishing even the most flagrant offenders of its own rules. Business failure is neither adequate nor sufficiently dependable as a measure or a punishment for unethical business practices. It is a person's sense of honor that must be put into play, and for those who don't understand or scoff at this notion, the old tribal practice of exile (federal minimum security prisons will do) serves an extremely necessary function in the survival of the business community.

The opposite of honor is *shame*. Aristotle lists, with some discomfort, shame as one of the virtues, not because it is good to be ashamed but rather because, as in that Ethiopian proverb, "where there is no shame, there is no honor." Thus John Rawls is not entirely wrong when he insists that shame is the opposite of self-esteem, since honor can be the criterion for self-esteem.[3] But not all societies are honor societies and not everyone's self-esteem is tied to their sense of honor. But shame is not, as Rawls says, failing to live up to one's potential; it is, much more

---

3. John Rawls, *A Theory of Justice* (Cambridge: Harvard University Press, 1971), pt. 3.

specifically, failing to live up to the standards of the group through which one gains one's self-identity. Of course, according to the Aristotelean approach to business ethics, failing to live up to one's potential may well be equivalent to failing to live up to the standards of the group, perhaps because he or she has made a commitment that cannot be kept or set a goal that cannot be met. But personal achievement and failure as such are not essential and often not relevant to honor and shame. What one fails to *be* is acceptable to the group and, accordingly, acceptable in terms of one's own essential sense of identity. To feel shame (not quite the same as our "being ashamed") is quite literally to fail oneself, but only in the context of one's larger self.[4]

It is in this sense that shame is contrasted to guilt, and it is guilt that defines the appropriate attitude in our non–honor society, not shame. Shame is always defined in a group context; guilt is born by one alone. Once again, this is suggestive of the religious origins of much of our talk about morality (in which guilt and sin play a large role) and the naturally more secular framework of business (and Aristotelean) ethics. It is not surprising that the Scriptures talk mainly of sin and guilt when concerned with an individual's wrongdoing before God. Guilt is an emotion that permeates the personal self, but other people, one's peers, play no clear role in its workings. We feel guilty, not shamed, for failing to live up to our own goals and standards. We feel guilty, not shamed, for breaking the rules or commiting a moral infelicity. Guilt is appropriate to isolated individuals; shame is possible only in groups. Guilt ties in nicely with the traditional concept of the individual soul; shame is essentially a tribal emotion. It has often been said (by Nietzsche and Freud most famously) that there is too much guilt in our society. I would like to suggest that, while this is probably true, there isn't nearly enough shame. Indeed the payoff for public humiliation in current-day America seems to be a fat book advance and profitable public appearances, not repentance, apology, and retribution. We may have more guilt than we ought to have, but part of the reason may be that we don't have enough room for honor—or shame.

What all of this amounts to is the idea that business ethics is at once more personal and more social than it is usually thought to be. It is not enough to teach principles and policies much less the theories of the great, dead, mostly white male philosophers. Business ethics require

4. On the other hand, *not* to feel shame may be the most offensive evidence of unethical attitudes and the lack of virtue. Last year, a 100-million-dollar settlement was denied to Exxon by a judge who rightly suspected that such an amount would be no more than the usual "cost of doing business" for the giant oil company. Indeed, the preceding week chairman Lawrence Rawl announced to the stockholders that "it will not have a significant effect on our earnings." After the judge's action *Newsweek* commented, "It may be the world's biggest oil company, but Exxon could learn a trick or two from a common street criminal: if there's one thing a judge wants to see when a miscreant makes a plea, it's remorse" (May 6, 1991, p. 54).

the cultivation of the civic virtues, not something possible in an isolated business ethics course—on this, at least, the critics are correct—but nevertheless, as Aristotle himself surely would have argued, something absolutely necessary for the health and well-being of the business world itself. What business ethics does and what business ethics courses do is not to "teach" ethics to business managers and students but to remind us all that there are standards and virtues at issue in business without which the enterprise will not and does not deserve to survive.

21

Competition, Caring, and Compassion

No man is devoid of a heart sensitive to the sufferings of others
. . . whoever is devoid of the heart of compassion is not human.

MENCIUS

Howsoever selfish man may be supposed, there are evidently some
principles in his nature, which interest him in the fortune of others,
and render their happiness necessary to him, though he derives
nothing from it except the pleasure of seeing it. Of this kind is pity
or compassion, the emotion which we feel for the misery of others.
. . . The greatest ruffian, the most hardened violator of the laws
of society, is not altogether without it.

ADAM SMITH, *The Theory of the Moral Sentiments*

Competition, we keep hearing, is the fuel of free enterprise. According
to the Aristotelean approach to business I have been defending, cooperation, not competition, the desire for excellence and not just the need
or desire to win, are what moves and motivates business. People act in
order to impress and win the respect of their peers, not just in order
to "beat" them. People may welcome a challenge, but not all challenges
are competitive and virtually all competitions presuppose an under-
girding of mutual acceptance and respect. Moreover, since business activity in corporate life is by definition cooperative, the presuppposition
of mutual acceptance and respect (as opposed to grudging acceptance
of necessity) is essential to the very nature of the corporation. But the
best corporations do not stop there. Mutual respect is a minimal affection that may be suitable for strangers but is inadequate for colleagues
and people who work together as much as fifty or sixty hours a week.
Mutual acceptance is important for temporary teammates but it is hardly
adequate for people who work together for five, ten, twenty, and even
forty years or more. Competition may be important in picking the most
promising executives and, within the organization, for determining the
best performers for promotion. But the glue that holds the corporation

225

together and keeps it from fragmenting into brooding pockets of fear, envy, and resentment is a deeper sense of affection that is often expressed (sometimes hypocritically) as the idea that the corporation is "family." That glue is *caring*, a genuine sense of attachment and belonging that gives employees and managers a real sense of security and belonging and, consequently, a very real reason for sticking with the company and caring about its well-being in return.

"Caring" is not a word that makes executive hearts beat faster or stronger. It does not get the adrenalin flowing or the muscles flexing the way "competition" and "the profit motive" do. Instead, it conjures up very uncorporate images of the nursery, the hospital, and for those obsessed with costs it immediately suggests enormous increases in health and retirement benefits. It certainly does not suggest an organization requiring hard work and hierarchical authority. But much of the uninspiring imagery of caring has to do with the overly military and otherwise macho metaphors that have dominated so much of business thinking in this century. And caring, of course, is not even incompatible with such thinking, for surely one of the marks of a successful military commander is that he cares for his troops. And in Darwinian thinking, one of the often neglected aspects of natural selection is the immense evolutionary value of caring, among those species (most mammals and birds) that raise a frew offspring caringly rather than give birth to tens of thousands, most of whom are soon devoured (like some amphibians and most insects). Indeed, when one thinks of the "survival of the fittest" imagery applied to the corporation, it becomes obvious that the fittest corporation will be one that cares for and nurtures its employees and managers rather than one that leaves them to fight it out amongst themselves. Nevertheless, caring is too often thought to be too "soft" to be good for business, while internecine squabbling, no matter how destructive, is somehow accepted as a sign of health and strength. Nothing could be further from the truth, or as bad for business.

Caring in the corporation consists of a fundamental attitude. That attitude is one of mutual affection and obligation. This does not mean mawkish sentiment, and it does not suggest that the best executive is one that treats or thinks of his or her employees as children. It does mean that the recognition and treatment of one's employees as people, full of fears and jealousies and other unbusinesslike emotions, is essential to the bonding that corporate life requires. It involves the recognition that a resentful employee is a minimally cooperative and potentially destructive employee, and that a fearful employee—especially if the fear is for his or her job—is an employee who cannot, despite appearances and efforts to the contrary, be expected to be a loyal and dedicated employee. When the tie to one's job becomes evidently contingent, one's devotion to the job becomes cautious, calculated, and merely contingent too. And when one is plagued by fears for the future, the threat of sickness or financial ruin, one cannot expect adequate focus on the present or on the job at hand. Executives who see health and retirement benefits simply as a "perk" or, worse, as a wasted but unfortunately necessary expenditure on the future of those who will then no longer be productive employees, are greatly missing the point. Caring is not just charity, and it is not represented by selfless generosity. Caring is the unity and the health of any ongoing organization. It is the dynamic of the present as well as an investment in the future.

There are limits to caring. Caring is a relatively intimate emotion, appropriate for those in the family and the community but stretched thin when extended to the world at large. It is true and important that one can care about and (more obviously) care *for* strangers, but at a certain distance it becomes more appropriate to talk about a less intimate emotion, the sentiment of *compassion*. Compassion literally means "feeling with," and thus it is often confused with empathy or "putting yourself in the other person's shoes." But empathy is often over-interpreted as an elaborate excercise in moral imagination. Compassion is a much more direct sense of shared urgency. It differs from pity in just this directness; pity involves a distance, a detachment (perhaps even moral censure) that compassion lacks. Compassion requires understanding, but it would be a mistake to think that this need involve any great psychological insight or that it necessarily requires excessive tolerance. It doesn't take much of a psychological genius to recognize that another person is in pain or difficulty, and one need not approve (or refrain from disapproving) of the behavior that brought about the pain or difficulty. Within the corporation, compassion is often called for—once one looks up out of the ledger books or over the computer screen—for an employee who has a sick spouse or child, for a manager who just received an ominous medical report, for a colleague who manifests the signs of serious depression or a drinking problem. Compassion, of course, can be exepensive—giving time off, paying for medical or counseling expenses, taking time off from work to express one's concern—but what is less obvious is the enormous expense of not having or expressing compassion, in further lost time and the distraction that comes of suffering through hardship alone, in the insecurity and consequent lack of devotion of not only the employee in question but of everyone around, in seething resentment. Compassions, like caring, is not merely a humanizing embellishment in the otherwise businesslike life of the corporation. It is essential to the very life of that corporation as a human community.

Care, like the moral sentiment theorists' sympathy, encompasses almost all emotions, insofar as one must care about the world in order to feel anything else about it. We can restrict our characterization of care, however, to include just a certain set of "positive" feelings about another being (or any number of other beings) such that one "wishes them well" and is moved to act (where possible) on their behalf. But note that "being moved" is not the same as acting, and we often care for or about someone whose fate is quite out of our hands. A good executive cares about his or her employees even when there is nothing to be done about them. Such "positive" feelings about a person are no guarantee of continued "niceness"; caring always sets up the possibility of ingratitude and betrayal, and though the limits of tolerance may sometimes be stretched remarkably far (between employer and employee as well as between parents and their young children) that possibility is always there. Indeed, one might hypothesize that the more intensive the care and the more the limits of tolerance are stretched, the more violent the reaction should those limits be violated. Caring about anyone or anything sets up a zone of dangers and threats that promote aggressive defensiveness and hostility. One would not long think that an employer cared about his employees if he made no effort to save them from litigation or arrest for following the orders of their superior. To care for is to be prepared to fight for. (The standard sweet image of women caring for the world the way mothers have always cared for their children should be juxtaposed with the not-so-sweet image of a mother defending her children against the dangers and offensiveness of the outside world. Campers and backpackers know that there is nothing more vicious or dangerous in nature than a female animal protecting her young.) To "care for" someone ultimately means to be concerned about him, perhaps "to help him grow and actualize himself."[1]

Compassion, on the other hand, is more specific emotion than care, and so it may be much easier to define and delimit. The most obvious specifying feature of compassion ("suffering with") is that the object of one's concern is somehow in pain. One does not feel compassion for a friend who has just won the local lottery (except, of course, in a very unusual set of circumstances). One might well feel compassion for a friend who is getting divorced, but it would be inappropriate, at least, to feel compassion for friend who was getting married. (Again, one makes exceptions for the unusual and unfortunate instance.) It is often suggested that (as the prefix might suggest) in compassion one *suffers with* the other, but one need not actually feel his or her pain in any sense oneself; indeed, compassion suggests that one somehow stands safely "above" the misery of the other, affording one the luxury of

1. Milton Mayeroff, *On Caring* (New York: Harper and Row, 1971). See also Nell Noddings, *Caring* (Los Angeles: University of California Press, 1984). The foremost defender of care and compassion, however, is certainly Adam Smith, who defended the centrality of what he called "sympathy" in his *Theory of the Moral Sentiments* sixteen years before he wrote *Wealth of Nations*.

commiseration. A student who has just flunked his exams does not feel compassion toward a fellow student who has also flunked his exams. They just feel miserable together. It is the student who has passed her exams with flying colors who is in a position to feel compassion for the other two, though the giddiness of her own success may make it difficult to do so. It is compassion, this ability to feel for those less fortunate than ourselves, that composes the cornerstone passion of our sense of justice.

It makes good sense, but it can be deeply misleading, to say that compassion, pity, and sympathy are "feelings." They are indeed aspects of consciousness and not action or activities, but they are also engagements in the world, instances of involving if not identifying oneself with the circumstances and sufferings of other beings. Compassion and its kin are above all else *motives:* they move us to act (whether or not it is evident what we should do). They are not simply self-enclosed sensations, like a headache or a gouty toe, that focus our attention within ourselves and distract us from the world. Compassion and its kindred emotions focus our attention on the world, on the person or creature who is suffering. Compassion, pity, and sympathy are feelings but they are not "mere" feelings. Moreover, they are not, as John Rawls sometimes seems to say, disposition to instantiate a theory or principle of justice. This is backward. One may be moved to accept a theory or a principle of justice on the basis of strong feelings of compassion, which the principle or theory seems to address. The feeling of compassion may be elegantly articulate, as in some of the best socially conscious poetry and journalistic prose, but it can also be "dumb" and only felt. Indeed, I have no reservations about ascribing compassion to nontalking animals and very young children, although they may often be confused or have no way of knowing exactly what is going on. What I do not want to allow is for compassion (and related emotions) either to be dismissed as "mere feelings" or to be co-opted by an overly intellectualistic account such that they become nothing more than applied abstract beliefs. To say that they are feelings makes them vulnerable to the first danger but clearly saves them from the second. But so long as we keep in mind a healthy cognitive picture of the passions, we should not feel tempted to minimize the significance of our feelings.

It is one of the more disturbing features of the popular social philosophy of our time that there is this pervasive, confident contempt for "do-gooders," a contempt that is often confused with "toughness." What could possibly be wrong with a kind emotion and the actions that go along with it, whose only aim is to help other people? The problem is that compassion, by itself, is often ill-informed, even stupid, vaguely directed, and self-serving (though it pretends to be the very opposite). It is true that compassion typically prompts kindly action. (It also inspires the search for ways of helping where none was evident before.)

But compassion often prompts precipitous action, or makes more difficult the sort of cold, professional behavior that may be necessary (for example, in a medical emergency). Larry Blum points out that compassion may make worse an already hopeless situation and may hurt its recipients by concentrating too much on [their] plight.[2] It can be "misguided, grounded in a superficial understanding of the situation." Indeed, we all can think of examples where being too "caught up" in a tragedy makes us less rather than more capable to cope with it, and other examples where "superficial understanding" of someone else's plight has led us to intrude where we were not welcome, intervene where we were not competent, interfere where we were not wanted. But the limitations of compassion hardly undermine its virtue or the overall utility of compassionate actions. Blum rightly concludes that, "because compassion involves an active and objective interest in another's welfare, it is characteristically a spur to deeper understanding than rationality alone could insure. A person who is compassionate by character is in principle committed to as rational and as intelligent a course of action as possible." Compassion without intelligence is no virtue, and intelligence without compassion is not good management—indeed, it may not be management at all (rather, engineering). And finally, care and compassion are not antithetical to hardheaded management nor incompatible with being "tough"; they are rather the preconditions of that toughness that is respected and is recognized as tough rather than simply meanspirited (as in "tough love"). My aim is to put these gentle sentiments back where they belong, at the core of our sense of ethics and business life.

2. Blum, "Compassion," in *Explaining Emotions,* ed. Amelie Rorty.

22

Justice: The Ultimate Virtue of Corporate Life

Justice is the first virtue of social institutions, as truth is of systems of thought."

JOHN RAWLS, *A Theory of Justice*

Fairness, justice, whatever you call it—it's essential and most companies don't have it.

ROBERT TOWNSEND, *Up the Organization*

Justice makes Aristotle's list as one of his basic virtues—indeed, he sometimes suggests (as did Plato) that it is *the* basic virtue.[1] In the corporation, justice is not only a virtue. It is an utter necessity. Justice, as "fairness," holds the institution together. As fairness, it is the fact and perception that all members of the organization and everyone connected with it is "getting their due." In particular, this means that people get recognized for what they do and are properly rewarded with commendations, bonuses, and promotions, that people are hired into positions they deserve and given duties commensurate with their abilities and salary, that they are treated in times of crisis no differently than their peers and, of course, that they are paid and paid on time. The bond between the individual and the organization cannot be maintained on the basis of affection alone, nor can it be understood as a merely contractual arrangement. It is a bond that involves a person's very identity (as well as the identity of the corporation) and so includes a myriad of expectations and demands so varied that they cannot possibly be reduced to caring alone or summarized in a contract no matter how complicated. Justice is the demand that one is recognized and respected for what one is, that one is not neglected or short-changed, that one is not exploited or abused. Justice is the sense that one is being treated fairly, and this requires due diligence on the part of the cor-

1. The discussion of justice in this chapter is adapted from ch. 4 of my *Passion for Justice*, with the kind permission of Addison-Wesley, Inc.

poration, for whether or not the organization is attentive, one can be sure that the individual employee or manager will be. Nothing fosters resentment faster than the perception that we are being paid less or given less recognition for our accomplishments than someone else, and nothing fosters negative competition more readily than the perception that someone else is getting the rewards that we ourselves deserve.

Although the dimensions of justice are many and complicated, the first rule of justice in business ethics must be "equal work, equal pay." But this is easier said than implemented, not only because of the political and social pressures that influence every financial decision in the corporation but because of traditions that are anything but egalitarian (for example, the gargantuan difference between top executive and employee salaries, sometimes thirty-to-one in some industries) and prejudices that one would think belong strictly to the past (the still shocking 40 percent differential between men's and women's salaries for the same job and experience). There are subtler concerns as well, of course, the most evident of which is the not-at-all-easy determination of what "equal work" amounts to, or how one weighs and evaluates jobs that are clearly unequal. Even in the simplest case, there are such questions as whether it is hard work or results that count more, how much to reward potential rather than actual accomplishment (why else would M.B.A.s fresh out of school deserve those bonuses?), how much "personal" factors should be counted in, and how the various members of a team (in which one cannot assume equal effort) should be recognized and rewarded. What this means is that every act and decision involving justice also involves a sophisticated personal *judgment,* not a routine application of some formula or decision procedure. And this is what makes justice not only essential, but both difficult and central to any conception of corporate virtue.

In the context of the corporation and in business in general, justice is part of a tradition that precedes business life as we know it by many centuries. It goes back to the ancient Aristotelean and medieval conception of the "just wage" and the "fair price" and the more abstract "labor theory of value" that was embraced by both Adam Smith and Karl Marx. The basic idea is that justice has much to do with *merit*—giving each student what he or she *deserves* on the basis of effort and accomplishment. Insistence on merit is, in part, insistence on personal responsibility, and built into any merit system is the demand that factors that are irrelevant to the task and beyond a person's control are not to be taken into consideration. So managerial ability and performance, hard work and intelligence are relevant to one's evaluation, but hair and sex and skin color and family fortunes are not. But within the context of merit, there is considerable room for disagreement. Should hard work be rewarded regardless of actual performance? What about those routine but necessary office and management jobs that allow for no displays of brilliance but just demand to be done? Should brilliance be rewarded even if it is effortless? What about the young hotshot who spends his day schmoozing by the coffee machine, distracting other employees but dependably producing a good idea every week? Should a person who does well in a business boom be rewarded more than someone who manages to hold his or her head above water in a time of economic disaster? There are no easy answers to these questions, and they are properly left up to the judicious manager for his or her personal and professional judgment. Judgments regarding justice are almost always like this, not applications of an abstract formula to concrete cases but rather a closely considered and felt engagement with the situation and the people involved in it, in which conflicting criteria and concerns are sorted and sometimes singled out.

There are *dimensions* to justice and their appropriateness depends on the context. The more specific and well-defined the context, the more confident and spontaneous our judgments. It is not so much that the situation is simple; it is rather that experience has already digested and synthesized the various competing concerns and considerations. In most established games, for example, the limits and boundaries and the realm of fair play have become polished and virtually second nature for any seasoned manager. In the realm of the law, the accumulation of precedents serves much the same purpose, so that daily conflicts in law are almost always well defined and clearly embedded in a framework in which a myriad of considerations have already become codified. (Supreme Court and World Court decisions, by contrast, concern those that are not so well defined or clearly embedded. So, too, the decisions that arrive on the desk of the corporate attorney or the CEO). But the reason we have judges, magistrates, and referees and not merely personal computers on the bench or on the sidelines is because justice, even so well defined, requires sensitivity and experienced judgment and not merely the mechanical grinding out of an already established decision procedure.

This is not to say that justice is merely relative or subjective, or that there is no agreement whatever that will carry us along from one case to another. Ever since Plato, there seems to be almost universal agreement on at least three points:

1. Justice is not merely a matter of "might makes right." Strength and power may be essential to defending justice, but they do not constitute justice. The fact that one of your employees has threatened to beat the stuffing out of you if she doesn't get a big bonus is not an argument on her behalf.

2. *Irrelevant* considerations should not enter into our deliberations. For example, the fact that one employee is a woman and the other a man, or that one is Chicano and the other Chinese, is irrelevant to the question of how large a bonus each should receive. But, of course, the

question What is relevant? can be just as hard to answer as the question What is just?—in fact, it is pretty much the same question. Is the fact that one works harder a relevant consideration? (Probably not in a high-pressure business where it is only results that count.) How about the fact that one is smarter than the other? Or the fact that one has been with the company five times as long? The fact that one is charming and pleasant looking while the other is a perpetual grump and slob? The fact that one is heavily in debt? And, perhaps hardest of all, the fact that you *like* one better than the other? To treat your employees differently for no reason is obviously unfair, but to treat them differently for the wrong reason is also unfair, and so is treating them similarly without regard for relevant differences.

3. The most obvious way to reconcile the demand for equal treatment with attention to differences is to insist on *equal standards*. But here, of course, is where the idea of dimensions of justice becomes most problematic. Which standards do we use, and are they the appropriate standards? We could evaluate the lifetime athletic performance of Joe Namath and Wilt Chamberlain by comparing the total points earned by each for their respective teams, but this would hardly be a fair and appropriate measure, even if we are using the same standard for both of them. A company could evaluate all of its managers by measuring their various contributions to the bottom line, but such a measure would be dubious for some of the most essential departments of the corporation.

Among the various dimensions of justice, the two most basic considerations are merit and equality. In the corporation, we consider an employee's or manager's motivation, effort, and accomplishment, and we ask whether he or she *deserves* our attention or support. In terms of merit, everyone is ostensibly different, and it is almost impossible to imagine what it would be for everyone—even in the most routine tasks—to have equal abilities, to be equally productive, and to make equal contributions. On the other hand, the presupposition of our evaluations of merit seems to be the principle of equality, such that if two people are doing the same work, putting in the same effort, and getting similar results, they deserve to be treated the same, and insofar as two people are to be rewarded differently it is the *difference* between them that is essential. Thus Aristotle takes it as the primary, irrefutable demand of justice that "equals should be treated as equals; unequals should be treated unequally." But, of course, there is a sense in which everyone is equal to everyone else, in the most innocent and uncritical sense: "We are all human beings." We all have feelings. We all have *needs*. We all have interests, fears, affections. Thus there is the familiar argument that everyone's needs and interests should be taken equally seriously, whatever their abilities or accomplishments. In this sense, it is our sameness and not our differences that are in question, and one person's interests and concerns are of equal weight to anyone else's interests and concerns. It is here that the demand for equality runs counter to the recognition of merit, and many of the most personally difficult decisions managers have to make involve those cases in which an employee's personal needs are enormous (because of serious illness or family problems, for example) but his or her accomplishments are minimal (in part, naturally, because of those problems).

The idea that justice has dimensions—that it is not a single measure—is not at all new. But we resist the idea that these various dimensions cannot be reduced to one, or weighed and balanced in a single grand formula that will suffice in every circumstance. Thus the history of ideas about justice, since the time of Plato and Aristotle until the present-day theory of John Rawls, is filled with efforts to reduce the bewildering number of considerations of justice to a single formula. But in addition to equality and merit there are many other considerations. We have already mentioned the presence of special *needs*, notably the plight of sick and disadvantaged people for whom merely equal treatment is insufficient. There is also the notion of *entitlement*—what a person has a *right* to, quite apart from questions of equality, merit, or need. The most straightforward example of such a right is the result of an explicit contract; an agent of the corporation promised Jones (in writing) that the company would pay him twenty thousand dollars to redesign the corporate boardroom. Jones completed the job and now he has a right to payment. It does not matter if, afterward, some top executive doesn't like the design, or thinks that the price was too much, or decides that he just doesn't like Jones. So, too, there are those social and legal guarantees that we call "civil rights" that are the result of a "promise" of sorts made by the society as a whole, eventually canonized in law or the constitution. Much more abstract but clearly central to our thinking about justice are "human rights," which may or may not be spelled out explicitly but nevertheless override the customs and even the laws of any particular society or culture and provide the most basic constraints for any corporate discussion of justice. We cannot even conceive of justice today without the notion of such rights, despite the fact that they played little role in social thinking before just a few centuries ago. Freedom of political speech, for instance, is one of those bedrock human rights that precedes any particular government promise or state charter and remains a basic right for any employee or manager. Thus employees and managers often discern a deep injustice when the company extracts contributions from them for political causes or candidates that they do not themselves support. Indeed, I have found that the resentment that accompanies such corporate policies often runs deeper than personal slight or gripes about salaries. Not all speech is protected by the right to political free speech, of course; giving away company secrets is hardly an exercise in First Amendment rights and bad-mouthing the company holds only a debatable claim to protection. (Here we enter difficult territory, for what seems like bad-mouthing the company to top management may well seem to outside observers and sympathetic colleagues to be whistle-blowing, an act of integrity rather than disrespect.) Freedom of speech, we are constantly reminded by the news, is a right embedded in a context that qualifies and occasionally contradicts it.

One of the central rights in our capitalist conception of justice is the right to have and hold private property. Part of our sense of justice is the sense that one has a right to hold onto whatever wealth and material goods one has in possession, however (legally) acquired and whether or not one in any sense deserves them. The notion of rights is often held up as the hallmark of egalitarianism, but the emphasis on property rights runs directly counter to the idea of equality. So, too, merit is opposed to equality (if we assume that people's talents and achievements are not equal) and one cannot wholly support one without violating the other. And so, despite our popular emphasis on rights, equality, and merit, it is important to appreciate just how *inegalitarian* our sense of justice is. We may believe that everyone is, in some abstract sense (and not just before the law) equal; but we also believe that people need, deserve, and have a right to unequal portions of the rewards of the world.[2]

A very different dimension of justice enters into our considerations with that extraordinary institution we call "the market"—that disorganized system of bargaining that defines not only capitalism but much of our sense of fairness as well. To listen to the most vocal defenders of the free market, one would think that the market is just a measure of merit, because hard work, efficiency, and inventiveness will almost always win in the competition for dollars and the respect and admiration that comes with success. Sometimes, of course, merit and the market cooperate entirely, and to foster the illusion of their total compatibility we favor stories about the young, bright, hard-working entrepreneur who invents a product of enormous value and becomes wealthy as his or her reward. But, then again, there are those other inventors of equally valuable products, who worked equally hard with similar inspiration, who reaped only a nominal honorarium for their efforts or nothing at all when some conglomerate snatched up the patent and made its fortune through marketing. True, the original inventors may have been incompetent as businessmen and could never have so successfully marketed their products. But the scenario nevertheless strikes us as a gross injustice, and we have to recognize that market thinking ultimately stands distinct from both equality and merit.

2. For a good discussion of comparative versus noncomparative conceptions of justice, see Joel Feinberg, "The Nature and Value of Rights," *The Journal of Value Inquiry* 4 (1970).

One consideration that cannot be left out of any discussion of justice is "the public good." Indeed, we have already defined a sense of justice as, in part, concern for the well-being of the whole community. Not surprisingly, egalitarians argue that a society of equals tends to be less torn by envy and strife, and defenders of merit argue that encouraging people to do their best will guarantee a better society for all. Defenders of the unregulated free market almost always base their defense on the (historically contingent) claim that freedom in the market all but inevitably produces prosperity for all. Indeed, without this defense, our belief in the desirability of a market economy would be shaky indeed, the entrepreneurial "freedom" of a small number of wealthy individuals notwithstanding. But the public good is not always best served by either equality, merit, or the market, and there are those few notorious cases in which the good of a society on the whole depends on the grossest injustice against one or more of its members. The ancient rituals of human sacrifice made this point quite evident, but our modern system of celebrities and scapegoats may well work in much the same way. We can hardly talk about justice without taking into account the good of all, but this cannot by itself be the key to justice either.

The notion of "dimensions of justice" is not an easy idea for us to accept, for what it means is not just that our sense of justice is complex but that it is riddled with contradictions and conflicts. We almost all agree that equal respect for people as human beings is in some sense imperative, but when it gets down to most particular cases it is not at all clear what that is supposed to mean. We all tend to agree that people should get what they deserve, but once this formula is taken out of its merely formal mode and applied to real people who differ in all sorts of different ways in terms of their talents, their ambitions, their conscientiousness, their accomplishments, and their contributions, we are not at all agreed how these different considerations are to be weighed, or how they are to be weighted against needs, or how much we should simply leave these difficult decisions up to the impersonality of "the market," where the skill of marketing suddenly takes top priority and the needy, who have nothing to sell, are systematically disadvantaged. (The Nobel Prize in economics usually goes to the scholar who can hide this obvious fact under the econometrics of a formal theory.)

Let's consider an everyday issue of justice in which most of us are involved, one way or the other, the distribution of "merit" money for the work we have done. Imagine yourself in the position of a supervisor of two employees, with a fixed bonus of one thousand dollars to distribute between them. What are the considerations, the dimensions of justice, that you have to take into account, eliminating *irrelevant* considerations such as the fact that one employee is a woman and the other a man, or that one is Chicano and the other Chinese? Presumably we should insist on an equal standard—that is, whatever we decide is relevant to the evaluation in question, we should use the same criterion for both employees. But, as in our decision concerning what is relevant, the hard part is deciding whether the two cases are sufficiently similar as to warrant the same standard. It is far from obvious that it is fair to evaluate them in the same way. Indeed, one can list at least a baker's dozen considerations that may enter into this seemingly simple decision:

Equality. Ignore all differences, give them five hundred dollars each, split down the middle. (The illusion is that such even splits provoke no resentment and require no justification.)

Merit (results). Who has actually produced more? (Of course, deciding how to measure production is already half the concern.)

Merit (effort). Who has worked harder? As any fair-minded employer knows quite well, results are important but they do not always reflect true merit. Charlotte may get the credit for a discovery whose groundwork was 95 percent completed by Carl.

Ability. How much "promise" a person shows. (How long does one have to be "promising" before only results have to count? Is it really fair to reward promise as such?)

Need. Does the fact that one has two sick children and another in college while the other is single with a substantial trust fund enter into our deliberations at all? Does justice on the job always have to be job-related?

Rights. Are there any outstanding agreements or legitimate expectations that already commit you to paying a certain bonus to either of them? (Can one have a right to a "bonus"?)

The public good ("utility"). What would have the best effects for the most people, for the rest of the employees, for the company, for the larger community?

Duties and responsibilities. How much of a "burden" are we compensating them for? (Why does a CEO make so much more than his or her hard-working employees? Is any of this a psychological question? How much is a matter of tradition?)

Market value. Could one of them get another job with higher pay? Better pay what it takes to keep 'em. But if one of them is especially loyal to the company and wouldn't consider taking another job, even for higher pay, is this fair?

Risk and uncertainty. We pay more for a dangerous job, whether or not it requires more skill and whether or not it involves a greater contribution than a safe job. We reward investors who put their money at risk, quite apart from any question of their time and effort spent and any skills they might have. Marx was surely wrong in insisting that the fruits of an enterprise belong solely to those who actually do the physical labor. (Of course, *how much* of a return on risk is a matter of serious debate.)

Seniority. How long has a person been with the company? Does this in itself give him or her special status, apart from skill and accomplishment?

Loyalty. Not the same as seniority (though seniority may be a sign of loyalty). It is worth noting the recent difficulty surrounding the concept of loyalty, as more and more young executives "fast track" and jump from company to company, as more and more companies fire their older rather than more recent employees (often just months before benefit packages kick in). But this, I suggest, is a symptom of a much deeper problem, which is the very way we tend to see ourselves in our jobs and institutions as well as in society as a whole, as individual contractors rather than as participant members.

Moral virtue. We sometimes think it worth rewarding people for simple trustworthiness or honesty, even when this does not necessarily benefit the company (as loyalty does). "Congeniality" is often included in this category, but so too are the more dubious considerations of personal affection and "liking" someone. Are such personal considerations fair. Is virtue itself a personal consideration?

Tradition. Finally, no institution exists in a historical vacuum, and surely it is relevant to people's expectations that bonus money has in the past always been distributed a certain way, whether this is strictly egalitarian or always unequal (say 750:250), and then in favor of the older employee or the newer one, the harder worker or the most productive, the needier of the two or the more demonstrably virtuous. One can buck tradition, of course, but that in itself requires some special justification in terms of one (or more) of the preceding concerns.

There are other considerations, even in this simplified domestic case of justice. But the point has been to show that, even in the simplest cases, justice is not simple. It requires judgment, not a decision procedure, and it involves a broad range of considerations. Trying to divide the thousand-dollar bonus fairly between our two employees, we try to apply some sort of fair and consistent standards and take into account their very different contributions (and, perhaps, very different *kinds* of contributions) to the company, how hard they work, their abilities, their personal needs, their duties and the responsibilities they shoulder, and their rights. We take into account the length of time they have been with the company, their loyalty to the company, their virtue, and, quite simply (unfairly?) how much we like them. We try to strike a balance between these various considerations, and most of the time our judgment is fair and reasonable. But the point is that there is no possible formula, and consequently no possible theory, that will tell us how to judge such cases. Justice is contextual, and it virtually always involves conflicting considerations, different dimensions of justice, any of which itself may also involve internal contradictions and conflicts.

Of course, we might also use the bonus to send a message—to warn, to reward, to punish, to praise—but we might also use it to correct a previous inequity or to admit some prior mistake of our own. But the point is not that justice is a kind of stew with lots of different ingredients and spices, much less an incomprehensible clash of contradictory claims and demands. An employer who agonized over the "simple" distribution of a thousand dollars' bonus money would not be virtuously conscientious or philosophical but incompetent and indecisive. The fact is that the various dimensions of justice fall into order rather readily, not because of a theory of justice (which most often seriously distorts such decisions) but because of practice and participation in the context and the institution in question. It is thus our acquired as well as natural *sense* of justice that is critical, and it is only in special cases—often called tragedies—that two or more dimensions of justice clash or contradict one another in such a serious and unusual way that we are forced to rely on extraordinary deliberations and negotiations. The familiar appeals to incommensurability, inconsistency, and undecidability are more often than not rejections of the wisdom of our pretheoretical sense of judgment, if not sophistries in defense of some possibly vicious ideology.

It has recently been suggested that what is missing from the standard analyses and theories of justice is an adequate sense of care and compassion. This is, I believe, true and important. Even so pivotal a figure as John Rawls, whose liberal credentials and sense of compassion are not in question, finds it necessary to dress his sentiments in the formal costume of an impersonal deduction of rational principles, and most of the literature that has followed him has shown far more enthusiasm for his form than for his feelings. (Perhaps that is why so much of social philosophy today resembles a debate in game theory rather than an expression of concern for human suffering, even if "the needy" and "the least advantaged" often appear as players.) Justice is, first of all, a sense of compassion. But this is no Kierkegaardian "either/or," impersonal justice *or* personal concern. The kindly sentiments represented by care and compassion cannot by themselves explain the enormous range or the profound depth of the passions that constitute our sense of justice, including our often vehement and not at all kindly sense of *in*justice. Sentiments alone cannot solve or account for the large policy issues that are (or should be) the ultimate concern of those theories of justice, but any sense of justice whatever begins with caring—about ourselves and our reputations, about those whom we work with and for, about those whom we feel akin to and responsible for, about the world. Without that care and concern, there could be no sense of justice. Why else would any of this matter to us—the well-being of the company, the distribution of rewards, fair and equal treatment? Justice begins with and presupposes our emotional engagement, and justice in the corporation cannot be separated from the personal virtues of caring and compassion, loyalty, and one's sense of honor—and, of course, the six parameters of the Aristotelean viewpoint, a sense of community, a demand for excellence, a sense of belonging and responsibility, a keen sense of one's own integrity, a penchant for good judgment, and a view of the whole instead of a narrow focus on one's own little world and interests.

23

Envy and Resentment: Corporate Poison

[The man of *resentment*] loves hiding places, secret paths and back doors, everything covert entices him as his world, his security, his refreshment; he understands how to keep silent, how not to forget, how to wait, how to be provisionally self-deprecating and humble.

FRIEDRICH NIETZSCHE,
On the Geneaology of Morals

The executive suites of thousands of corporations in the United States are filled by men who have become professional eunuchs. The drive and potency they once possessed has been spent . . . they spend their days doing things that often seem meaningless.

O. WILLIAM BATTAGLIA
AND JOHN J. TARRANT,
The Corporate Eunuch

No discussion of the Aristotelean virtues would be complete without some discussion of the vices. We have already discussed a number of Aristotelean vices, of course, in particular the notion of "abstract greed" and that ancient personality disorder called "the profit motive"—known to the ancients and medievals as the sin of avarice. But Aristotle condemned all commercial activity, and so is a tentative guide at best to the virtues and vices of business as such, since he thought that business consisted of virtually all vices. But applying Aristotle to the concept of the corporation as community, we can benefit a great deal from his perspective. Whatever renders a community more harmonious and productive is a virtue; what weakens its bonds and sets one person against another is a vice. If justice is the chief virtue of the corporation, it is injustice that will prove to be the most vicious vice. For the products of injustice perceived are the nasty twin sentiments of *envy* and *resentment*, two emotions that act as corrosives on any joint enterprise or organization.

Envy and resentment are corporate poison. They affect the health of the organization the way a slow acting poison affects the health of an

242

individual, working its way through the veins and eating away at the tissues that provide cooperation and loyalty and good feeling. Envy and resentment are both obsessed with the idea that one has been slighted or denied his or her due. The difference between them is that envy desires what it does not have—usually power, position, or material goods—whereas resentment is aimed at the person, the process, at the justice of the matter. As such, resentment is deeply condemnatory, not just because of a sense of deprivation but because of a sense of outrage. Envy, on the other hand, does not involve outrage, only covetousness. Indeed, envy is typically aimed at positions and perks it has not earned, which it may even know that it does not deserve. Resentment, by contrast, involves the belief that one has been cheated, that the game is rigged or otherwise unfair. Whereas envy includes lust and scheming, resentment prompts us to dig much deeper and condemns, builds a case, feigning cooperation but in fact sowing the seeds of disruption. Accordingly, envy, while perhaps the greater personal vice (because not based on any legitimate claim), is the lesser danger. Indeed, it has even been suggested (wrongly, in my opinion) that envy is a goad, a source of motivation that is good and healthy for the corporation and for capitalism in general.[1] But envy is not just covetous: it is also malicious and potentially destructive. It does not encourage cooperation (except by way of a tentative strategy) and it tends to be blinded to the good of others and the needs of the organization by its own desire. Resentment, however, is worse than noncooperation. It is subversive. Whereas envy is self-interested, resentment is often ideological and prompts us to get the person or organization we perceive as the offender. Resentment is the ultimate corporate poison, and its source is almost always the presence of injustice—even if slight. Accordingly, it can and must be avoided, though the antidote must be supplied early if the corporation is not to suffer long-term damage.

Resentment is often born of fear. Corporations that suffer repeated "downsizing," made more traumatic by prior assurances that this would not happen (again), are breeding grounds for resentment. This weakens their solidarity just at the time when they are most needful of team effort and dedication. Of course, fear is also a powerful motivator, but it is an illusion to think that the kind of energy evident as a result of fear is devotion or that a sense of ominous contingency is conducive or compatible with loyalty. The survivors of a severe cutback may initially feel relieved, even grateful, but those posttraumatic feelings are typically replaced by second thoughts, of colleagues that are no longer there, of added duties and a sense of disorientation, a nostalgia for the comparative calm and order of the "old" organization. These lead in turn

---

1. Helmut Schoeck, *Envy: A Theory of Social Behaviour* (New York: Harcourt, Brace and World, 1970).

to a sense of deprivation, a reminder that one could be the next to go, that the company is still in trouble, that those who suffered were not, after all, to blame, that there has been a pervasive injustice perpetrated on oneself and one's colleagues. The result is not a drawing together, a sense of shared urgency, but a psychological scattering, "everyone out for themselves," the busy preparation of résumés during company time, serious lunchtime conversations with outside contacts and recruiters. When the fear turns to resentment, the result may be subtle sabotage as well, as childish as some stolen office equipment or a padded expense voucher or as serious as disaffected clients and lost accounts.

The usual case of resentment poisoning, however, requires nothing so dramatic as a corporate trauma. It is rather part and parcel of everyday operations, a bit of neglect here, a passed-over promotion there, a missed compliment for good work, a mistaken promotion for the departmental schmooz. It arises because managers no longer have a sense of mission or purpose, because it seems to them that they spend their time in pointless activity. Even where this is not true, it is the fault of their managers in turn, who have failed to inform them of the importance of their tasks. Resentment arises because someone feels stuck in a position, unappreciated, and hopeless. Indeed it is hopelessness rather than fear that breeds the most vicious resentment, because the latter still seeks to save itself whereas the former acts as if it has nothing to lose. Resentment arises in a particularly malevolent form when the delegation of responsibility is not coupled with adequate authority to see it through, a truly hopeless situation that is the bane of many a manager's job. On the other hand, feeling that one's talents are wasted or ignored is also a breeding ground for resentment. A bored employee or an underemployed manager will very likely turn his or her unused energies to resentful thinking and subversive acts of compensation and revenge.

The causes of envy are usually simple and straightforward: a too-lavish display of "perks" and power at the top, too many empty promises, too little satisfaction with what one actually has and deserves. The causes of resentment, however, are as varied as the possibilities of injustice, yet many of these causes involve a single theme, which is not the supposedly unjust action itself but a failure of communication—or worse, outright pretense or fraud. Sensitive decisions are too often made without adequate explanation, and threats and trauma are too often soft-pedaled before the fact and down-played after, despite the obvious results for the employees and management of the company. A company trumpets its meritocracy, and then gives raises to only those managers who cause the least "trouble" (that is, do not disagree with the boss). A company touts its regard for quality but then fails to reward those responsible for the product and gives all of the goodies to the sales and marketing force. A company claims to be caring but isolates and abandons a manager in trouble for enforcing company policy. A company insists on improving quality but does not provide the resources to do so, or it encourages better teamwork but implements a system of increased competition among employees in doing so. A company gives bonuses to its top executives as employees and managers are being let go. Or a company invites its employees and managers to make suggestions about how things can be improved, and systematically ignores them. And in every case, the sense of offense begins to spread, first among those directly affected, then by word of mouth, then as a rumor that may last for years, long after the situation has been corrected, long even after all the originally affected employees are gone. Resentment probably causes more damage to corporations than the most malicious competition, but yet most companies seem to accept it as the "natural" disaffection of a few employees. Resentment is highly contagious, and it can only be stopped by shutting off its sources. The virtue of justice—and the elimination of injustices—is the one and only way to prevent corporate poisoning.

24

The Charismatic Virtues: Saints, Heroes, Clowns, and Rogues

I want a hero, an uncommon want,
When every year and month sends forth a new one
GEORGE BYRON, *Don Juan*

Most of the virtues we have discussed are virtues of "congeniality," virtues that have to do with how people get along with one another, virtues that aid cooperation and team effort, virtues that minimize antagonistic self-interest and emphasize care and concern for others and for the organization. But there is a set of corporate virtues that do much more, virtues that provide a company with not only good and productive citizens but with leaders and exemplars. There are also virtues that provide creative energy, eccentricity, and—not to be neglected—the Aristotelean virtue of a sense of humor. The virtues we have been stressing modify individualism in order to allow for a dedicated sense of community and shared purpose, but there are also room and the need for extreme individuality in every corporation. The mistake is thinking that such virtues are needed by everyone in the organization—"everyone an entrepreneur" or "every manager a leader." The truth is that such uniformity of individuality would make organization and cooperation impossible. To take but one lighthearted example, I will argue in this section that people who properly deserve the unofficial job designation as "clowns" are essential to every group or institution, but one does not have to stretch his or her imagination very much to picture what it would be like if an entire organization were composed of clowns. (*Monty Python* once presented a skit entitled "The Village Idiots' Convention.") So, too, an organization entirely composed of heroes or saints or creative eccentrics would not long be an "organization" at all. The character that used to be called (in now outmoded sexist language) "the company man" is absolutely essential to the workings of any even modestly complex institution. He or she is the source

246

of solidity, organization, and cooperation. But just as a company would not be much of a company if it were composed only of such solid citizens, a company cannot be much of a company at all without them.

Much of what is discussed under the title of "morality" has to do with fulfilling obligations, with doing one's duty—what one *ought* to do. But what one morally ought to do is often limited and much of morality rather consists of prohibitions rather than positive recommendations or ideals for action. We have already noted that one problem with a conception of morality that is limited to obeying the rules of the "thou shalt not" variety is that a perfectly good person might also be an absolute bore, a moral prig whose behavior benefits no one and inspires no one. The consequence of such a conception is that morality becomes a dreary, quite boring, and tedious affair. The "antimoralist" Nietzsche thus suggests that morality is essentially a "leveling" device intended to lop off the peaks of human excellence as well as to raise up the "herd" to a "higher" form of behavior. Extraordinary behavior, heroic and saintly deeds, would be ignored in such a conception, and, indeed, moral theorists in the Kantian mold have been hard-pressed to give an adequate account of those who go far beyond their moral duties to display such extraordinary behavior. A special term has been provided for such behavior, which is "beyond the call of duty": *supererogatory*. But any word in ethics that is seven syllables long is suspicious; this one converts those exemplary acts and people making up the very heart of ethics into a curious and problematic set of exceptions. We would be far better advised to take Nietzsche's "antimoral" advice, not to do wrong knowingly but rather to break beyond the bonds of mere obedience to do something bold and creative, to be leaders rather than followers. Indeed, I once considered entitling this entire project an introduction to "Nietzschean Management," but given Nietzsche's reknowned but undeserved reputation as a "destroyer" and an "antichrist," I thought his name might more prudently be reserved for the back pages. In fact, however, Nietzsche's urgings have much in common with Aristotle, as I have often suggested elsewhere.[1]

What Nietzsche has in common with Aristotle is that critical concept of *excellence*. We can better understand the nature of these inspiring examples in the terms of virtue ethics rather than the terms of morality and obedience to principles. Indeed, it is the primary datum of ethics, not a set of exceptions, that there are people who go far beyond the rules, not breaking them but far exceeding their demands. The good man, for Aristotle, is not just one who obeys the rules; he also excels in what he does. This is not to say that he disobeys the rules and laws of

1. E.g., in my essay, "A More Severe Morality: Nietzsche's Affirmative Ethics," in *From Hegel to Existentialism* (New York: Oxford University Press, 1987). Some of the arguments in this chapter have been adapted from that essay and from pt. III of my *Ethics: A Short Introduction* (Madison: Brown and Benchmark, 1992).

Athenian society; he just does not often think of them—they are "second nature" to him. What he concentrates on is excelling. He is expected not only not to flee from battle; he is expected to fight to the best of his ability. He is not only expected not to lie (which is easy enough if you keep silent); he is also expected to be witty and clever and informative, if not as brilliant as Socrates. From ancient times, we have had the heroes of the *Iliad;* the Bible is full of heroes. We are inundated daily (on television, at least) with examples of personal excellence and exceptional virtue in which the pronouncement of principles plays but a small role. Such examples may be far more personal and powerful than the abstractions of morality, and we may well want to agree with Nietzsche that the ethics of heroism is far more inspiring than the mundane world of morality. Ethics, in other words, needs not be confined to obedient mediocrity. It is also the demand for excellence—and more. In the corporation, it is the demand for integrity and leadership.[2]

This idea of going *beyond* morality, beyond the "call of duty," is nowhere more evident than in those special people whom we designate as *saints* and *heroes.* I have tried to minimize my mention of these special characters in the preceding pages, because I wanted to avoid the impression that Aristotelean or virtue ethics is not part of ordinary life for ordinary people. But a virtue is also an ideal, and it has ideal representatives and ideal types. A saint is not just someone who is perfectly good in the easy sense of not sinning (perhaps because there have been no opportunities); a saint is extraordinarily good, resisting temptations that we cannot imagine resisting and doing good deeds that are far beyond the demands of duty or charity. Similarly, a hero or heroine is a person who does not do just what is commanded, but much more—indeed, much more than anyone could have expected. One cannot command saintliness or heroism, and it is no one's duty to be a saint or a hero or heroine. Nevertheless, our ethics would be impoverished without such concepts and if we did not aspire to *be* such persons. This aspiration inspires the best in us and the best of what we call our morals. Refraining from a forbidden act because of fear of punishment or anticipation of guilt may still count as "moral," but it is nothing like, and does not feel at all like, that sense of what Nietzsche calls "nobility," which motivates our best actions. Acting from a sense of duty may be motivated and accompanied by a comforting sense of righteousness, but that is something less than even the beginning of sainthood or heroism, for it is typical of the saint and the hero that they do not even

2. In *Corporate Cultures* (Reading, Mass.: Addison-Wesley, 1982), A. Kennedy and T. Deal say that "Heroism is a leadership component that is all but forgotten by modern management. Since the 1920's, the corporate world has been powered by managers who are rationalists, who do strategic planning, write memos and devise flow charts. . . . Managers run institutions; heroes create them."

think of what they are doing in such terms. Indeed, it is in part that naiveté, devoid of self-doubt and deliberation, that may make them saints and heroes.

Saints and heroes have the virtues appropriate to their cultures; these will not, obviously, all be the same. The Christian saints had different virtues from those of Buddhism, and Francis of Assisi had different virtues from Mohammed's. Achilles and Alexander the Great had very different virtues from those of Gandhi and Martin Luther King, and Einstein, who was a popular folk hero in America, had a different set of virtues from those of Giordano Bruno, who was burned at the stake in 1600 for his scientific speculations. But the virtues of the saints and heroes are not just the ordinary virtues that make a "good person"— honesty, trustworthiness, a sense of humor; indeed, their virtues may be such as to eclipse some of those more ordinary and domesticated virtues altogether, particularly in times of moral turmoil when saints and heroes are particularly prevalent. It is far more important to the sainthood of Augustine that he was extremely devout than that he had a sense of humor, and it is far more important to the heroism of Beowulf that he could slay terrifying monsters than that he should be a nice guy.

The occasional contradiction between virtues and moral rules, between the virtues themselves and in particular between the more ordinary virtues and the extraordinary virtues of saints and heroes helps to explain our fascination with the character we call the "rogue." Rogues are familiar heroes and heroines in contemporary American literature and culture, even if they have not yet made a noticeable appearance in ethics as such. The rogue is almost always a likable figure, often played in movies by such charming stars as Burt Reynolds, Richard Pryor, and Goldie Hawn, for example. In the movies, the rogue character breaks the law, or at least is at odds with the law, having robbed a bank or undertaken some devious, daredevil plot, which more often than not, includes breaking no fewer than several dozen traffic laws within a ten-minute chase scene. In literary criticism, such a character is often called the "antihero," a term that expresses some ethical confusion about the fact that the person has the status but not the morals of a hero. In the corporation, one does not expect law-breakers but nevertheless there is a familiar American character we call the "outlaw," who may within the bounds of legality nevertheless show how far the bounds of propriety may be creatively challenged.[3]

3. "Perhaps no other situational hero fires the imagination of employees more than the outlaw or maverick: Billy the Kid, Patton, bad boys with a heart of gold. This hero is necessary when the company needs some degree of creativity for a challenge to existing values. Outlaws can symbolize the darker side of an organization, yet their bizarre behavior will release the pent-up tension everyone feels" (T. Deal and A. Kennedy, *Corporate Cultures*).

Why should such a character be mentioned in ethics at all, except perhaps as an unfortunate popular example of rampant immorality? Because, first of all, like it or not, these are the "heroes" and "heroines" who now provide the moral examples for millions of American children. (Burt Reynolds was voted both the most popular and the most admired male in America in several youth polls over the past few years— not Reynolds the private individual, of course, but Reynolds as the "bandit" persona of the movies.) Second, such examples illustrate quite clearly the complexity of our actual morals and moral conceptions, which are not limited to universal rules and obedience but, quite the contrary, include a distinctive admiration for those who dare to be different—so long as they are also charming and attractive. Third, it points out the enormous range of the concept of "character" in ethics, which is not restricted to the traditional "man (or woman) of character" of Victorian novels—a person who is honorable, trustworthy, and a good mate; it also includes eccentrics and rogues who may not be "moral" in the narrow, traditional sense.

It would be misleading, however, to leave the example of the rogue in the hands of American moviemakers, as if the sole occupation of such characters were the perpetration of financially rewarding felonies.[4] There is a far more honorable history of roguery, in which the compensating virtues go beyond superficial charm and attractiveness and provide rewards for society for generations to come. This history includes many of the great artists of past centuries who were famously difficult people and often selfish and immoral as well. (Whether they had to be so to be great artists, or became so because they were great artists, are two much-celebrated but dubious hypotheses that we need not explore here.) Beethoven, for example, scandalized most of Viennese society with his lack of manners and the absence of any sense of trustworthiness. The great French author Balzac motivated himself to write by plunging deeply in debt with high living. Picasso's moral eccentricities have been much publicized in recent years, but his behavior is not very different from that of a great many famous artists—male and female—in the bohemian culture in which the arts have flourished for the past century or so. In the realm of the intellect, Freud and Jung have often been accused of inconsiderate if not immoral behavior toward their psychoanalytic colleagues. And in the world of business, the most well-known heroes have often been known for their bossiness, their crudity, even their miserliness, but yet their status as rogues and heroes

4. In fact, the role of businessmen and -women as such in the media has often been documented and shown to be unflattering, to say the least. A study several years ago showed that some 80 percent of the representative executives on television were depicted as fools, crooks, and pompous tyrants. When a businessman breaks out of his mold to become a hero or a rogue, he usually jettisons his business role as well (The Media Institute, 1981).

(rarely as saints) outlasts the gossip and slander surrounding them. The importance of these characters is also to remind us that acts of creativity and courage often consist in following one's own sense of integrity rather than thoughtless obedience, and inspiring others rather than following them. The hero today is rarely the most ferocious fighter; he or she is more likely the persistent, original thinker who pursues an idea to its fruition.

Finally, a word should be said about the clown. Every office has (or needs) one. Like the rogue, the clown releases tension and often indicates real weaknesses in the company and in its leading personalities. (A witty imitation of the boss can do more toward departmental reform than a thousand complaints and memos.) The clown is, no doubt, a source of inefficiency in an office, and that, perhaps, is his or her greatest virtue. The more a company runs like the proverbial machine, the less human it will be and the less inspired the humans in it will be. The clown, like the rogue, reminds us all of the place of our jobs in our lives and our business in the world, something that humor—even silliness—can do better than any sermon or book on business ethics. Some of the virtues most prized in our society—independence, humor, initiative, and a kind of courage—are too often left out of the management books on efficiency and effectiveness and the strategic planning books and corporate reports. To think of the entrepreneurial rogue as simply "immoral" or the corporate clown as simply silly is to miss an extremely important ethical point and present us with a fraudulent portrait of both business and ethics.

25

Theories in Practice:
Ethical Styles

> Outstanding achiever[s] not only had a different executive style,
> but [were] inconsistent in personal style. Paradoxically, successful
> implementators have many styles. They are regularly inconsistent.
>
> W. SKINNER AND W. SASSER,
> *Harvard Business Review*

The variety of virtues and the contextual nature of so much of business
ethics too readily raise the awesome (but innocent) specter of "relativism" or, worse, utter indecisiveness. In the conflict-resolution-minded
context of practical problems, twenty-five-century-old disputes do not
appear promising, and, even given some semblance of a generally agreed
upon if banal principle, practical application is often difficult, or at least
debatable. Not surprisingly, many of the people to whom our ethical
theories are being applied retreat, in the name of efficiency, to dog-
matism or existentialism; in the imminently practical words of a classic
gangster movie, "Ya takes yu's choice and ya takes da consequences."
But where our tradition perhaps fails us most in the realm of practice
may be our age old conviction that there must be a "right" (if not "true")
way of thinking about ethics, rather than a variety of ways, each of
them "ethical." We are still captivated by the image of Moses bringing
down the Ten Commandments from Mount Sinai, a single set of ethical imperatives. Or, more philosophically, we are enamored of the Pla-
tonic image of a single great Good, written in the heavens and discov-
erable, just possibly, through human reason. What we tend to deny is
that people are different, even within the same organization and seemingly with the same values and same projects and purposes. In other
words, we might say that there are different *ethical styles*, just as there
are different management styles.

"Ethical styles" is a phrase and an idea that would have been utterly
unacceptable until a few years ago—except, perhaps, to Nietzsche and
Oscar Wilde. It smacks of relativism of an odious sort. It suggests not

only subjectivism (which at least can be "deep" and supported by extensive reasons and reasoning) but superficiality as well—ethics and ethical behavior as fashion, a matter of personality or worse, a costume of thoughts and actions that may be put aside as easily as it can be put on. Of course, different ethical styles would have very different advantages and disadvantages, and it may well be that an ethical style is no more easily changed than other life-long traits of character such as thoughtfulness, recklessness, or spontaneous generosity. Nevertheless, the idea that the rule utilitarian and the Kantian deontologist are just expressing personal differences, rather than arguing—once and for all—about what is really "right" grates against our philosophical sensibilities. Is the categorical imperative really just a Kantian fashion, perhaps typical of certain personality types, and not the key to "morality" after all?

But the fact is that promoters of applied ethics have been forced into a recognition of ethical styles, albeit very much against their own philosophical judgment. This is evident, for example, at the beginning of the large majority of applied ethics textbooks, which begin by rehearsing once again—but probably for the first time for the future executives, physicians, engineers, or lawyers in the classroom—the time-honored disputes among utilitarians, deontologists, and, perhaps, libertarians, with mention of a few metaethical theorists thrown in for good measure. With considerable embarrassment, the ethicist seeking to apply these theories will suggest, "Now an act utilitarian would say that . . ." The "applied" context is not the place to dispute the ultimate superiority of one or another ethical school, to show that rule-governed (or deontological) arguments do indeed involve utilitarian considerations, or that utilitarianism, despite all clever qualifications, cannot adequately deal with the question of justice with desert island examples or the gleeful sadist. The case itself demands discussion—be it the responsibility of pharmaceutical companies to stop drug abuse in the streets, euthanasia for the dying, bridge bid rigging, or criminal-client confidentiality. The audience wants a resolution, the perennial philosophical dispute, quite frankly, be damned. And so they hear "Well, a libertarian would no doubt see it this way . . ."

In the context of that long classical tradition in ethics, which we conveniently but somewhat arbitrarily trace back to Socrates, such answers are indeed inadequate and embarrassing. In the applied context, on the other hand, they are in some equally embarrassing sense necessary. Disputes between utilitarians and deontologists are not restricted to professional philosophy. They are a very real part of the arguments that go on daily in offices and boardrooms across the country. Indeed, philosophers thrown into practical contexts are often surprised—with mixed feelings—to see just how well the "nonphilosophers" have mustered up not only evidence but arguments for their positions. It sometimes appears that all that there is for the philosopher to do is to give these positions their proper names—an exercise of dubious practical importance but in any case considerably less than the traditional view of philosophy as a conceptual peacemaker would prescribe.

And yet, the recognition of such large ethical differences can be of enormous practical importance, even in the absence of a knock-down argument for one ethical position and against all of the others. Philosophers may be frustrated by the lack of resolution to the classical disputes, but they are at least well informed about what is in dispute and practiced in the art of clarifying what is at stake in this position or that one. The fact is that a great many practical disputes, in which the relevant evidence has been made available and the prominent arguments have been formulated and exhausted, turn out to be identical to the classic philosophical disputes (if a bit more crude and less filled with jargon). But the philosopher who is waiting for the final solution in ethics is not going to be in an enviable position to resolve practical disputes involving the same unresolved philosophical questions. In practice, if not in theory, ethical styles is all there is.

In practical disputes, it is not clear to the participants how differences in ethical style are to be treated, partly because there is usually not the recognition that the dispute is, in part, a conflict of ethical styles. Once accounted for, however, differences get treated as options or as possibilities to be resolved through negotiation. What is much worse, however, is when the discussion takes on the same direction as most philosophical debates and stops only with the unacceptable conclusion that "it's a complicated issue." However philosophically gratifying, that conclusion is the worst one possible, if our experience in business ethics is a fair indication. It doesn't teach conflict resolution but rather the importance of ignoring philosophy.

The classic and most familiar clash of ethical styles is the seemingly irresolvable conflict between the rule-governed deontologist and the utilitarian. It is worth repeating, but in style-minded terms, what the nature of that conflict tends to be in practice. The deontologist believes in the letter of the law, and in the office or in the boardroom he or she will very likely cite the rules of the institution or principles from a professional handbook. It may not matter that the rule in question is outdated or impractical. It may not matter that it became a matter of law or policy under another administration now out of office. It may not matter that the rule will no doubt be changed some day. The deontologist believes that one should obey rules, laws, regulations, and policies, whatever their origins and whatever the consequences. Any other way of thinking, from his standpoint, is amoral.

The utilitarian, on the other hand, is self-consciously practical. Rules serve a purpose, and they are to be obeyed just because—but only because—they serve that purpose. A rule that proves to be impractical no longer deserves our respect or obedience. A rule that was formulated under very different circumstances or was legislated by a different administration should be carefully scrutinized and not given too much weight. The utilitarian makes his decisions on the sole ground that a certain course of action has the best consequences for everyone involved. If that fits the rules (as it usually does), then so much the better. If it does not, then so much the worse for the rules—and so much too for the deontologist, who because of sheer obstinacy or perhaps for some unfathomable personal reason refuses to see the point.

We know how this little scenario tends to go, from departmental meetings if not from arguments in ethics: the deontologist considers the utilitarian an opportunist, an amoral deviant, a man who does not respect authority and the rules. The utilitarian considers the deontologist to be utterly unreasonable and impractical if not neurotic and "impossible." When general utility conflicts with an established rule, the utilitarian and the deontologist are sure to misunderstand one another. There can be no compromise because each of them considers his own position to be beyond negotiation and neither can understand the other, except, perhaps, in the terms of moral pathology.

Some practical disputes get more fine-grained; arguments between deontologists and between varieties of utilitarians are not difficult to find. Of course, not every attitude in ethics constitutes an ethical style. There are, however, many ways of being ethical. We have mentioned the two most common of them, deontological and utilitarian. Some others are variations on these; some are insightful, some degenerate. More often than some philosophers suppose, "metaethical" theories appear as ethical styles, typically defining normative content as well. But what is most important is that all of these deserve to be called "ethical" and perhaps "moral" approaches to practical problems, though they differ considerably and have different advantages and disadvantages in terms of simplicity, clarity, applicability, and scope. Here I have outlined seven distinct ethical styles of thinking and acting, but without any claim to completeness, in order to give some sense of the sorts of attitudes and approaches that appear to be most prevalent in practical situations (no doubt one could make up many more on an a priori basis:

1. *Rule-Governed:* thinking and acting on the basis of rules and principles, with only secondary regard to circumstances or exceptions.
2. *Utilitarian:* weighing probable consequences, both to the company or the professional and to the public well-being. Principles are important only as rules of thumb. "The greatest good for the greatest number of people" is the ultimate test for any action or decision.
3. *Loyalist:* evaluating all decisions first in terms of benefit to the profession, the institution, the company, and its reputation. In business, "the company man."
4. *Prudent:* long-term self-interest through identification with the

profession, and the institution, the company, or the larger social good, but always aware of the only contingent connection between self-interest and the larger interests one serves.

5. *Virtuous:* every action is measured in terms of its reflection on one's character (or the profession, institution, or company reputation) without immediate regard to consequences and often without paying much attention to general principles.

6. *Intuitive:* making decisions on the basis of "conscience" and without deliberation, argument, or reasons. Intuitive thinkers tend to be extremely impatient with more deliberative deontological and utilitarian types. It is a style that flourishes at the top of the decision-making hierarchy, if only because of an obvious history of natural selection. (Errors in intuition, unlike errors in deliberation and calculation, cannot be readily explained or rationalized.)

7. *Empathetic:* following one's feelings of sympathy and compassion. "Putting oneself in the other's place" is the modus operandi of the empathetic style, whether the "other" be a competitor ("How would we like it if he . . .") or a client ("I can easily imagine how it would feel to be . . .").

With this list as our basis, perhaps it would be worth mentioning a few degenerate styles which are not uncommon variations on these:

1. *Rule-governed* [degenerate form] *compulsive:* being so caught up in principles that even the point of the principles is lost from view.

2. *Utilitarian* [degenerate form] *perplexed liberal:* finding so many possible consequences and complications that action becomes impossible and inaction ("pending investigation") the only moral course. The source of most committees.

3. *Loyalist* [degenerate form] *hominoid:* in office circumstances, the ("yes-man") technician who has lost all sense of social context and even of his or her own well-being.

4. *Prudent* [degenerate form] *gamesman:* thinks of a profession solely in terms of self-advancement and treats all rules and laws—including moral principles—as mere boundaries of action. "Free enterprise" rhetoric in business often adopts this stance. Ethical problems for the gamesman are mainly obstacles, opportunities, challenges. Not uncommon in legal ethics, frowned upon in medicine.

5. *Virtuous* [degenerate form] *heroic:* in which every action is self-consciously a reflection of extraordinary virtues and abilities and in which any course of action that is routine or ordinary is not to be seriously considered.

6. *Intuitive* [degenerate form] *mystical:* making decisions on the basis of invariably cosmic intuitions, often with cloudy references to the "whole earth" or "cosmic harmony," without further justification and with

as little reference to practical realities as possible. Eccentricity is taken to be a virtue (prosaic intuitions are a sign of sheer heteronomy).

7. *Empathetic* [degenerate form] *sentimental* or *maudlin:* having so much sympathy that it becomes impossible to look after one's own or the profession's (institution's, company's) self-interest. A "bleeding heart" and a very short career in business or law, a nervous breakdown in medicine. (In the press, often used as a conflict of hard-hearted professionals against ethics and sensitivity.)

Perfectly proper ethical styles can also go wrong. One way is to be inappropriate. Whatever one's preferred style of thinking, there are contexts in which some styles are clearly appropriate, others clearly inappropriate. For example, with a religious group, a prudential or utilitarian style will be disastrous. At a sales meeting or among a group of young surgeons, on the other hand, a deontological style will sound abstract, pompous, and beside the point. Philosophers sometimes talk as if moral considerations (of the deontological variety) are always appropriate, in any practical context. The fact is rather that ethical styles—and style of any kind—are context sensitive. The idea that some peculiarly tedious styles are appropriate everywhere has caused many a philosopher to be left off the guest list. (Kant's popularity as a dinner guest in Königsberg makes one wonder.) Whether or not there is a "true" ethical theory, there is always a place—or not a place—for certain ethical styles.

The discussion of ethical styles is not intended as a part of—much less to replace—traditional ethical arguments and debates. But for the philosopher who tries to apply ethics <u>and</u> for whom that means something more than hanging our laundry in the seminars of professions other than our own, it is a concept of considerable value. To talk about ethical styles is, first, to say, that many of the positions and arguments that have defined the history of ethics also define practical positions and arguments used by people who have never taken or thought of taking a philosophy course, and, second, to emphasize the importance of respect for ethical differences—which we may take for granted but are not easily recognized by most people in the midst of an argument. It is in times of conflict or crisis that differences in ethical styles become prominent, and it is in those times that such differences must be understood and negotiated instead of—as so often—allowed to make a bad situation that much more explosive.

26

Moral Mazes, Moral Courage, and the Problem of Integrity

> What is right in the corporation is not what is right in a man's home or in his church. What is right in the corporation is what the guy above you wants from you. That's what morality is in the corporation.
>
> ROBERT JACKALL, *Moral Mazes*

The Aristotelean framework of community and personal virtue is, I believe, just what most corporations need in these difficult days. The new emphasis on toughness and competition can be healthy, but only so long as toughness if properly understood and not opposed to integrity and competition is similarly not contrasted with cooperation. But I do not want to promote the Aristotelean approach to business as if it were the answer to end all answers in corporate ethics. Communities can be chaotic and demeaning, suffocating and even dangerous as well as cooperative, productive, and fulfilling. The personal virtues will wither or become self-defeating if not nurtured in a climate that recognizes and rewards virtue and is itself virtuous. Even the search for excellence can lead to arrogance and elitism as well as to quality and teamwork. What's more, the presence of alternative ethical styles suggests that, even in the best corporations with the best people, internal dissension will be the rule rather than the exception.[1] But it is in the midst of cooperative and creative commotion (also known as "chaos") that the virtues show their stuff. Without a sense of community and cooperation, there will be no corporation. Without individual as well as corporate virtue, all success—if it is success—will be empty. But that means that business ethics cannot be limited to a description and a celebration of the virtues; it must also take a part in cultivating them—and in creating the kinds of organizations in which they flourish.

1. See, notably, Stuart Hampshire, *Morality and Conflict* (Cambridge: Harvard University Press, 1983).

Discussions of the virtues have been hamstrung since Aristotle by a kind of wishful thinking and a certain chauvinist narrow-mindedness. The chauvinism is the presumption that one's own community and culture represent the ideal, imperfect, perhaps, but on the right track—as opposed to all of those philistines and barbarians "out there." The wishful thinking is the unexamined assumption that one's own community and culture are coherent, that there is, accordingly, a unity of the virtues, a happy harmony that the virtuous man or woman will enjoy. What is notoriously missing in Aristotle, accordingly, is any reformist impulse, any attempt to view his community and culture as possibly not only imperfect but deeply flawed. In retrospect, of course, we can rightly despise the fact that the prosperity of Athens weighed heavily on the backs of its slave population, however much historical understanding we might put into that perspective. In a milder manner, we can criticize Aristotle's limited view of the role of commerce and speculate, without much difficulty, that an unmodernized Athens, despite its many accomplishments, would today be a largely underdeveloped civilization. But, to get back to our own corporate communities and cultures, we too easily presume that we are on the right track, even if imperfect, and that our institutions are coherent. The truth is that our entire corporate system is currently being forced to reexamine and perhaps even reinvent itself.[2] It is not at all clear that we are on the right track or on any established track at all, he may have to clear a new uncharted way. Nor is it at all evident that there is, in Aristotle's phrase, a "unity of the virtues." That is why so much of business and business ethics has been concerned with internal dissension and ethical dilemmas. Too often doing right is tantamount to threatening one's job, and too often doing what one is supposed to do is also doing wrong.

The Aristotelean thesis of the unity of the virtues is, put crudely, the view that, if one (truly) has one virtue, he or she will have all of them. The virtues do not and will not conflict. I believe experience proves this to be just plain false, and one of the most obvious discoveries of any empirically minded or practical virtue ethics is that there is often a conflict of virtues, a clash of loyalties, a disharmony of equally valued values. I can readily hear a pressured sales manager arguing that too much dependability and forthright honesty can undermine one's skills in negotiation and, in a sense, the business enterprise itself. In a recent Dudley Moore movie, an advertising executive decides that his agency will only tell the truth. The chaos that follows is predictable and instructive in this regard. It is clear that loyalties often conflict on the job, particularly in a politicized company or institution—and that probably doesn't leave anyone out. One's duty to superiors may well conflict with one's obligations to subordinates, and in any but the best-organized

2. John Naisbett, *Reinventing the Corporation* (New York: Bantam, 1983).

company there is always the possibility of conflicting, even contradictory, but equally obligatory orders from two different superiors. One's sense of loyalty to an aging and no longer effective manager who provided one's job opportunity in the first place may well clash with a more general sense of obligation to the company. There is no unity to the virtues, and as Nietzsche in particular argued—against Aristotle—the pursuit of one virtue may well eclipse or even maim others.[3] The pursuit of excellence in business puts pressure on the corporate community as well as consolidates its mission, and the pursuit of personal integrity often runs against a corporate wall of resistance when corporate mandates contradict personal or other company values.

The seriousness of these conflicts and clashes is documented in detail by Robert Jackall in his *Moral Mazes.*[4] I think that he ultimately makes too much of the clash between morality and corporate politics and fails to appreciate both the multitude of ethical styles and the importance of compromise rather than purity in ethics.[5] As Tom Peters, a notable Aristotelean, has said, "a 'pure' ethical stance in the face of most firms' political behavior will lead you out the door in short order. . . . The line between ethical purity and arrogant eccentricity is a fine one."[6] In any less than perfect organization or society, there will be no guaranteed unity of the virtues no matter how much integrity you have, and there is no easy distinction between virtue and the duties of one's job or position. Virtues are context-bound, and contexts overlap and clash with one another. In any organization, there are overlapping and concentric circles of identity and responsibility, and a virtue in one arena may conflict with a virtue in another—indeed, it may even be a vice. This is a painful realization, and it may even tempt some to declare an Aristotelean ethics to be impossible. My reply, however, is that even Aristotle realized that the search for a perfect world was futile, that one did the best with what one had, and ethical ideals were nonetheless

3. Nietzsche, *Thus Spoken Zarathustra*, Book I (New York: Viking, 1954). See also Lester Hunt, *Nietzsche and the Virtues* (New York: Routledge, 1990).

4. Jackall, *Moral Mazes*, pp. 191–92: "Bureaucracy breaks apart the ownership of property from its control, social independence from occupation, substance from appearances, action from responsibility, obligation from guilt, language from meaning, and notions of truth from reality." In place of morality and merit, "bureaucracy makes its own internal rules and social context the principle moral gauges for action."

5. Jackall suggests an unbridgeable gap between morality and bureaucracy and argues that a "bureaucratic" ethic comes to replace the old work ethic, our lost "economy of salvation," once rich with powerful religious and symbolic meanings. Finally giving up the facade of social science neutrality that he has been maintaining throughout the earlier chapters of the book, Jackall preaches that we find ourselves in "a Calvinist world without a Calvinist God" (ibid., p. 193). "In such a world, notions of fairness or equity that managers might privately hold, as measures gauging the worth of their own work, become merely quaint" (198). Ultimately, he concludes, it is "a society where morality becomes indistinguishable from the quest for one's own survival and advantage" (p. 204).

6. Tom Peters, "The Ethics Debate," *Ethics Digest* (Dec. 1989): 1–2.

essential. Not only institutions but people were naturally flawed. What after all, were all of those Greek tragedies about?[7] But then again, this is not to say that we should retreat in desperation, pretend a false sense of integrity that is too detached or divorced from the realities of one's role identity in the company—as philosophers and business theorists, standing on the outside, are too prone to do—or to encourage total absorption in one's company or community role so as to be incapable of seeing beyond it (Aristotle's own tendency and a favorite strategy of authoritarian managers). But there is no such easy answer. We always wear multiple hats and have potentially competing responsibilities. Thus, by way of conclusion, we must again emphasize the importance of judgment and integrity, which means, among other things, keeping the big picture in mind. But this isn't just a matter of vision; it is also a cultivated virtue, comprised of a balancing act and a sense of corporate and personal diplomacy that might well be compared to juggling.

The balancing-act and juggling metaphor puts a spin on the problem of the disunity of the virtues that is, I think, far more constructive than the ultimately despairing picture of "moral mazes" that emerges from Jackall's detailed study. It is not as if we are lost or trapped so much as we find ourselves in positions of increasing complexity in which holding it all together—in other words, integrity—is what ultimately counts. But Jackall has rightly identified what is surely the most serious threat to that integrity, and that is the problem of *embeddedness*. People get embedded in their jobs, their positions in the company, and they have trouble seeing beyond the pressures that they face in the company. The result, however, is a problem much like we diagnosed in our opening case of the overzealous bond trader. It is a kind of blindness, cut off from the larger view. Business ethics means looking beyond the walls of one's department or company and beyond (or above) the "bottom line." Unfortunately, this is a perspective easy to encourage but difficult to adopt when one is in the midst of a company crisis, and it is the rare executive or manager who can see the bigger picture in the middle of such circumstances. We have all seen corporations sacrifice their best people in the face of a financial downturn, and we have all worked with those "survivors" who, while contributing very little (and often slowing things down) manage to remain in the company through the harshest reductions. The secret of their success, it seems, is their embeddedness, their insinuation in a protected pocket under some patron or guardian who may also succeed through similar insinuation. Those who get fired, on the other hand, may so suffer just because they are too visible and not sufficiently embedded, despite (or because of) their accomplish-

7. Aristotle's "tragic flaw" theory is found in his *Poetics*, but for a mind-bending account of Aristotle's effort to ultimately deny tragedy on behalf of an idealist concept of integrity, see Martha Nussbaum, *The Fragility of Goodness* (Cambridge: Cambridge University Press, 1989).

ments. They make the mistake of serving the purpose of the practice instead of, as current vulgarity has it, practicing "C.Y.A." Indeed, as Robert Jackall puts it (summarizing Thorsten Veblen): there are "no intrinsic connections between the good of a particular corporation, the good of an individual manager, and the common weal."[8]

Robert Jackall has described the problem of embeddedness in depressing detail, showing how executives and employees of a variety of corporations sacrifice their sense of personal values and kowtow to the political, sometimes manipulative, and even sadistic whims of their superiors. Some of them hope that they too may one day get to be manipulative, whimsical, and sadistic to others. Most of them just want to get by, to "get along by going along," to survive the next company or division upheaval and keep their jobs and their paycheck. He shows how they get embedded in system, walled in without a view or, worse, blinding themselves to the obvious in the name of "reality" and taking loyalty and loyalty alone as their mandate. "What is right in the corporation is what the guy above you wants from you." It is not all that clear how an individual employee or manager, embedded in the corporation, can do more than do his or her job well and fairly.

We earlier distinguished (with considerable qualification) between the purposes of a practice and its intrinsic goals and rules. The ethics of a practice, I suggested, consisted not only in honoring the rules and pursuing its goals but in trying to fulfill the ultimate purpose of the practice, which in the case of business is general prosperity and a version of distributive justice, reward according to merit. But there is an unavoidable shift from ultimate purposes to internal goals, and the danger is that specific tasks and duties will eclipse the overall purposes of business altogether. Most of the time, of course, this is not an ethical problem, for the tasks and duties of a job in a well-organized corporation will already be fine-tuned to the fulfillment of the corporate mission and ideals. But in a sleaze-bag corporation, fulfilling one's tasks and duties as instructed is surely not enough. My student who quit her job as a "telemarketer" for the company that sold nonexistent surgical equipment is an apt and common example. Perceiving the violation of ethics and the wrongness of fulfilling her tasks and duties in such a case did not require any great ethical sensitivity, but it did require a certain amount of sacrifice and courage. "But I really needed the job," my student complained. And so do we all. The complicity between one's own tasks and duties and less obviously unethical corporate behavior, however, is always an open question, and it is thus always essential to see one's particular job and role in an organization in the larger ethical context, even if (especially if) one "really needs the job."

If corporate life were (as it often proclaims) a matter of merit, if

8. Jackall, *Moral Mazes*, p. 198.

success really were the natural result of innovation, hard work, and good results, embeddedness would be at worst a distraction and, more often and much better, a welcome camaraderie in which to pursue joint projects and shared goals and interests. But in many if not most managerial positions, one's accomplishments are wholly dependent on the actions of others, including those over whom one has no supervisory capacity and no control. And so, one gets desperate, seeking out misleading measures and false security, and loses sight—or one's boss looses sight—of the ultimate goals and purposes of the organization. When sight gets blurred, the idea of excellence loses its meaning, to be replaced by a more rigid and often pathological sense of community—"teamwork" in that cynical sense that every manager recognizes as "play ball or get out." In other words, shut up and keep your ethics to yourself. Thus the disastrous tendency to measure results by "the bottom line" and ethics by costs and benefits and the pressure to compromise not only one's personal values but also the values fostered by the corporation and the inevitable temptation to office politics.

What is the answer to Jackall's gruesome and all-too-real portrait of many corporations in trouble? Cooperation, in this case, is part of the problem, and integrity, in the face of conflicts of the virtues, is the challenge rather than the answer. The answer, in two words, is *moral courage*. But, again, this often lauded virtue has more often than not been misunderstood and miscast. Moral courage is not just another warrior virtue, transposed from the battlefield into the more civilized realm of the corporation. It is not the same as toughness, although toughness can be, as we noted earlier, a form of moral courage. Moral courage is not self-sacrifice; indeed, this tendency to confuse the virtues with altruism and self-sacrifice is one of the confusions we have been fighting for the past few chapters. Moral courage is not self-righteous obstinacy and it is not all opposed to compromise. Indeed, moral courage more often consists in the willingness to compromise than in the refusal to do so.

In his *Vanguard Management,* O'Toole calls moral courage "the *sine qua non* of greatness."[9] But what O'Toole seems to have in mind is not moral courage at all, but rather a general concern for what he dubiously calls the "conservative" concern for (quoting John Adams), "a passion for the public good." But no matter how noble and virtuous it may be, philanthropy is not courage, and O'Toole's tendency to throw all of the virtues together into one large undifferentiated pot is disturb-

9. James O'Toole, *Vanguard Management* (New York: Doubleday, 1985), ch. 12. What is particularly remarkable about O'Toole's chapter, however, is that despite the bold claim in his title, as if it were a banner to be waved, he says virtually nothing about moral courage at all. Indeed, he does not even employ the phrase again until the penultimate page of the chapter, and what he talks about is nothing more specific than the usual grab-bag of virtues that fall under the now-tired heading of "social responsibility."

ing, to say the least. But if he never gets clear about his subject matter, O'Toole is nevertheless right in his titular pronouncement. Moral courage is the *sine qua non* not only of greatness but of ordinary integrity as well. Indeed, it *is* integrity, proving itself under tough circumstances. Moral courage includes an understanding of the big picture, the purpose(s) of the organization, and the ways in which the organization or some part of it thwarts its own best intentions. It means sticking with those best intentions, heeding a higher loyalty than one's immediate superiors or, on occasion, even the chief executive officer. The price may be high, but the usual celebration of the sad case of the whistleblower and the company martyr is often overdone here. The truth is, as O'Toole points out in his examples, that moral courage is often successful as well. But it is not, as he suggests, just a virtue for leaders and leadership. It is, under pressure, the virtue that puts the others to the test. Moral courage is integrity under fire.

If Jackall's diagnosis were generally true, the consequences for business ethics would be ominous. The prognosis for the survival of American business—or at any rate the survival of the corporation—would be bleak. If business is to pursue its purpose, if the market is to provide any sort of meritocracy, it must preserve more than the illusion that hard work and contribution are rewarded. Once the practice collapses and no longer serves its purpose, once the goals of a practice become purely self-protective, such essential underlying values of fairness and cooperation also start to break down. In a world where only politics and not productivity counts, politics and not productivity will indeed come to dominate. In a world where success is measured *only* by whom one knows and pleases and goals are defined *solely* by reference to the internal hierarchy, one's sense of integrity and purpose do indeed start coming apart. Jackall asks rhetorically, "How does one act in such a world and maintain a sense of personal integrity?"[10] for he makes it all-too-clear that there is no integrity within a corporate world of pervasive mediocrity, with no fixed criteria for merit and an obsession with "teamwork" (rather than work) and a preference for short-term solutions that hide problems rather than admit and solve them.

But even in those momentary (but very painful) periods of transition, which often precede the bankruptcy of the organization, there are always outside forces that will, eventually, remind the most corrupt corporation of its ultimate purposes and its social responsibilities.[11] Whether

10. Jackall, *Moral Mazes*, p. 194.
11. It is extremely unfortunate that one of the current shibboleths of some top management thinking is that such "shake-ups" are healthy and bring out the best in people. True, a newer, "leaner and meaner" organization may be more competitive in a fast-changing market, but the results of continuous upheaval are more often than not precisely the pathology that Jackall so well describes. But most organizations most of the time are not in a period of shake-up, nor could they be. It is precisely the presumption

or not the consumer is "sovereign," the customer still has a lot of clout, and whatever upheavals and political battles may be fought within the corporation the bottom line is still out there in the marketplace. Someone has to be producing and selling something. Indeed, the viciousness of corporate political battles is often not due to financial exigency or "fighting for a smaller piece of the pie" but to continued success. No one fights to be captain of a sinking ship. The abusiveness and intrusiveness of office politics have their limits, and those limits are set by the need to produce and make a profit. To put the point bluntly, if there were no market, there wouldn't be anything to fight about. The obvious truth is that there is (and must be) considerable correlation between corporate cooperation and contribution in the marketplace. Integrity in business is, accordingly, paying attention to those ultimate powers of the marketplace rather than just the immediate pressures of one's job situation. Thus it is that integrity and success are not so much opposed as mutually supportive. It is a healthy organization that recognizes this and makes sure that it permeates every level and is sought and cultivated in every member of the institution.

What Jackall describes in *Moral Mazes* is the dark side of corporate ethics: "the deep anxiety created by organizational upheavals that jumble career plans, or the troubling animosity generated by intense rivalries that pit managers against one another in struggles for prestige and say-so, or the emotional aridity caused by continually honing one's self to make hard choices with ambiguous outcomes."[12] My aim in this book has been to provide an antidote to these anxieties and pressures. If the problem with Michael Lewis's traders was that they lost sight of the larger picture and purpose of business because they became so flushed with their own success, the problem for the average corporate manager is losing any secure sense of how he or she fits into that larger picture. In one sense, the two cases are the very opposite of one another: the trader enjoys clear-cut goals and immediate feedback while the typical manager suffers from the lack of both well-defined goals and meaningful feedback. But for our purpose here the differences are of less importance than the similarities, conceptual isolation that blocks our vision and destroys any sense of ultimate purpose and of the larger community and makes personal integrity impossible.

Jackall asks rhetorically, "How does one act in such a world and maintain a sense of personal integrity?"[13] But things aren't always or even usually as bad as the corporations in crisis that Jackall describes,

---

of stability that allows large organizations to operate and the people within them to identify themselves and their goals with the organization. Like any good pathologist, Jackall has a keen eye for disease but therefore tends to seek it out while ignoring the healthy organism.

12. Ibid., p. 4.
13. Ibid., p. 194.

and corporate life is not hell even if it is not an invitation to heaven (*a la* the Puritan ethic and Jackall's "economy of salvation"). True, life in a rotten organization does threaten and can corrupt a person's integrity, but there are a lot fewer bad corporations out there than the pessimists believe and a lot more integrity than the critics of business would allow. Indeed, as the first full century of corporate business draws to a close one would like to think that there is at least as much hope as there is cause for despair, that in the competition for corporate survival that will rock many industries in the next few years one of the most important ingredients for success as well as survival will be the Aristotelean virtues—a sense of community and cooperation and not the legalistic fiction of the corporation as a competitive money-making machine, the search for excellence and not just short-term profits, the importance of integrity in both the individual and in the company and that larger picture, which, despite the still routine references to Adam Smith, has seemingly been lost from sight. I think that it is also being rediscovered. The corporation is no longer (if it ever was) the soul-destroying monolith that eliminates all individuality and extinguishes personal integrity. There is a new generation of corporate citizens, no longer addicted to the fast-tracking greed of the Eighties and no longer willing to tolerate the unquestioning obedience expected back in the Fifties. Then there are the survivors, in the Nineties, who have seen themselves betrayed and watched the old rules crumble. They understand that most Aristotelean business guru Tom Peters, when he says, "Each of us is ultimately lonely. In the end, it's up to each of us and each of us alone to figure out who we are and who we are not, and to act more or less consistently on those conclusions."[14] Together, we are reinventing the corporation and trying to create a business world that is not only prosperous and productive but personally and spiritually rewarding as well. Ethics and excellence, community and integrity, are not mere means to efficiency and effectiveness. They are the ends without which the corporation will have lost its soul.

14. Tom Peters, "The Ethics Debate," p. 2.

Bibliography

Abrahamsson, Bengt. *Military Professionalism and Political Power*. Beverly Hills, Calif.: Sage, 1972.

Ackerman, B. A. *Social Justice in the Liberal State*. New Haven: Yale University Press, 1980.

Andrews, Kenneth R. "Can the Best Corporations Be Made Moral?" *Harvard Business Review* (May–June 1973).

———. "Ethics in Practice." *Harvard Business Review* (Sept.–Oct. 1989).

Andrews, Kenneth R., and C. Roland Christensen. *Business Policy: Texts and Cases*. 6th ed. Homewood, Ill.: Irwin, 1987.

Aristotle. *Nichomachean Ethics*. In *The Works of Aristotle*. Trans. T. Irwin. Indianapolis: Hackett, 1985.

———. *Politics*. Trans. B. Jowett. New York: Modern Library, 1943.

Arrow, Kenneth. *Social Choice and Individual Values*. New Haven: Yale University Press, 1970.

Axelrod, Robert. *The Evolution of Cooperation*. New York: Basic Books, 1984.

Baier, Annette. *A Progress of Sentiments: Reflections on Hume's Treatise*. Cambridge: Cambridge University Press, 1991.

Barth, John. *Giles Goat-Boy*. New York: Fawcett, 1974.

Battaglia, O. William, and John J. Tarrant. *The Corporate Eunuch*. New York: Crowell, 1973.

Beauchamp, T., and N. Bowie, eds. *Ethical Theory and Business*. Engelwood Cliffs, N.J.: Prentice-Hall, 1983.

Bellah, Robert, et al. *Habits of the Heart*. Berkeley: University of California, 1985.

Bentham, Jeremy. *Introduction to the Principles of Morals and Legislation*. Oxford: Oxford University Press, 1948.

Bergman, Frithjof. "The Experience of Values." In *Revisions*, ed. Hauerwas S. and A. MacIntyre. Notre Dame: University of Notre Dame Press, 1983.

Berman, Martin. *Splitting the Difference*. Lawrence: University Press of Kansas, 1990.

Blum, Lawrence A. "Compassion." In *Explaining Emotions*, ed. Amelie Rorty. Berkeley: University of California Press, 1980.

———. *Friendship, Altruism and Morality*. London: Routledge and Kegan Paul, 1980.

Bonevac, Daniel, and Thomas Seung. "Conflicts of Values." *Philosophical Studies* (1988).

Bowie, Norman. *Business Ethics*. Engelwood Cliffs, N.J.: Prentice-Hall, 1982.

267

———. "Business Ethics as a Discipline: The Search for Legitimacy." In *Business Ethics: The State of the Art*, ed. R. Edward Freeman, New York: Oxford University Press, 1990.

———. "The Profit Seeking Paradox." In *Ethics of Administration*, ed. N. Dale Wright, Provo, Utah: Brigham Young University Press, 1988.

Brandeis, Justice Louis. "Competition." *American Legal News* 44 (Jan. 1913).

Brandt, R. B. *A Theory of the Good and the Right*. Oxford: Oxford University Press, 1979.

Brickman, Philip. "Models of Helping and Coping." *American Psychologist* 37, no. 4 (April 1982): 368–84.

Burrough, B. *Barbarians at the Gate* (New York: Harper Collins, 1990).

Calhoun, Cheryl H. "Feeling and Value." Ph.D. Dissertation, University of Texas, 1981.

Calhoun, Cheshire. "Justice, Care and Gender Bias." *Journal of Philosophy* 83 (Sept. 1988).

Campbell, Joseph. *The Power of Myth*. Ed. Betty Sue Flowers. New York: Doubleday, 1988.

Carnegie, Andrew. "Wealth." *North American Review* (June 1889). Reprinted in *Ethical Issues in Business*, by T. Donaldson and P. Werhane. Engelwood Cliffs, N.J.: Prentice-Hall, 1983.

Carr, Alfred. "Is Business Bluffing Ethical?" *Harvard Business Review* (Jan.–Feb. 1968).

Cicero. *De Officiis*. New York: Macmillan, 1913.

Ciulla, Joanne. "Casuistry and the Case for Business Ethics." In *Business and the Humanities*, 1989 Ruffin Lectures, ed. E. Freeman. New York: Oxford University Press, 1990.

———. *Honest Work*. New York: Random House, 1992.

Coleman, Jules L. "Market Contractarianism and the Unanimity Rule." In *Ethics and Economics, Social Philosophy and Policy* 2, no. 2 (Spring 1985).

———. *Markets, Morals and the Law*. Cambridge: Cambridge University Press, 1988.

Collard, David. *Altruism and Economics*. Oxford: Oxford University Press, 1978.

Collins, Denis. "Aristotle and Business." *Journal of Business Ethics* 6 (1987):

Cooper, John. *Reason and Human Good in Aristotle*. Indianapolis: Hackett, 1977.

Copp, David. "Morality, Reason and Management Science: The Rationale of Cost-Benefit Analysis." *Ethics and Economics, Social Philosophy and Policy* 2, no. 2 (Spring 1985).

Cropsey, Joseph. *Polity and Economy*. Westport, Conn.: Greenwood Press, 1957.

Daniels, Norman. "Merit and Meritocracy." *Philosophy and Public Affairs* 7 (1978): 206–23.

Davidson, Greg, and Paul Davidson. *Economics for a Civilized Society*. New York: Norton, 1989.

DeGeorge, Richard. *Business Ethics*. New York: Macmillan, 1982.

———. *Ethics, Free Enterprise and Public Policy*. New York: Oxford University Press, 1978.

———. "The Status of Business Ethics: Past and Future." *Journal of Business Ethics* 6, no. 3 (April 1987).

Derry, Robbin. *Moral Reasoning in Organizations: A Study of Men and Women Managers*. Ann Arbor, Mich.: University Microfilms, 1987.

Dion, Michael. "Corporate Ethics and Human Values." Paper presented at the University of British Columbia Applied Ethics Conference, June 1990.

Donaldson, T., and Werhane, P. *Ethical Issues in Business.* Engelwood Cliffs, N.J.: Prentice-Hall, 1983.

Donaldson, Thomas. *Corporations and Morality.* Engelwood Cliffs, N.J.: Prentice-Hall, 1982.

———. *International Business Theory.* New York: Oxford University Press, 1990.

———. "The Third Wave," *Ethics Digest* 6 (March 1989).

Douglas, Mary. *How Institutions Think.* Syracuse: Syracuse University Press, 1986.

Downie, R. S. *Roles and Values.* London: Methuen, 1971.

Drucker, Peter. "Ethical Chic." *Forbes,* Sept. 14, 1981, pp. 160–73.

———. *Management.* New York: Harper and Row, 1974.

———. "What is business Ethics?" *The Public Interest* 63 (Spring 1981).

Dunfee, Thomas. "Business Ethics and Extant Social Contracts." *Business Ethics Quarterly* (Jan 1991).

Elster, John. *The Cement of Society: A Study of Social Order.* Cambridge: Cambridge University Press, 1990.

———. *Solomonic Judgments.* Cambridge: Cambridge University Press, 1990.

———. *Ulysses and the Sirens: Studies in Rationality and Irrationality.* Cambridge: Cambridge University Press, 1989.

Elster, John, ed. *Rational Choice.* Oxford: Blackwell, 1986.

Epstein, Edwin M. "The Corporate Social Policy Process." *California Management Review* 29, no. 3 (Spring 1987).

Etzioni, Amitai. *The Moral Dimension: Toward a New Economics.* New York: Free Press, 1989.

Fanning, Deirdre. "Will Boilermakers Replace M.B.A.s?" *International Herald Tribune,* March 5, 1990.

Feinberg, Joel. "The Nature and Value of Rights." *Journal of Value Inquiry* 4 (1970).

———. *Social Philosophy.* Engelwood Cliffs, N.J.: Prentice-Hall 1973.

Firth, Roderick. "Ethical Absolutism and the Ideal Observer." *Philosophy and Phenomenological Research* 12 (1952): 317–45.

Flew, Anthony. *The Politics of Procrustes.* Buffalo: Prometheus, 1981.

———. "The Profit Motive." *Ethics* 86 (July 1976): 312–22.

Flores, Carlos F. *Management and Communication in the Office of the Future.* Berkeley: Logonet, 1982.

Frank, Robert H. *Passions within Reason: The Strategic Role of the Emotions.* New York: Norton, 1989.

Freeman, R. Edward, ed. *Business Ethics: The State of the Art.* (New York: Oxford University Press, 1991.

Freeman, R. Edward, and D. Gilbert. *Corporate Strategy and the Search for Ethics.* Engelwood Cliffs, N.J.: Prentice-Hall, 1988.

Freeman, R. Edward, and Jeanne Liedtka. "Corporate Social Responsibility: A Critical Approach." *International Association for Business and Society Proceedings,* 1991.

French, Peter A. *Collective and Corporate Responsibility.* New York: Columbia University Press, 1984.

———. "The Corporation as a Moral Person." *American Philosophical Quarterly* 16, no. 3 (1979).

———. "Responsibility and the Moral Role of Corporate Entities." In *Ruffin Lectures II,* ed. R. Edward Freeman. New York: Oxford University Press, 1992.

French, Peter A., ed. *The Spectrum of Responsibility.* New York: Martin's, 1990.

French, P., T. Uehling, and H. Wettstein, eds. *Ethical Theory: Character and Virtue.* Midwest Studies in Philosophy 13. Minneapolis: University of Minnesota Press, 1988.

———. *Social and Political Philosophy.* Midwest Studies in Philosophy 7. Minneapolis: University of Minnesota Press, 1982.

Friedman, Milton. "Adam Smith's Relevance for 1976." In *Selected Papers of the University of Chicago Graduate School of Business,* no. 50. Chicago: University of Chicago Graduate School of Business, 1977.

———. "The Social Responsibility of Business Is to Increase Its Profits." *New York Times,* Sept. 13, 1970.

Friedman, Milton, and Rose Friedman. *Free to Choose.* New York: Harcourt Brace Jovanovitch, 1979.

Fullinwider, Robert K. *The Reverse Discrimination Controversy.* Totowa, N.J.: Rowman and Littlefield, 1980.

Galston, William. "Equal Opportunity and Liberal Theory." In *Justice and Equality: Here and Now,* ed. F. Lucasch, pp. 89–107. Ithaca: Cornell University Press, 1986.

———. "Toughness as a Political Virtue." *Journal of Social Philosophy: Virtues in Social Theory* (Summer 1991).

Gautier, David. *Morals by Agreement.* New York: Oxford, 1986.

Geertz, Clifford. *The Interpretation of Cultures.* New York: Basic Books, 1975.

Gellerman, Saul. "Why 'Good' Managers Make Bad Ethical Choices." *Harvard Business Review* (July–Aug 1986).

Gibbard, Allan. *Wise Choices, Apt Feelings: A Theory of Normative Judgment.* Cambridge: Harvard University Press, 1990.

Gillespie, Norman C. "The Business of Ethics." In *Ethical Issues in Professional Life,* ed J. Callahan, New York: Oxford University Press, 1988.

Gilligan Carol. *A Different Voice.* Cambridge: Harvard University Press, 1982.

Goodpaster, Kenneth and John Matthews. "Can a Corporation Have a Conscience?" *Harvard Business Review* (Jan.–Feb. 1982).

Goodpaster, Kenneth. "Ethical Imperatives and Corporate Leadership." In *Business Ethics: The State of the Art,* ed. R. Edward Freeman. New York: Oxford University Press, 1991.

Greenwood, Ernest. "Attributes of a Profession." In *Man, Work and Society,* ed. S. Nosow and W. Form. New York: Basic Books, 1962.

Griswold, Charles L. "Adam Smith of Virtue and Self-Interest." Paper read at the American Philosophical Association, Dec. 1989.

Hadreas, Peter. "Money: A Speech Act Analysis." *Journal of Social Philosophy* 20, no. 3 (Winter 1989).

Hampshire, Stuart. *Innocence and Experience.* Cambridge: Harvard University Press, 1989.

———. *Morality and Conflict.* Cambridge: Harvard University Press, 1983.

Hampshire, Stuart, ed. *Public and Private Morality.* Cambridge: Cambridge University Press, 1978.

Hartle, Anthony E. *Moral Issues in Military Decision-Making*. Lawrence: University Press of Kansas, 1989.

Hartman, Edwin. "Virtues and Rules: A Reply to Robert Solomon." In *Ruffin Lectures II*, ed. R. Edward Freeman. New York: Oxford University Press, 1992.

Harwood, Sterling. "Affirmative Action Is Justified. Paper read at the American Philosophical Association, 1990.

Hegel, G. W. F. *The Phenomenology of Spirit*. Trans A. V. Miller. Oxford: Oxford University Press, 1977.

———. *The Philosophy of Right*. Trans. T. Knox. (Oxford: Oxford University Press, 1967.

Hennig, M., and Anne Jardin. *The Managerial Woman*. New York: Doubleday, 1977.

Henry Mintzberg. "The Manager's Job: Folklore and Fact." *Harvard Business Review* (July–Aug. 1975).

Hobbes, Thomas. *Leviathan*. New York: Hafner, 1926.

Hoffman, Martin L. "Empathetic Emotions and Justice in Society." *Social Justice Research* 3, no. 4 (Dec. 1989).

Horniman, Alexander B. "Whatever Happened to Loyalty?" *Ethics Digest* (1989).

Hume, David. *A Treatise of Human Nature*. Oxford: Oxford University Press, 1978.

Hunt, Lester. *Nietzsche and the Virtues*. New York: Routledge, 1990.

Jackall, Robert. *Moral Mazes*. New York: Oxford University Press, 1988.

Kant, Immanuel. *Grounding of the Metaphysics of Morals* trans. J. Ellington. Indianapolis: Hackett, 1981.

Kant, Immanuel. *The Metaphysics Elements of Justice*. Trans. J. Ladd. Indianapolis: Bobbs-Merrill, 1965.

Kant, Immanuel. *The Philosophy of Law*. trans. W. Hastie. Edinburgh: Clark 1889.

Keeley, Michael. *A Social Contract Theory of Organizations*. Notre Dame: University of Notre Dame Press, 1988.

Kennedy, A., and T. Deal. *Corporate Cultures*. Reading, Mass.: Addison-Wesley, 1982.

Kinsley, Michael. "Stock Response." *New Republic,* Aug. 20, 1990.

———. "Two Japanese Myths." *New Republic,* Jan. 29, 1990.

Koestenbaum, Peter. *The Heart of Business*. Dallas: Saybrook, 1987.

Kohn, Alfie. *Beyond Selfishness*. New York: Basic Books, 1990.

Kristol, Irving. "Ethics Anyone? Or Morals?" *Wall Street Journal*, Sept. 15, 1987.

———. *Two Cheers for Capitalism*. New York: Basic Books, 1978.

Ladd, John. "Morality and the Ideal of Rationality in Formal Organizations." *The Monist* (October 1970.

Lakoff, George, and Mark Johnson. *Metaphors We Live By*. Chicago: University of Chicago, 1980.

Levin, Michael. "Ethics Courses Are Useless," *New York Times,* Nov. 27, 1989.

Lewis, Michael. *Liar's Poker*. New York: Norton, 1989.

Lindholm, Charles. *Charisma*. Oxford: Blackwell, 1991.

Longnecker, J., and C. Pringle. *Management*. 5th ed. Columbus: Merrill, 1981.

Luce, R. D., and Howard Raiffa. *Games and Decisions*. New York: Wiley, 1957.

Maccoby, Michael. *The Gamesman.* New York: Pocket Books, 1975.

MacDonald, John. *The Game of Business.* New York: Doubleday, 1977.

Machiavelli, Niccolo. *The Prince.* Trans. C. Detmold. New York: Airmont, 1965.

MacIntyre, Alasdair. *After Virtue.* Notre Dame, Ind.: University of Notre Dame, 1981.

———. *Whose Justice: Which Rationality?* Notre Dame, Ind.: University of Notre Dame, 1988.

———. "Why Are the Problems of Business Ethics Insoluble?" In *Proceedings of the First National Conference on Business Ethics.* Waltham, Mass.: Bentley College, 1977.

Marx, Karl. *Selected Writings.* Ed. David McClellan. Oxford: Oxford University Press, 1977.

Mayeroff, Milton. *On Caring.* New York: Harper and Row, 1971.

McClennen, Edward F. "Justice and the Problem of Stability." *Philosophy and Public Affairs* (1988).

———. "Morality as a Public Good." Paper read at the Society for Business Ethics, 1988.

McFall, Lynne. "Integrity." *Ethics* 98 (October 1987).

McGregor, Douglas A. *The Human Side of Enterprise.* New York: McGraw-Hill, 1960.

———. "The Human Side of Enterprise." *Management Review* (Nov. 1957).

Mencius. *Mencius on the Mind.* Trans. P. Lau. New York: Penguin, 1970.

Menken, Daniel L. *Faith, Hope, and the Corporation.* St. Paul: Phrontisterian, 1988.

Mertzger, "What is a Profession? *Seminar Reports* 3, no. 1. New York: Columbia University Press, 1975.-

Mill, John Stuart. *On Liberty.* Indianapolis: Hackett, 1978.

Mill, John Stuart. *Utilitarianism.* Indianapolis: Hackett, 1981.

Miller, David. *Social Justice.* Oxford: Oxford University Press, 1976.

Moyers, Bill. *The World of Ideas.* Vols. 1 and 2. New York: Doubleday, 1989, 1991.

Nagel, Thomas. "Ruthlessness in Public Life." In *Public and Private Morality,* ed. Stuart Hampshire. Cambridge: Cambridge University Press, 1978.

Naipul, V. S. *A Bend in the River.* New York: Vintage, 1989.

Naisbett, John. *Re-inventing the Corporation.* New York: Bantam, 1983.

Nash, Laura. "Business Ethics without the Sermon," *Harvard Business Review* (Nov.–Dec. 1981.

Newton, Lisa H. "Reverse Discrimination as Unjustified." *Ethics* 83 (1973).

Nietzsche, Friedrich. *Beyond Good and Evil.* Trans. W. Kaufmann. New York: Random House, 1967.

———. *Genealogy of Morals.* Trans. W. Kaufmann. New York: Random House, 1967.

———. *Thus Spoke Zarathustra.* Trans. W. Kaufman. New York: Viking, 1954.

Noddings, Nell. *Caring.* Los Angeles: University of California Press, 1984.

Nozick, Robert. *Anarchy, State and Utopia.* New York: Basic Books, 1974.

Nussbaum, Martha. *The Fragility of Goodness.* Cambridge: Cambridge University Press, 1989.

O'Toole, James. *Vanguard Management.* New York: Doubleday, 1985.

Oldenquist, Andrew. "Loyalties." *Journal of Philosophy* 79, no. 4 (April 1982).

Ouchi, William. *Theory Z.* New York: Avon, 1986.

Paine, Lynne Sharp. "Ethics as Character Development." In *Business Ethics: The State of the Art*, ed R. Edward Freeman. New York: Oxford University Press, 1990.

————. "Ideals of Competition and Today's Marketplace." In *Enriching Business Ethics*, ed. Clarence Walton. New York: Plenum, 1990.

————. "Utilitarianism and the Goodness of Persons." In *Foundations of Morality*, ed. L. Rouner. Notre Dame, Ind.: University of Notre Dame Press, 1983.

Pastin, Mark. *The Hard Problems of Management.* San Francisco: Jossey-Bass, 1986.

Peters, Tom. *In Search of Excellence.* New York: Harper and Row, 1982.

Pincoffs, Edmund. *Quandaries and Virtues.* Lawrence: University Press of Kansas, 1986.

Plato, *Republic.* Trans. C. Grube. Indianapolis: Hackett, 1974.

Rapaport, Anatole. "Escape from Paradox." *Scientific American* 217 (1967).

Rawls, John. "Justice as Fairness." *Philosophical Review* 62 (1963)

————. *A Theory of Justice.* Cambridge: Harvard University Press, 1971.

Rescher, Nicholas. *Unselfishness.* Pittsburgh: University of Pittsburgh Press, 1975.

Rorty, Amelie. *Explaining Emotions.* Berkeley: University of California Press, 1980.

Royce, Josiah. *The Philosophy of Loyalty.* New York: Macmillan, 1908.

Samuelson, Robert J. "Competition: Tried and True." *Newsweek,* June 11, 1990.

————. "The End of Economics." *Newsweek,* July 24, 1989.

Sandel, Michael. *Liberalism and the Limits of Justice.* Cambridge: Cambridge University Press, 1982.

Sartre, Jean-Paul. *Being and Nothingness.* New York: Philosophical Library, 1956.

————. *Dirty Hands.* In *No Exit and Three Other Plays.* New York: Vintage, 1946.

————. "The Wall." In *The Wall and Other Stories.* New York: New Directions, 1948.

Scheler, Max. *The Nature of Sympathy.* Trans P. Heath. London: Routledge, 1954.

Schelling. T. C. *The Strategy of Conflict.* Cambridge: Harvard University Press, 1960.

Schlick, Moritz. *Problems of Ethics.* Trans. D. Rynin. New York: 1939.

Schoeck, Helmut. *Envy: A Theory of Social Behaviour.* Trans. M. Glenny and B. Ross. (New York: Harcourt Brace and World, 1970.

Schopenhauer, Arthur. *The Basis of Morality.* Trans. Payne. Indianapolis: Bobbs-Merrill, 1841.

Schwartz, Barry. *The Battle for Human Nature.* New York: Norton, 1989.

Sen. Amartya. "The Moral Standing of the Market." *Ethics and Economics, Social Philosophy and Policy* 2, no. 2 (Spring 1985).

————. *On Ethics and Economics.* Oxford: Blackwell, 1989.

Sheaffer, Robert. *Resentment against Achievement.* New York: Libertarian Books, 1987.

Shorris, Earl. *The Oppressed Middle.* New York: Doubleday, 1976.

Silk, Leonard, and David Vogel. *Ethics and Profits.* New York: Simon and Schuster, 1976.

Singer, Peter. *Practical Ethics.* Cambridge: Cambridge University Press, 1979.

Smith, Adam. *An Inquiry into the Nature and Causes of the Wealth of Nations.* New York: Hafner, 1948.

————. *The Theory of Moral Sentiments.* London: George Bell, 1990.

Solomon, Robert C. "The Emotions of Justice." *Social Justice Research*, 3, no. 4 (Dec. 1989).

―――. *Ethics*. Madison, Wis.: Brown and Benchmark, 1992.

―――. "Ethics and Economics." *Business and Society Review* 46 (Summer 1983).

―――. *Passion for Justice*. Reading, Mass.: Addison-Wesley, 1990.

―――. *The Passions*. New York: Doubleday, 1976.

Solomon, Robert C. and Hanson, K. *Above the Bottom Line*. New York: Harcourt Brace Jovanovitch, 1983.

Solomon, Robert C. (with K. Hanson). *It's Good Business*. New York: Atheneum, 1985. Reprinted, Harper and Row, 1987.

Stocker, Michael." Aristotle on Teleology." In *Essays on Aristotle's Ethics,* ed. Amelie Rorty. Berkeley: University of California Press, 1980.

―――. "The Problem of Dirty Hands." In *Plural and Conflicting Values* Oxford: Oxford University Press, 1990.

Stone, Christopher. *Where the Law Ends: The Social Control of Corporate Behavior*. New York: Harper and Row, 1975.

Stone, Oliver. *Wall Street* (Twentieth Century-Fox, 1987).

Suits, Bernard. *The Grasshopper*. Toronto: University of Toronto Press, 1978.

Tawney, R. H. *Religion and the Rise of Capitalism*. New York: Harper and Row, 1952.

Taylor, Gabriele. *Pride, Shame, and Guilt*. Oxford: Clarendon, 1985.

Thomas, Laurence. *On Being Moral*. Philadelphia: Temple University Press, 1989.

―――. "Morals, the Self and Our Natural Sentiments." In *Emotion*, ed. G. Myers and P. Irani, pp. 144–63. New York: Haven, 1983.

Thurow, Lester. *The Zero-Sum Society*. New York: Basic Books, 1980.

Toqueville, Alexis de. *Democracy in America*. New York: Knopf, 1945.

Toulmin, Stephen. *Cosmopolis: The Hidden Agenda of Modernity*. New York: Free Press, 1989.

Townsend, Robert. *Up the Organization*. New York: Knopf, 1970.

Turnbull, Colin. *The Mountain People*. New York: Simon and Schuster, 1974.

Ungar, Robert. *Passon: An Essay on Personality*. New York: Free Press, 1984.

Urmson, J. D. "The Interpretation of the Moral Philosophy of J. S. Mill." In *Theories of Ethics*, ed. P. Foot (Oxford: Oxford University Press, 1967).

Velasquez, Manuel G. *Business Ethics*. Engelwood Cliffs, N.J.: Prentice-Hall, 1982.

von Hayek, Friedrich. *Mirage of Social Justice*. London: Routledge and Kegan Paul, 1976.

von Neumann, John, and Oscar Morgenstern. *Theory of Games and Economic Behavior*. Princeton: Princeton University Press, 1944.

Walton, Clarence C. *The Moral Manager*. Cambridge: Ballinger, 1988.

Walzer, Michael. *Spheres of Justice*. New York: Harper and Row, 1983.

Weber, Max. "Politics as a Vocation." In *From Max Weber: Essays in Sociology*, ed. H. Gerth and C. Mills. New York: Oxford University Press, 1946.

Weber, Max. *The Spirit of Protestantism and the Rise of Capitalism*. New York: Macmillan, 1977.

Werhane, Patricia. *Ethics and Economics: The Legacy of Adam Smith for Modern Capitalism. Oxford: Oxford University Press, 1991.*

―――. *"Moral Character and Moral Reasoning." Ruffin Lectures II,* ed. R. Edward Freeman. New York: Oxford, 1992.

Williams, Bernard. *Ethics and the Limits of Philosophy.* Cambridge: Cambridge University Press, 1985.

Williams, Bernard. *Morality.* New York: Harper and Row, 1972.

———. "Politics and Moral Character." In *Moral Luck.* Cambridge: Cambridge University Press, 1981.

———. *Problems of the Self.* Cambridge: Cambridge University Press, 1973.

Wolfe, Art. "Game Metaphors." *Business Horizons* (1989).

Wolfe, Tom. *Bonfire of the Vanities.* New York: Farrar Strauss and Giroux, 1987.

Wolgast, Elizabeth. *A Grammar of Justice.* Ithaca: Cornell University Press, 1988.

Yeo, Michael. "The Myth of Amoral Business Ethics." Paper read at the University of British Columbia Applied Ethics Conference, June 1990.

INDEX